# The
# TEDDY BEAR
# Craft Book

Teddy bears come in all sizes, shapes, and materials, from the small bear in the front to the big zoo bear to the crocheted bear on the left.

# The TEDDY BEAR Craft Book

CAROLYN VOSBURG HALL

VNR VAN NOSTRAND REINHOLD COMPANY
New York · Cincinnati · Toronto · London · Melbourne

Printed in the United States of America
Designed by A. Christopher Simon

Published by Van Nostrand Reinhold Company Inc.
135 West 50th Street
New York, New York 10020

Van Nostrand Reinhold Company Limited
Molly Millars Lane
Wokingham, Berkshire, England RG11 2PY

Van Nostrand Reinhold
480 La Trobe Street
Melbourne, Victoria 3000, Australia

Macmillan of Canada
Division of Gage Publishing Limited
164 Commander Boulevard
Agincourt, Ontario M1S 3C7, Canada


16 15 14 13 12 11 10 9 8 7 6 5 4 3 2



**Library of Congress Cataloging in Publication Data**

Hall, Carolyn Vosburg, 1927–
    The teddy bear craft book.

    Includes index.
    1. Soft toy making.   2. Teddy bears.   I. Title.
TT174.3.H34      1983        745.592′4        83-5752
    ISBN 0-442-23616-6

# Acknowledgments

Bear hugs to:

Mary Zdrodowski for drawings
Alice Avedisian for editorial assistance
Margaret DeGrace for information
Bob Vigiletti for color photography and advice
David Fry for lighting assistance

Claudia and Doug Stroud for art and wood works
Jim Balmer, John Reddy, and George Woods for
    bear data
My artist friends for making teddy bears
And to Cap and Garrett Hall for forbearance

# Contents

This classic early teddy bear, given to owner Charles Kass as a baby present in 1904, has typically long arms and feet, shoe button eyes, and movable joints. Much of his excelsior stuffing has sifted out as sawdust over the years. Note his serious expression.

# Introduction

"Who owns a teddy bear?" I asked. Every hand in the kindergarten class shot up. Then each child began to tell me about his or her particular bear and what made it so special

There's no doubt about it. Teddy bears occupy an important role in our lives. In compiling information for this book, I learned just how important they are. It is the rare individual who doesn't fondly recall a beloved bear from childhood. Bears are not just soft toy animals; they are best friends and secret-keepers. Psychiatrists describe bears as "transitional objects" chosen by the child to help make the change from total dependence on parents to self-determination. The teddy bear fills this role admirably well: he's a small animal friend who is not quite human enough to give away the child's secrets. What's more, little boys feel free to love their bears as much as little girls do. This even spills into adulthood. Many adult teddy bear lovers laughingly agree that they still need their bears. An August 1982 issue of the *Wall Street Journal* showed a cartoon of a harried executive who called his wife to say, "Please bring my teddy bear to the station. I've had a rough day."

The teddy bear patterns included in this book evolved from my research on teddy bears as historic and folk art objects. They express some of the magic and mystery of a culture. The teddy bear has been evolving since the beginning of this century, and I have tried to represent the various stages of its development in my patterns.

The official history of the teddy bear begins in the United States in 1902 with the creation of the first toy bear named Teddy, after Theodore Roosevelt, and was based on a Clifford Berryman political cartoon. Curiously, a toy bear was invented earlier that year in Germany but only later called a teddy bear. (For further details on the controversial invention of the teddy bear, turn to page 36.)

From 1860 to 1914 (referred to as The Golden Age of Toys by authors Jac Remis and Jean Fondin in their book by the same name) all manner of exquisite toys evolved. Many were so elegant that children weren't allowed to play with them. Perhaps to combat this trend, two toy designers on different continents invented a small bear-person for children to love. This anthropomorphized figure had the same soft body and movable joints as dolls, but was covered with furry mohair plush. These teddys were small-eyed, serious little fellows, quite different from many of the comical characters manufactured today.

But the main characteristic that separates the old bears (and some expensive new ones) from the average teddy bear made today is "articulated" joints. These fully movable joints allowed separate parts of the bear to rotate completely. Teddy bears were not the first toys to be made using this system. Many dolls had "tube" legs attached by disks and cotter pins to "bag" bodies. Toys of this era had the firmly stuffed bodies necessary for this type of joint.

Examine an old bear or a new jointed bear to feel the firm round disks inserted at his neck,

Early teddy bears were distinguished by their disk-and-pin articulated joints. Another feature of Virginia Debenam Rogers' 1935 jointed bear is its fur, which "grows" in all directions.

By 1945 many teddy bears were made with sewn joints and more childlike proportions, as shown by Randall Hall's inherited bear. The beady-eyed look on his celluloid movable eyes has dimmed from wear.

shoulders, and hips. Each disk has a matching one sewn into his head, arms, and legs. The early bear's disks were made of wood and were padded with leather to diminish wear on the fur fabric covering. They were held together with cotter pins, long metal fasteners with prongs that twist into loops to hold the disks together yet allow full rotation.

Using hand tools, the teddy bear maker worked through the open seam in the bear's back to twist the pins firmly in place. Companies that still make disk-and-pin bears have improved their methods and techniques, but it's still an expensive, time-consuming process. (Complete directions for making this type of bear and obtaining disks appear for Carolyn's Teddy Bear on page 22.)

Manufacturers began to develop teddy bear designs that avoided this manual process. One less expensive solution was to use buttons anchored together with elastic or wire through the bear's body for fully articulated joints, but exposed buttons. (Directions for the "homey" version of this appear for Flat Foot Bear on page 29.) Small versions of this bear can be assembled with a sturdy sewing thread (there are directions on page 34 for Small Bears). The imaginative Chinese produce a tiny bear with sets of snaps for joints. These allow not only full movement, but also change of placement—you can snap his legs on backwards, his arm on his neck. . . .

It was around 1940 that a manufacturer made a teddy with prestuffed arms sewn into the body seam. The legs were cut with the body. They flexed because no stuffing was placed in this joint. Rag dolls had flat sewn joints before this but the development was new to bears.

By cutting and machine sewing mobility into the bear, the manufacturer acheived several results. The bear could be more softly stuffed, which made it ideal for taking to bed. It was now lighter in weight. Most importantly, the teddy was cheaper to manufacture and involved less hand work.

Not all changes in the teddy bear's appearance resulted from technology. Collectors may insist that the only authentic ones resemble the 1902 teddys, but in fact, the shape of the bear you loved as a child usually determines your conception of a "real" teddy bear. Over the years gradual changes in the toy's shape occured as a result of many influences, our society's emphasis on youth, stylized versions of people and bears in movie cartoons, individual toy designers' creativity, and other cultural influences. As a result, teddy bears began to have larger heads and more widely spaced eyes, perched on smaller bodies for a more childlike effect. When the newly designed bear with the "cute" look of a child arrived, the younger audience was willing to agree that this was a "real" teddy bear.

From this point on teddy bear making changed forever. Both commercial and homemade bears were created in all manner of configuration and called teddy bears.

Some manufacturers emphasized economics over creativity and produced inexpensive, characterless teddy bears. Other companies, such as Steiff in Germany, deplored the shift from tradition and continued to emphasize traditionally shaped bears in ever more elegant and expensive fabrics.

A new teddy bear boom is underway, with imaginative bears being created in novel forms, particularly by the Gund toy company. Teddy bear imagery now reflects many influences—cartoon characters, real bears, old-time bears, story book characters, and new fabrics.

My goal in writing *The Teddy Bear Craft Book* was twofold: I wanted to design a collection of bears that reflected the evolution of the teddy bear from 1902 to the present; I also wanted to create "the perfect teddy bear," one who would embody all that is expected of a good bear. The first project in the book, Carolyn's Teddy Bear, is the result of this effort.

There are more than 25 projects in the book, ranging from cuddly teddy bears, to a teddy bear chair, to a soft teddy bear quilt. Each project comes with appropriate patterns, diagrams, photographs, and directions. Before beginning the projects, however, read The Bear Essentials for basic how-to information that should help you along the way. Scattered throughout the projects in the book are what I call The Bear Facts, tidbits of information about teddy bears and their role in our society.

The more I learned about teddy bears the more mysterious their enormous appeal became. "Why bears, why not cats or elephants?" the curious-minded ask. "Why indeed!" huffs any true teddy bear lover, "everyone *knows* why teddy bears are special."

Lacking an answer to this question after all my research, I put it aside and poured all my new knowledge and old affection for teddy bears into creating these designs. I hope these warm feelings enfold you as you read the book and then make teddy bears for your own pleasure

The "Teddy Bear Room" shows teddy bears to make in a variety of forms. Try your hand at a rug, a quilt, a headboard, curtains, a chair, or any of the toys.

# The Bear Essentials

Complete instructions accompany each teddy bear project, but some additional information will be helpful. Information on scaling up and tracing patterns and templates, choosing fabrics, stuffings, stitching fur fabrics, and teddy bear faces appears in this section for your convenience. Read the entire section for general background, or refer back as needed while making a teddy bear.

## SCALING UP TEDDY BEAR PATTERNS

Most of the teddy bear patterns in this book appear full-sized. You need only trace or photocopy them for use. But there are nine larger patterns that appear in reduced size, most on a grid. These and other patterns may be scaled up or down to the size you want or the size indicated.

To enlarge, draw a large grid on paper, making the same number of squares as on the paper. All grids in this book, unless otherwise stated, were reduced from 4-inch squares, so to draw them full-sized, make the large grid squares 4 inches each. Then copy the drawing square by square. For other sizes change the large grid squares to suit your needs. To make the pattern half this size, for example, make 2-inch squares, and to make it twice the size, make 8-inch squares.

There's an easy way to enlarge or reduce the other patterns in this book. Draw a 1-inch grid over the pattern. On a large piece of paper, draw a right angle in the lower left-hand corner. Measure up the vertical line to the finished size you want: to make the pattern twice as big, for example, measure twice the distance of the pattern up the side. Make a horizontal line at this point. Lay the first drawing with the 1-inch grid over the right angle, aligning it at the corner. With a ruler, draw a diagonal line from the lower left-hand corner through the upper right-hand corner of the small drawing and continue the line until it meets the top horizontal line. Draw a vertical line down to the base line from this point.

Divide this larger rectangle into the same number of squares as the smaller square. Copy each square on the larger grid. (For a smaller pattern, follow the same instructions but make the height of the vertical line shorter than the rectangle height. Resulting squares will be smaller than the 1-inch grid of the original.)

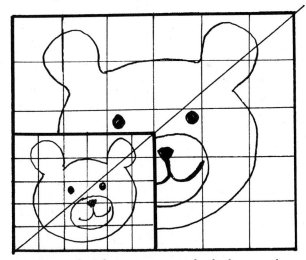

To scale up, place drawing on perpendicular lines you have drawn on a piece of paper or the lower right-hand corner of the paper. Measure up the vertical line to the desired new size and draw a horizontal line at that point. Draw a diagonal line through the drawing from the lower right to the opposite upper corner, continuing until it intersects the horizontal line. Draw a vertical line at this point, divide into the same number of squares, and transfer the drawing, square by square.

When you have produced the new pattern, mark pattern information on each piece: direction of fur, darts or clip marks, number of pieces to be cut, and which need to be reversed. It's not necessary to draw the seam line, but keep an even seam allowance as you stitch to avoid distorting the pattern.

Mechanical means can be used to increase or decrease pattern size. Use an opaque projector to shine the pattern directly on paper. Or photograph the pattern on slide film and project the slide on the paper. In both cases, draw a measured line for scale along one edge of the paper. Align the grid marks with the scale lining during projection to make sure that the image is not distorted. Carefully trace the design.

### TRACING PATTERNS

The two easiest ways to transfer a pattern to paper are to photocopy it and to trace it. Compare photocopies with the original since some machines distort the original considerably. To trace the pattern from the book use a paper through which you can see the lines. Work under good light, or hold the page up to a window to help illuminate the lines. Better-quality tracing paper makes good patterns since it resists tearing. You can find pads of it in art or office supply stores.

### TEMPLATES AND PATTERNS

To make a template—a cardboard pattern to trace around—find a suitably stiff paper, cardboard, or acetate sheet (clear plastic with one frosted side for accepting lines). You can trace the pattern on the clear plastic, but you will need to use carbon paper for opaque materials. To do this, lay carbon paper over the paper or cardboard, ink side down. Put both pieces, carbon paper side up, under the pattern page. Hold in place with masking tape if it appears to shift. Use a sharp point that leaves no mark to outline the drawing—a leadless pencil, a knitting needle, or whatever is handy. Cut the templates out carefully to keep a smooth edge and mark necessary information on the template. Keep the pieces in an envelope for storage or punch a hole through each and string them together.

### CHOOSING FABRICS FOR BEARS

A furry material is the most obvious choice for making a teddy bear, but you can choose between furs—real or fake—and fabrics. The bear projects in this book have been made from a wide assortment of materials.

Look for good color and texture first in picking a fabric. Most people use traditional honey-colored fake fur, but I've seen teddys in every color, including green! What's in fashion influences fabric availability. Choose plush for a traditional bear, calico for a country bear, denim for a western bear, and whatever you like for a modern bear.

Consider appearance, ease of handling, cost, and suitability to the pattern when selecting a fabric. If the bear is to be a gift for a child, consider washability, flame resistance, and durability. For humid climates, consider resistance to mildew and colorfastness. Fabric eaters such as moths may also be a problem.

Consider all these points if you plan to make a quality bear—a good teddy bear can be the next generation's treasure. More likely, however, you'll use what's on hand or available at the nearest fabric store—most teddys are loved to tatters soon enough anyway.

Among pile fabrics, "fake fur" usually looks best for a teddy bear. Most important is the appearance, length, and density of the pile. Patterns are usually designed for a particular length of pile. A teddy bear leg 2 inches wide in flat fabric, for example, will measure 3 inches wide in a ½-inch pile fabric. As a rule teddy bears look plumper in pile fabrics, and much plumper in long pile fabrics.

If you plan to make a small bear, choose a short pile with a firmly woven backing. Medium-sized bears look best in a ½-inch-length pile. For the larger bears a dense, ¾-inch pile is most suitable. Use a 2-inch shaggy pile for a lightweight costume, and the denser ¾-inch one for a more elegant outfit.

Nearly all pile fabrics and furs have a directional pile: the surface looks lighter when the light reflects off the side of the pile, and darker into the end of the pile. Stroke the fabric to determine pile direction. To avoid "shading," be sure all nap runs in the correct direction.

All pile fabrics from velvet to fur slide on each other when being machine stitched. You will need to anchor the pieces to each other carefully for stitching. Use dressmaker's pins, pinch clothes pins, or hand or machine basting, or guide the fabric with your fingers as you sew. Ease the pressure on the sewing machine presser foot if possible, or make other adjustments as suggested in your sewing machine manual.

Some upholstery fabrics are coated on the back to stabilize the fabric. Most backed fabrics sew well but a few of these backings may make the fabric too stiff to handle or hard to sew.

### Plush Fabrics

Real old-time teddy bears were made from mohair. Genuine mohair, from Angora goats, is a springy wool fiber usually woven into coating or upholstery plush. Around the turn of the century, this plush was called mohair no matter what the fiber content—Angora goat, silk, wool, or rayon. We now call "mohair" plush.

Woven upholstery plush comes in a variety of different grades. The better grades have rich colors, a dense pile, and firmly woven backing, and they come on wide bolts. Less expensive grades may be easier to work with and stitch, however, because they are thinner.

Plushes are woven in many fibers: nylon, rayon, wool, silk, synthetics, and combinations. Some wash, others need dry cleaning. Most can be sponged off with suds or upholstery cleaners. To find these fabrics, look in fabric and upholstery stores or order from their swatch books.

### Velvet and Velveteen

Closely related to the plushes, the velvets have a short-napped, directional pile with a woven backing. Velvet has shiny fibers made from silk, rayon, or nylon. Velveteen, which is cotton, has less sheen, but it does have a rich softness. Both are considered luxury fabrics. The cut edge of softly woven velvet may fray, so use Fray-No-More "glue" or overcast the seams.

Velvets and velveteens come in rich colors and appear in fabric stores mainly during the winter. Heavier upholstery grades, however, are available throughout the year.

Both of these fabrics handle like plush and need careful control during stitching. They also shed bits of pile along cut edges. Velveteen washes, but some velvets water spot or mat. Check the care instructions on the bolt hang ticket.

### Corduroy

The country cousin of velvet and velveteen, corduroy has a shorter pile and is nearly always made of cotton. It has a characteristic "rib" in which the napped pile runs in rows. Pinwale corduroy has tiny rows, wide wale has wider rows,

and some corduroys have a combination of wide and narrow rows. Waleless corduroy, which resembles velveteen, has no visible rows. It lacks the smooth sheen but costs far less. (Most children know this fabric because of Don Freeman's book character, lovable Corduroy.)

### Real Fur

Furs come from many animals, but most have similar characteristics. Furs for clothing have thin, supple leather backings that can be sewn on the sewing machine. This leather is fragile and must be handled carefully. Rabbit, mink, muskrat, fitch, sheared opossum or beaver, and similar furs can be used to make teddys or bear rugs. Many furs are expensive and hard to contain. One ready source for furs is old coats.

Fur grows directionally, so the pattern must be cut accordingly. Choose a pattern with few seams for ease of construction and less wear on the fur. Fur makes an elegant but fragile teddy that needs good care to survive. For more details on handling fur, see instructions for the Bear Rug on page 46.

### Fake Fur

Most of the bears shown in this book are made from fake fur fabrics, the best choice for teddy bears. If they all look different it's because there is a wide variety of fake fur available. Fake furs differ from plushed in that most have a knitted backing. This provides flexibility, light weight, and easy care. Patterns for knitted fabrics need fewer seams since knits stretch and mold well to rounded shapes.

Fake fur fabrics are usually made from synthetic fibers: acrylic, polyester, modacrylic, and mixtures. The basic synthetic monofilament fiber can be shaped to achieve a variety of desirable characteristics. For example, the synthetic sheen that marked some early fabrics can now be avoided.

Gare's Bear on page 38 shows how elegant fake fur fabric can be in a combination of blended colors in acrylic fiber. These realistic fake furs are designed for coating and are relatively light weight, have subtle coloring, are easy to handle and are durable. With the heavy pile fabrics, however, multiple layers may make sewing difficult. See Gare's Bear instructions for help.

Carolyn's Bear on page 22 most resembles the traditional mohair in density of pile and color. The white version of Rand's Bear on page 66 has a much denser coat for a smooth, rich look. Both fabrics are known as robe fur, whether they have a stiffened backing or not.

The Koala Puppet's ears (page 91) require a 2-inch shaggy modacrylic fabric, which is most popular in black for gorilla suits. It's not my choice for a whole teddy bear but works wonderfully for these ears.

Fake fur fabrics tend to slide on each other less than the woven-backed plushes and velvets do. They are also forgiving of stitching errors—these hide in the pile.

Look in fabric and craft stores for fake fur fabrics. Availability changes with the season and the manufacturer's whim, but fall brings a good selection for holiday toy making. Take a look on the remnant table for small pieces since teddy bears don't take much fabric.

## Velour

The pile in some velour fabrics results from brushing the knitted surface vigorously to raise a soft nap. Other velours have a nub or pile incorporated in the knitting process. Velours have a soft, lightweight, flexible drape that makes them ideal for robes. This flexibility makes them difficult to sew because they stretch and shift. Use pins liberally to pin baste when stitching. Polyester velours wash easily and wear well. The color range in velours is varied and subtle and is related to the current fashion.

## Terry Cloth

In manufacturing terry cloth, a looped pile is woven into the fabric, usually on both sides. (Sheared terry cloth loops are called velour.) Terry cloth is nearly always made of pure cotton for wear, absorbency, and washability. Knitted terry cloth may contain spandex for added stretch.

Claudia's Bear Bag on page 152 was made from a towel. Thick towels are more difficult to sew than thinner or one-sided terry cloth. Stitch with care since the loops may catch on the presser foot.

Terry cloth teddy bears have a sturdy, textured look. If you use a preshrunk thread for machine embroidery and washable filler, they can make plenty of trips through the laundry cycle. This fabric can be found in fabric or linen stores. Colors, usually bright and soft, follow the fashion in sports and in decor.

## Leather and Synthetic Suede Cloth

Leather feet and paws look and wear well. Most leather takes special care and effort to sew. You may need a "leather" sewing machine with a tiny blade on the end. Wax the needle to help pierce the leather. Don't make stitches too close together since this may perforate the leather, causing it to tear.

Synthetic suede cloth has the best qualities of leather and it is easier to handle. During the manufacturing process, fibers are glued onto thin plastic sheeting. One brand of this elegant material is called Ultrasuede. It washes well and sews more easily than leather.

Neither leather nor "suede" is forgiving of mistakes. Make a needle or a pinhole and it's there to stay. The suede cloth has no "give" or stretch, so it's necessary to choose a pattern with the shape cut in. For details, see Teddy Bear Stuffing on page 17.

Suede cloths and Ultrasuede can be found in fabric stores. Look for quality leather in leather and fur stores, and for chamois in the hardware store.

## Denim and Calico

Flat fabrics like denim and calico, while easier to sew, make slender-looking teddys. For a plumper bear, add a little fullness to the side seams of the body, arms, and legs when cutting the pattern.

Denim is a tightly woven cotton fabric meant for hard wear. Its popularity has brought about new weights and surfaces. Some denim has polyester added for wash and wear. Another type has a brushed surface for a softer look and feel. Worn denim shows white fibers—a nice effect. Western Dressed Bear on page 76 has pants cut over a worn jeans seam. Flat Foot Bear (page 29) was cut from a different pair of old jeans.

The current popularity of quilting has brought a wonderful assortment of printed calico to stores and quilt shows. Calico is a plain-weave printed cotton of light weight. Added polyester reduces wrinkles and gives strength. The tiny traditional prints in muted country colors suit small toys and quilts well. For a calico quilt see the Teddy Bear Quilt, page 137 and for a calico bear, Rand's Bear, page 66, or small bear, page 34.

Calico lies flat enough for appliqué work, but machine satin stitching may cause any lightweight fabric to stretch and wrinkle. To prevent this, use a removable paper backing or a permanent interfacing backing, or use a machine embroidery hoop. For more details on appliqué see the instructions for the Teddy Bear Quilt and the Headboard Bear (page 144).

## Felt

Like leather or synthetic suede, felt is non-woven. It is made by compressing and adhering together wool, cotton, rayon, or other fibers. The best felt results from the natural felting characteristics of wool. This felt can be as hard as a man's hat or soft enough for a skirt. Most available felt, called craft felt, is made from rayon and cotton and is a thinner and less expensive material.

The best reason for using felt is its crisp, non-fraying cut edge. There is no need to turn the seams, as seen on the Decorated Bears (page 113), nor is there a need for any seams at all, the Felt Bears on page 128, for example.

Felt sews easily but does not have the strength of woven or knitted fibers. Use a good-quality felt for paws and feet. Craft felt is acceptable for simple projects. Felt can be found in fabric stores, craft stores, and some art supply stores.

## Knits

Single knitting produces the most flexible stretchy fabric of all. Notice how a stocking conforms readily to the shape of your foot. Teddy bears made from single-knit stockings need very few seams to achieve their shapes. The facial features stay in place on the Stocking Bear on page 62 by hidden hand stitching sewn into the stuffing. Joints are simply tied with thread or left unstuffed. Knit-and-purl stockings show a marked rib effect that you may wish to avoid.

Double-knit fabrics have crossed reinforcement threads. This results in a more stable knit that still maintains some of the stretch of knit.

## SEWING TOOLS AND SUPPLIES

Making teddy bears requires little more than the usual sewing equipment: a good pair of sharp scissors to cut fabric, a single edge razor blade for fur, a seam ripper to remove stitching, a dowel stick for stuffing, a tape to measure, a yard stick for straight lines, and needle-nose pliers to pull a reluctant needle through.

In addition, other hand tools are needed for certain projects: a staple gun, matt knife, coping or saber saw, hammer, screwdriver, drill and bits, and clamps. You'll need sandpaper, paint, and brushes for others. None require extraordinary strength, just care and practice in use.

Pins of several kinds are handy. To fold fabric for cutting or sewing, use 1-inch plastic head dressmaker pins. For heavier fabrics and fake furs, use regular pins or two 2½-inch pins. Use safety pins in layered fabrics to avoid losing pins, and for furs and leathers use spring clothespins to avoid pinholes.

Different types of hand sewing needles will be useful; these range from slim embroidery needles for sewing noses and hand sewing, to upholsterer's long or curved needles for closing seams on heavier fabrics. Keep an assortment of sewing machine needles on hand, suiting the needle to the thread and fabric. If you have difficulty stitching try these changes: use a new needle, a smaller needle, a "blade" edged leather needle, or a ball point needle (for synthetics). Wax the needle, or stitch through paper. Consult my book *The Sewing Machine Craft Book*, Van Nostrand Reinhold, for more specific advice.

Four kinds of thread are needed for good teddies. Use the standard cotton covered polyester for good strong seams. A thicker sewing machine embroidery thread is available for appliqué, but you can use double strands of regular sewing thread to accomplish a similar effect. To anchor button eyes, arms, and legs, use a tough nylon or polyester thread or button-hole twist. To embroider noses use six strand cotton embroidery floss or a more tightly twisted rayon or silk embroidery floss.

Useful adhesive products include Fray-No-More to stop fabric edges from fraying, Fabric Glue Stick to adhere appliqué patches, and Velcro snaps for ease of closing.

## TEDDY BEAR STUFFING

Stuffing a teddy bear presents a special problem. Two flat body pieces are expected to assume a nice, rounded shape when stuffed, and yet a similarly shaped football needs four seams to achieve the same roundness. How can flat change to round for a teddy bear head or body?

This requires two necessary factors: a fabric that can be molded to a curve and yet maintain its shape, and a firm stuffing. Some soft toys maintain their shape by the cut of the pattern. Early teddy bears grew round and smooth by having firmly packed stuffing. They were filled with shredded wood shavings, which resembled excelsior, a packing material. The softer bodies sometimes had a fluffy filler that came from kapok trees in Indonesia. Both shaved wood and kapok tended to deteriorate with time. Charlie Kass's 1904 bear has this problem, and I offered to restuff it. Charlie declined, thinking it might change its character.

Now most toys made at home are stuffed with polyester fiberfill because of its many good qualities, its availability, and its moderate cost. Fiberfill is a loose, short fiber that looks like bleached top-quality cotton fiber. This petroleum product has good loft and resists matting. It washes well and dries quickly since the fibers are nonabsorbent. Its light weight makes it ideal for toys.

Bonded polyester fiberfill, common for quilt batting, has coated fibers that adhere and do not shift. A quilt or toy may be lightly stuffed with this material.

Although fiberfill can be packed solidly, some bears may need an even firmer stuffing. Cotton fiber compacts more and is less resilient. Cotton stuffing is washable, but dries slowly due to its great absorbency. The popularity of fiberfill has cleared cotton off the shelves in many fabric stores, but it is still possible to find cotton quilt batting and cotton upholstery batting in thicker batts.

To fill teddy bears with fiber stuffing, carefully insert small, loose puffs, bit by bit, to fill the shape, as a sculptor would build a statue. Use tools—a dowel stick or your scissors tip (careful!)—if some spaces are too narrow for your fingers. For unwanted lumps, roll the pieces in your hands to redistribute the filler. If your bear doesn't look just right, take the stuffing out and start over. This provides a chance to reshape the bear by restitching seams if necessary. You can readjust the stuffing from the outside by using a yarn needle to poke into the stuffing and lever it into place.

Some teddy bear patterns do not require firm stuffing. Rand's Bear on page 66 has shape cut into the pattern and no disk joints, which require a firm base. This bear's legs flex at unstuffed joints, which remain open since cotton and fiberfill stay in place well. His neck, however, does need firm stuffing to remain erect.

Bonded batting stays in place even better, or

can be basted in place. This lightweight, non-shifting fiber is used in the head and the paws of Gare's Bear (page 38) and in the Teddy Bear Quilt (page 137). Do use caution in pressing since some bonding fuses under too much heat.

Some bears need a shifting filler. The remainder of Gare's Bear is filled loosely with shredded foam to achieve a floppy effect. Tiny bubbles are blown into a polyurethane mix to make foam rubber (this now no longer contains rubber, but has the same characteristics). Shredded foam comes from leftover bits of foam, which is torn into smaller pieces. If fully stuffed, shredded foam won't shift. Polyurethane foam lasts much longer than rubber foam, but any foam loses its elasticity and crumbles in time. Restuff with new material.

For perpetually shifting stuffing, use tiny pellets. The Bean Bag Bears are filled, not with dried beans, but with dried lentils of smaller size. They provide weight and movement in stuffing. A bean bag has a satisfying heft in your hand.

Many other stuffings can be used. I listed only those actually used in the bear projects. If you need an extraordinarily lightweight stuffing, say for a giant bear, use polystyrene pellets, the "peanuts" used for lightweight packing. Save your old nylon or other soft stockings for stuffing. You can also tuck leftover fake fur scraps into your bear along with the main stuffing. In addition to stuffing, add armatures if needed. The Dressed Bears (page 76) would stand more stiffly at attention with dowel sticks tucked inside the stuffing for added support, for example.

## HANDLING FUR AND PILE FABRICS

Since you will no doubt decide to make many of your bears in fur or pile, I thought it important to add a section about working with these fabrics.

Pile fabrics require special care in laying out the pattern and in cutting. Care begins with the pattern. Template patterns, with no seam allowances, are used for fabrics that shift, for heavy fabrics, and for patterns with many small pieces since the line traced around them on the fabric serves as a pinning and stitching guide to make the bear. Don't forget to leave enough space for seam allowance around each piece when you lay out the templates on the fabric.

Any pattern can be made into a template by cutting off the seam allowance. Conversely, templates can become patterns if you trace them on lightweight paper with seam allowances added. The main difference is that the template is for tracing around and the pattern is to be pinned on and cut around.

## Fur and Pile Fabric Preparation

Check the fabric before you buy it to see if there are any flaws. If you find flaws later, mark them on the back to avoid in cutting. If necessary, press the fabric on the back side to remove any folds or wrinkles, but avoid too much heat on synthetic fabrics. Press the pattern pieces flat if necessary.

Check to determine the direction of the nap. Most pile runs lengthwise with the grain of the fabric, but it can run across the fabric, or even change directions within one piece. Smooth your hand across the pile to test direction. "With the nap" is smooth and flat; "against the pile" stands up and appears darker in color. A few fabrics—some plushes and shaggy fake fur, for example—do not have a pronounced directional nap.

## Pattern Layout

Plan pattern placement carefully to conserve fabric, to make sure that all pieces follow directional arrows for the pile, and to cut enough pieces. Legs, arms, and ears usually take four of each. Remember to reverse duplicated pieces: arms, legs, body, and head sides. Make a pattern for every piece to help with pattern layout and to achieve a tight fit.

Trace around the templates with dark tailor's chalk on light fabric or with light tailor's chalk on dark fabric. Avoid using a marking pen—it may bleed.

If you use patterns, pin them in place with dressmaker's pins. Pin carefully, especially on thick pile, so the pattern pieces do not wrinkle or contract. Trace around the pattern pieces or make templates instead of pinning if this works better.

## Cutting Fur and Pile Fabrics

On fabrics such as corduroy, terry cloth, synthetic suede, velvet, velveteen, and plushes with a short pile, use large dressmaker's scissors and cut with long, smooth strokes. Medium length pile, such as real or fake fur, may require that the fabric be cut with small sewing scissors or as furriers do—using a razor blade. To cut fur, use a new single-edge razor blade and cut from the back. Follow the markings and slash carefully

through the leather backing. Do not apply so much pressure that you cut the pile fibers. Pull the edges of the cut apart, finishing any incomplete cuts. Also use this technique on long-pile fake fur fabrics for best results.

When using long-pile fabric, lift it slightly with your hand and use short sharp scissors to slide the blade under the pile as closely to the woven backing as possible. Cut the backing without clipping the pile. There are two good reasons for not cutting the pile: cut pile makes an indented seam that shows on the finished bear, and loose fur or pile fiber can irritate your nose and skin while you are working.

## Sewing Fur and Pile Fabrics

Machine stitching pile fabrics presents two problems not common to other fabrics: the piles placed face to face slide on each other, and they may stick in the seam.

Several techniques help to diminish sliding on pile. Try one or more to create a smooth seam. Surest, but most time consuming, is hand basting the seam first. To save time, pin baste by placing pins at right angles to the stitch line so you can stitch or hand wheel over them. For very slippery pile, machine baste with the longest possible stitch. This can be removed easily for adjustment, or can be overstitched to complete the seam. On thick fur, fake fur fabric, or materials that show pin marks, use clip clothes pins to hold the pieces together. Remove the clothes pins as you come to them.

Sewing pile fabrics requires your active participation in guiding the fabric. Use your fingers to get an even movement under the pressure foot. Friction of the presser foot on the top fabric may retard the foot and cause pulling. Push the top fabric along evenly with the bottom as you sew. Reduce the pressure from the pressure foot if possible, use an embroidery foot, or follow your sewing machine manual. Roller foot attachments were designed to prevent pulling on the top fabric, but they work better on long, straight seams than on short, curved teddy bear seams.

For leather, suede, back-coated fabrics, and flimsy fabrics that stick or slide on the feed dogs or throat plate, pin paper backing to the fabric for stability. If you are *really* having a hard time, sandwich the fabric between two pieces of tracing paper and stitch. The stitched line perforates the paper so it tears off easily.

## Seams

Teddy bears look best with unobstrusive seams. Yet when pile fabric sections are stitched, the pile flattens toward the edge, causing the ends to be stitched into the seam. This makes a wide, visible seam. To avoid this, brush the pile inward before you pin the seam and while you stitch. Keep poking the escaping pile inward by running a strong needle, or your finger, between the fabrics as you stitch. Don't rush this seam. You don't want to sew your finger!

It's much easier to prevent pile from being sewn into a seam than to remove it later. To remove pile ends, run a handneedle point across the trapped pile ends several times. This pulls the ends out more evenly than picking fibers out with the needle point. Use a wire dog-grooming brush vigorously on the seam to raise the fur pile. This also removes loose pile and bits of foam stuffing stuck in the fur.

For the longest pile furs, use the above care in stitching the seam, but use a machine-basting stitch for the first seam. Brush out the entrapped pile ends, then restitch the seam with shorter stitching.

For longevity, use a very strong, durable thread for your teddy bear seams. Cotton-wrapped polyester-core sewing thread and tough multifilament nylon thread are both good for this.

Use short stitches properly balanced for a sturdy seam. (Thread pulls out on one side of an unbalanced seam.) Reinforce stitch lines by overstitching with a second row for added strength. Reinforce corners and stress points particularly.

For the smallest bears, a 1/8-inch seam allowance is fine. This diminishes the need to trim. For added strength, increase the width of the seam allowance as the bears grow larger. Wider seam allowances keep fabric fibers from pulling loose at the seams.

Trim or clip seam allowances, particularly on inside corners. This seam allowance doesn't stretch around the corner when the bear is turned, causing a wrinkle in the "skin." Trim firm fabrics, and clip ones that might pull out or fray. To clip, make a series of short cuts almost to the stitch line along the curves.

To hand stitch a teddy bear's seams closed after stuffing, use a sturdy, matching double thread and knot it firmly. Sew with concealed stitching or use a baseball lacing stitch to close the seams. Sew a knot every few inches to hold remaining stitches in case of a break in the thread.

## MAKING THE TEDDY BEARS' EYES, NOSES, AND MOUTHS

Early teddy bears had black shoe button eyes, or glass-coated stickpin eyes. Shoe buttons were small black orbs with a metal shank on the back for sewing onto the shoe. These eyes glittered realistically and replacements were easy to obtain as long as button shoes were in style.

Stickpin eyes had a black head dipped in amber-colored glass on a 2-inch or 3-inch pin. The long pins were pushed into the bear's excelsior stuffing. Most were removed by careful mothers or curious little fingers and soon lost.

By the 1930s movable celluloid eyes had arrived. These eyes contained a small black disk within the flat hollow eye. They were attached to the bear's head by wires, shanks, or glue. These eyes rolled playfully whenever the bear moved, but weren't as elegant as glass eyes.

Eventually child safety laws prevented the use of the pin-backed eyes. Today plastic eyes are good replacements. Plastic eyes come in a wide variety of sizes, colors, pupil shapes, and configurations. They are attached by force-fitting a star-holed washer onto a post molded on the back of the eye. Don't make a mistake when you push on this lock washer because you'll need tools to remove it. (If you can't find these eyes at a local craft store, consult the list of mail order suppliers at the back of the book.)

Home teddy bear makers have produced innovative eyes. Most search the button box to try various buttons for size. Black, rounded, shank-back buttons look like old shoe buttons but have a molded shank. Brass embossed buttons give the bear a starry-eyed, military look. Handmade ceramic buttons harmonize with country calico.

Eyes may be embroidered on by hand or sewing machine—which makes them entirely safe. Quick eyes made from felt, leather, or fabric can be glued in place. Almost any small round object might do for eyes: beads, washers, sequins, or whatever you can find to suit.

It's not the eye alone, but the placement in combination with the other features that gives the bear expression. The smallest shift in features can make a difference. Early bears had small eyes placed close together at the juncture between their muzzle and head. As time passed, bear makers altered teddy bears to look "cuter" and more childlike. They added larger eyes spaced further apart on a larger head. Some cartoon-like bears have small eyes placed very close together, giving the bear a mindless look.

Authentic old-time teddy bears had hand-embroidered noses sewn on the tip of the muzzle in black pearl cotton. The satin stitching formed a fan or half-circle shape. The nose thread continued down one short stitch and bisected a long stitch sewn across the muzzle for a mouth. Every little variation of this formula produced a slightly different expression.

Noses, like eyes, now come in molded plastic of various sizes with a shank post and star washer. The shank has a hole for sewing the nose in place since the washer may flatten the muzzle too much when pushed in place. But for an authentic-looking bear, don't use a plastic nose.

To embroider a teddy's nose and mouth, begin with a knot in the middle of the nose. Cover the knot with solid satin stitching sewn over the tip of the nose. Sew the mouth with two long stitches that intersect, ending under the nose with a hidden knot.

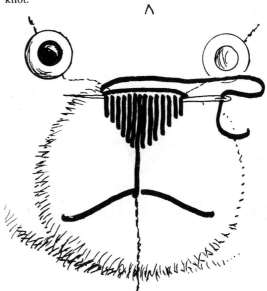

Sew fabric noses on the larger bears. Start with an oval twice as large as the nose. Stitch across the top, fold in the edges, then roll the nose under until it forms a padded nose shape. Sew the nose in place.

As you thumb through this book you will notice how many different eyes, noses, and mouths are shown. A variety of sizes, materials, colors, and placements results in a variety of expressions. Experiment by shifting features to see what looks best.

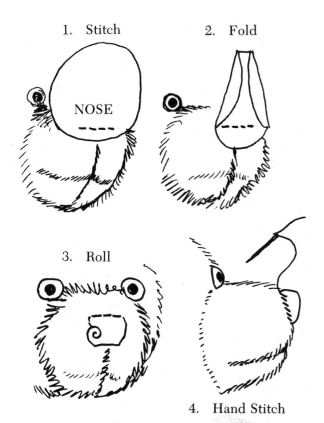

1. Stitch     2. Fold

NOSE

3. Roll

4. Hand Stitch

For a fabric nose, stitch a fabric circle on the tip of the nose for 1 inch. Fold the edges and roll under into a nose shape. Hand sew around the edges.

# Carolyn's Teddy Bear

Carolyn's Bear embodies the characteristics of the original teddy bear—articulated joints, embroidered nose and mouth, and a long-armed, bright-eyed look and shape.

Everybody loves teddy bears, especially old-time ones, with their understanding expressions and firm, cuddly bodies. This bear is "handmade" in the same painstaking way that the first teddy bears were. These early-1900s bears had movable joints so they could be dressed or assume various positions. As the popularity of the teddy bear grew, many companies began to manufacture them, each making changes to suit their particular idea of what a good bear looks like. Most eliminated the "hump" that appeared on the back of the earlier bears. Several shortened the arms to a more "human" length. Some made them fatter, some thinner.

In effect, Carolyn's Teddy Bear has the essential aspects of the early bears—"glass" eyes, an embroidered nose and mouth for a whimsical expression, articulated disk joints, small ears, long arms, long feet, and a ribbon—in addition to his distinctive shape.

Many of the original products for making these bears are not available now, but contemporary versions do exist and are specified in the instructions. Directions are given for making your own disk set with cotter pins, which you can find in hardware stores. (Also consult the list of mail order suppliers, at the back of the book.) Excelsior stuffing has been replaced with polyester fiberfill. Stickpin glass eyes have been replaced by similar plastic post-and-washer ones; these attach securely and are far safer than the sharp stickpin eyes.

This 18-inch bear is not hard to make if you follow the steps in order. Get help when twisting the ends of the cotter pin into place to hold the disks together if you aren't handy with pliers. The rest of the steps require only that you be accurate in cutting and stitching and careful in handsewing. The reward of producing this bear is well worth the effort!

## PATTERN PIECES

**A.** HEAD SIDE: cut 2, 1 reversed; fake fur
**B.** HEAD TOP (in 2 pieces): cut 1; fake fur
   *(see p. 24)*
**C.** OUTER ARM (entire piece): cut 2, 1 reversed (fake fur)
**D.** INNER ARM (minus paw): cut 2, 1 reversed (fake fur)
**E.** PAW: cut 2, 1 reversed (velveteen)
**F.** LEG: cut 4, 2 reversed (fake fur)
**G.** FOOT: cut 2 (velveteen)
   *(see p. 25)*
**H.** BODY: cut 2, 1 reversed (fake fur)
**I.** EAR: cut 4
   *(see p. 26)*

## MATERIALS

BEAR BODY:   24 by 30 inches of honey-colored fake fur fabric (usually comes in 60-inch widths; a 12-by-60-inch piece will do)

22

PAWS AND FEET:  6 by 8 inches of honey-colored velveteen
RIBBON:  24 inches of 1-inch-wide satin ribbon
EYES:  two 15-mm (5⁄8 inch) plastic post-and-washer eyes
THREAD:  black or dark brown embroidery floss, matching strong sewing thread, such as polyester-core cotton-wrapped
STUFFING:  1 pound of cotton and polyester upholstery stuffing, polyester fiberfill, or excelsior (ask an Oriental importer for shaved wooden strands used for packing)
JOINT DISKS:  eight 1½-inch disks, each ¼ inch thick; two 2-inch disks, each ¼ inch thick; five 2¼-inch cotter pins; ten 3-inch felt or leather padding disks; ten small washers to fit cotter pin heads.
SPECIAL TOOLS:  needle-nose pliers, possibly coping saw and drill

## TO MAKE THE BEAR

Lay all the pattern pieces so that the fur pile runs downward, which is how a bear's hair grows. (Follow the direction of the arrows on the pattern pieces.) Be sure to reverse the pattern for the opposite sides of the head, body, legs, arms, and paws. If you should miscut a piece, save it to use for smaller pattern pieces or a smaller bear. To cut fake fur, work from the back side, running the tip of the scissors under the pile. Make short clips to avoid cutting off the fur pile. Cut out all the pattern pieces.

## STEP 1: SEWING THE BEAR

*Note:* Use ¼-inch seam allowances.
**A.** Lay the EAR pieces face to face. Pin them, placing pins at right angles to the stitch line in case you plan to stitch over them. Tuck the fur pile inside with your fingers or a strong needle as you sew, so it doesn't catch in the seam. Stitch around the ears, leaving the bottom open. Trim the seam allowances to ⅛ inch. Turn the ears.
**B.** Pin the HEAD SIDE pieces face to face. Sew the CHIN seam. Open flat.
**C.** Pin the HEAD TOP to the HEAD SIDE section, aligning the center nose with the chin seam. Begin stitching at this center point to keep the piece even. Sew to the back of the head. Sew the other side, again beginning in the center. Leave the neck open. Trim the seam allowances.
**D.** Insert the plastic post-and-washer EYES. Old-

time bears wore their eyes close together, but they are a bit wider apart on today's bears.
**E.** Pin the BODY pieces face to face. Sew around the entire body, leaving a 4-inch opening in the center of the back for stuffing. Trim the seam allowances and turn.
**F.** Pin the PAW to the INNER ARM, face to face. Stitch across the joining, open flat.
**G.** Pin the INNER ARM and PAW section to the OUTER ARM, aligning the edges. Stitch around the edge, leaving a 1½-inch opening on the back of the shoulder. Trim the seam allowances and turn. Repeat steps F and G for the other ARM.
**H.** Pin the LEG sections together. Beginning at the heel, stitch up the leg back. Leave a 1½-inch opening at the back of the thigh. Continue to stitch the rest of the seam.
**I.** Position the FOOT in the foot hole on the leg bottom. Pin and stitch. Trim the leg seam allowances and clip the seam allowance at the ankle front so this seam will not pull when the piece is turned. Turn the piece. Repeat steps H and I for the other LEG.

## STEP 2: STUFFING THE BEAR

**A.** Begin with the HEAD. Push a wad of stuffing into the NOSE. Push small wads of stuffing into the HEAD, filling it firmly, bit by bit, to form the shape and keep the stuffing smooth. Fill the head as firmly as possible without distorting the fabric.
**B.** Thread a 2¼-inch cotter pin through a small washer, a 2-inch disk, and through a 3-inch pad. (The pad is always next to the fabric to diminish fabric wear on the disk corners.) Push the disk, pad, and pin into the neck opening, up against the stuffing, with the cotter pin ends protruding. Smooth the padding over the disk edges.
**C.** Hand stitch the opening closed around the cotter pin, pulling the fur fabric tightly over the disk. Be sure the fabric fits smoothly and lies flat over the disk. Trim off any extra fabric, if necessary.
**D.** Stuff the ARM, beginning with small wads in the PAWS. Fill the arm three-quarters full. Thread a cotter pin into a small washer, a 1½-inch disk, and through a 3-inch pad. Poke a small hole in the INNER ARM 1 inch down from the top as marked on the pattern.
**E.** Insert the disk, pad, and pin into the ARM slit, with the cotter pin ends protruding from the hole. Continue to stuff the arm to hold the disk in place until the arm is firm and full. Blind stitch the seam

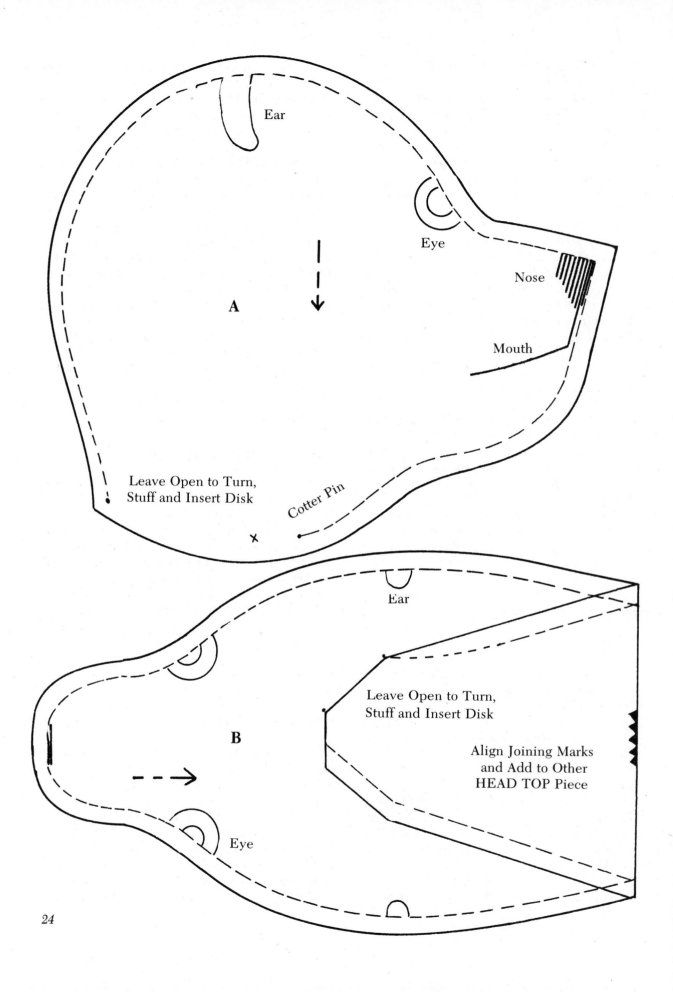

Ear

Eye

Nose

A

Mouth

Leave Open to Turn,
Stuff and Insert Disk

Cotter Pin

x

Ear

Leave Open to Turn,
Stuff and Insert Disk

Align Joining Marks
and Add to Other
HEAD TOP Piece

B

Eye

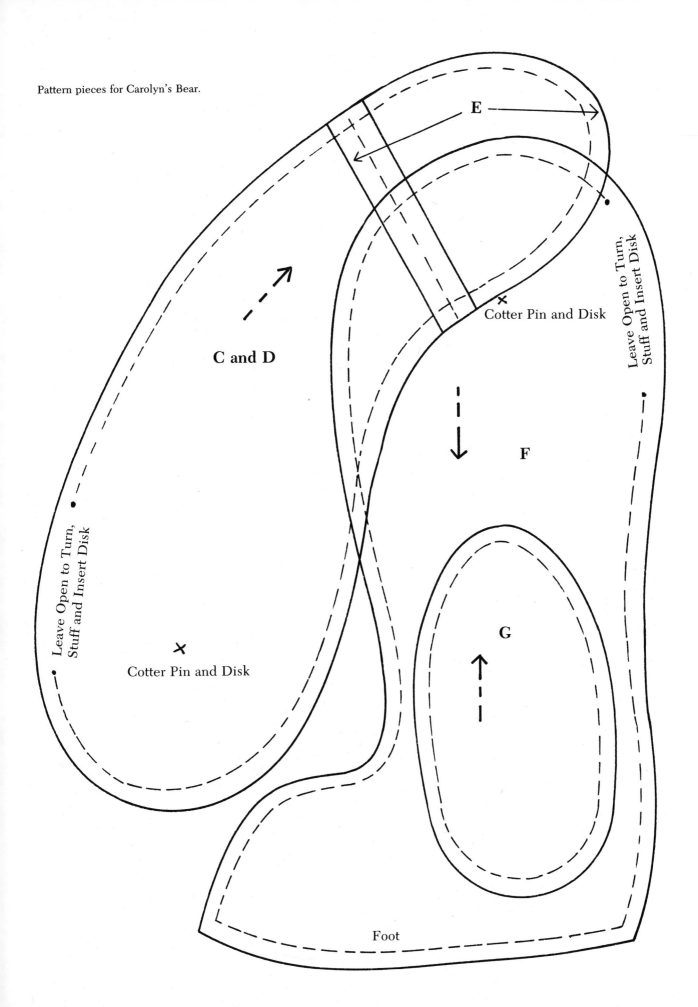

Pattern pieces for Carolyn's Bear.

C and D

Leave Open to Turn, Stuff and Insert Disk

×
Cotter Pin and Disk

E

Leave Open to Turn, Stuff and Insert Disk

×
Cotter Pin and Disk

F

G

Foot

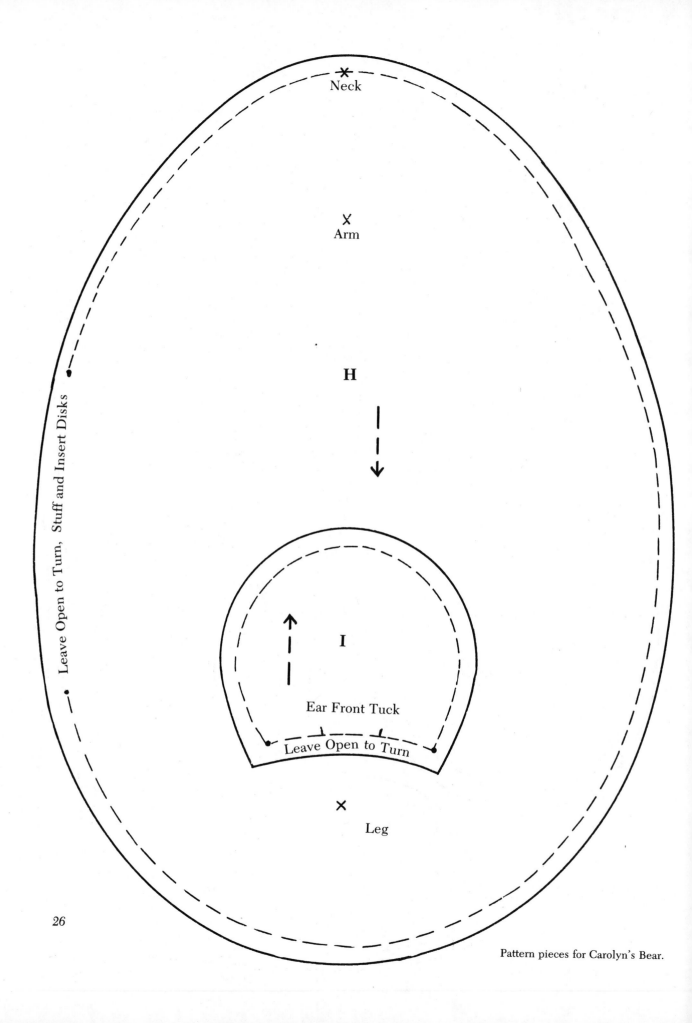

X
Neck

X
Arm

**H**

Leave Open to Turn, Stuff and Insert Disks

**I**

Ear Front Tuck

Leave Open to Turn

X

Leg

26

Pattern pieces for Carolyn's Bear.

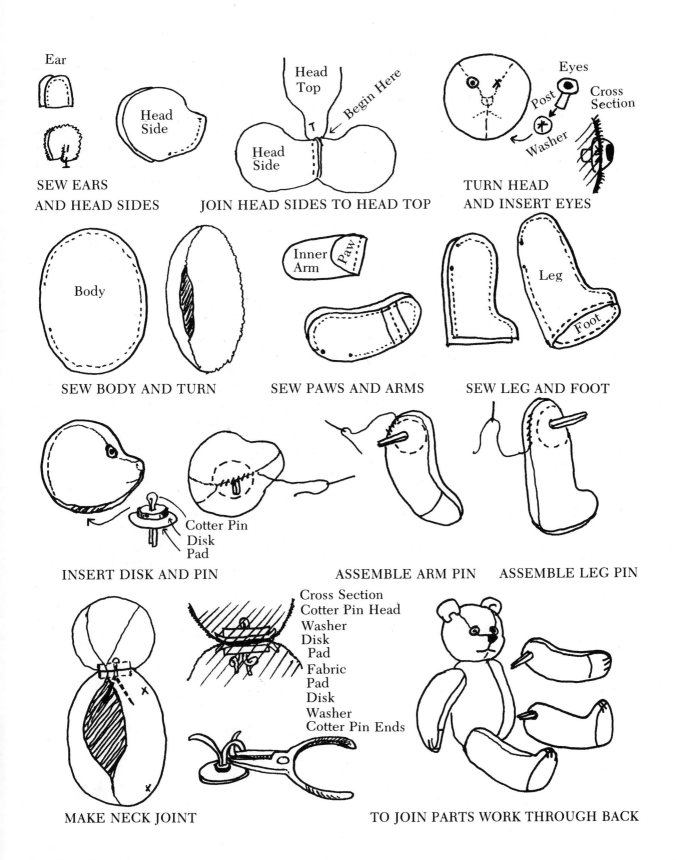

Ear

SEW EARS
AND HEAD SIDES

Head
Side

Head
Top

Head
Side

Begin Here

JOIN HEAD SIDES TO HEAD TOP

Eyes

Post

Cross
Section

Washer

TURN HEAD
AND INSERT EYES

Body

SEW BODY AND TURN

Inner
Arm

Paw

SEW PAWS AND ARMS

Leg

Foot

SEW LEG AND FOOT

Cotter Pin
Disk
Pad

INSERT DISK AND PIN

ASSEMBLE ARM PIN

ASSEMBLE LEG PIN

Cross Section
Cotter Pin Head
Washer
Disk
 Pad
Fabric
Pad
Disk
Washer
Cotter Pin Ends

MAKE NECK JOINT

TO JOIN PARTS WORK THROUGH BACK

Assembling Carolyn's Bear.

27

closed. Repeat steps D and E for the other ARM.

**F.** Fill the LEG nearly full, making sure the toes are firmly stuffed. Thread the small washer, disk, and pad with a cotter pin. Make a hole 1¼ inches down from the top seam in the center of the inner leg piece. Push a 1½-inch disk, pad, and pin into the leg, threading the cotter pin ends out the fabric hole.

**G.** Sew the LEG seam closed with blind stitching. Sew a knot every few stitches so if one stitch lets go, the whole seam will not open. Repeat steps F and G for the other LEG.

## STEP 3: ASSEMBLING THE BEAR

**A.** Poke a hole in the center of the top of the BODY (NECK). Insert a pad-covered 2-inch disk through the opening in the back.

**B.** Push the HEAD cotter pin end through the fabric hole and thread it into the pad, disk and washer inside the body.

**C.** Using needle-nose pliers, reach inside the body to twist the long side of the HEAD cotter pin away from the other side and into a loop. Force the loop down on the disk to tighten the head against the body. Twist the other cotter pin end in the opposite direction, looping the end in the same manner so it tightens the two disks to each other very firmly.

*Note:* Be sure you have placed the HEAD accurately. Cotter pins are very difficult to remove and impossible to reuse. The pins loosen with use, so seat them tightly.

**D.** Make a hole at the shoulder, 1½ inches down from the neck disk edge, in the center of one side of the BODY.

**E.** Working through the back, insert a pad-covered 1½-inch disk to match the hole. Thread the ARM cotter pin through the body fabric hole, then through the pad, the disk, and small washer. Twist the cotter pin ends firmly into loops, as described

in step C. Repeat steps D and E for the other ARM.

**F.** Measure up 1½ inches from the bottom of the BODY, and poke a hole centered between the seams.

**G.** Insert the pad-covered 1½-inch disk through the back to cover the LEG hole. Thread the leg cotter pin ends through the body, pad, disk, and small washer. Twist the cotter pin ends very tightly into loops. Repeat steps F and G for the other LEG.

**H.** Stuff the BODY firmly, tucking wads in carefully around the disks to keep them in place. When the body is tightly stuffed, blind stitch the back seam, knotting every few stitches to hold firmly.

## STEP 4: FINISHING THE BEAR

**A.** TURN a ¼-inch hem into the EAR bottom. Sew the ear in place on the head side and top as marked, curving the ends slightly forward. Repeat for the other EAR.

**B.** For the NOSE and MOUTH, insert the needle threaded with black or dark brown embroidery thread ¼ inch down on the middle of the nose to conceal the knot end. Satin stitch the nose over the nose/chin seam downward, as shown in the diagram on page 21, making the stitches solid so no fabric shows through. Sew two long intersecting stitches for the mouth as shown in the same diagram, using a double thread so it will show well. Sew the expression carefully to achieve the look you want. Use sharp scissors to clip away fur that may cover the mouth and eyes. Clip carefully since it won't grow back!

**C.** With embroidery floss, sew three long claw stitches on each PAW and FOOT, going ½ inch into the velveteen and ½ inch into the fur.

**D.** Tie the ribbon in a bow knot on the finished bear's neck. Brush the seams with a dog-grooming brush to pull any fur out of the seams.

# Flat Foot Bear

The Flat Foot Bear, a homey version of the original teddy with button eyes and joints, can be made with stiff flat soles to stand well.

Carolyn's Bear is the most authentic old-time bear I was able to devise. This bear is the easy home version. His articulated joints move by a simpler mechanism—buttons and thread. His eyes are not the hard-to-find glass or plastic "real" eyes, but come straight out of the button box. His body may look as if all the fur has been "loved" off, but the fabric came from an old pair of blue jeans and there's some added calico trim. At 12 inches tall, this bear takes a small amount of fabric, little time to make, and is just the right size for a child to carry. (Be sure to sew the buttons on with unbreakable nylon or polyester thread if this is a gift for a child.)

## PATTERN PIECES

**A.** OUTER ARM (entire piece): cut 2, 1 reversed (denim)
**B.** INNER ARM (minus paw): cut 2, 1 reversed (denim)
**C.** PAW: cut 2, 1 reversed (calico)
**D.** STIFF SOLE: cut 2 (firm material)
**E.** FOOT: cut 2 (calico)
**F.** BODY: cut 2, 1 reversed (denim) *(see p. 30)*
**G.** HEAD SIDE: cut 2, 1 reversed (denim)
**H.** HEAD TOP: cut 1 (denim)
**I.** EAR: cut 2 (denim), cut 2 (calico)
**J.** LEG: cut 4, 2 reversed *(see p. 31)*

## MATERIALS

BODY:   12 by 24 inches of blue denim or one leg of used jeans fabric

PAWS, FEET, EARS:   4 by 9 inches of blue calico print fabric (but ear backs are denim)
RIBBON:   24 inches of trim ribbon
BUTTONS:   four 1-inch blue buttons with 2 holes; two ½-inch white or cream buttons, with 4 holes
THREAD:   black embroidery floss, blue polyester or nylon thread
STIFF SOLES:   4 by 6 inches of firm material, such as interfacing, cardboard, plastic, or Masonite
STUFFING:   less than 1 pound of polyester fiberfill

## TO MAKE THE BEAR

Cut out all pattern pieces. Cut out the FEET SOLES from the stiff material.

### STEP 1: SEWING THE BEAR

**A.** Place the calico EARS on the denim EARS, face to face. Pin and stitch with small stitches. Trim the seam allowances and turn.
**B.** Fold a tuck in the EAR FRONT and pin the ear to the front side of the EAR SLOT in the HEAD SIDE, raw edges aligned, leaving a ¼-inch seam allowance at the end of the head seam. Fold the back side of the ear slot to cover the ear end. Be sure the ear angles upward. Stitch this seam. Repeat for the other EAR.
**C.** Pin the HEAD SIDES face to face and stitch the chin seam.

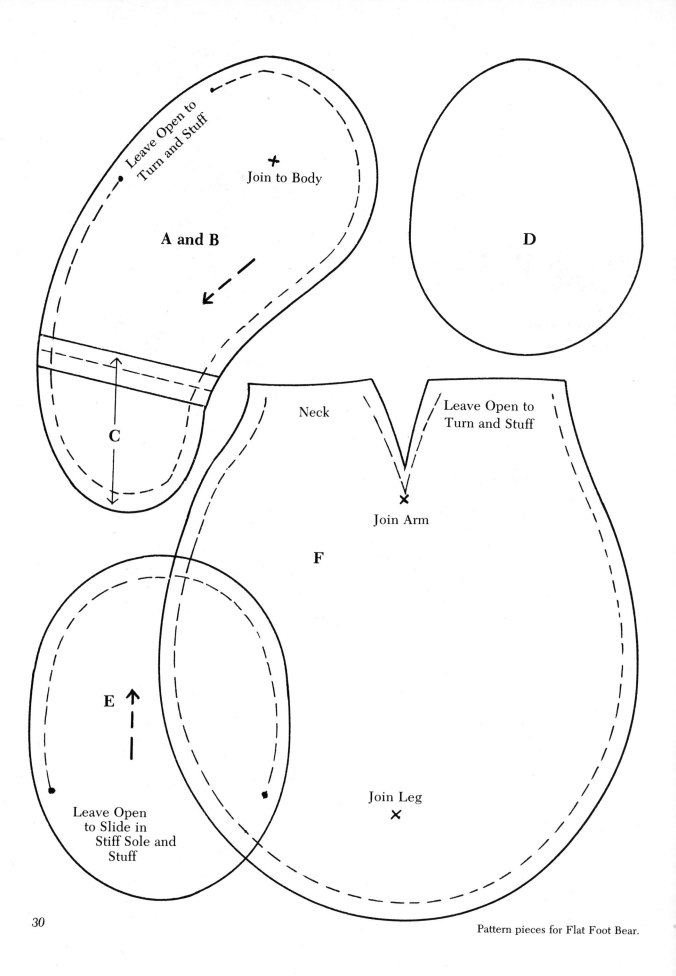

Leave Open to Turn and Stuff

Join to Body

**A and B**

**C**

**D**

Neck

Leave Open to Turn and Stuff

Join Arm

**F**

**E**

Leave Open to Slide in Stiff Sole and Stuff

Join Leg

Pattern pieces for Flat Foot Bear.

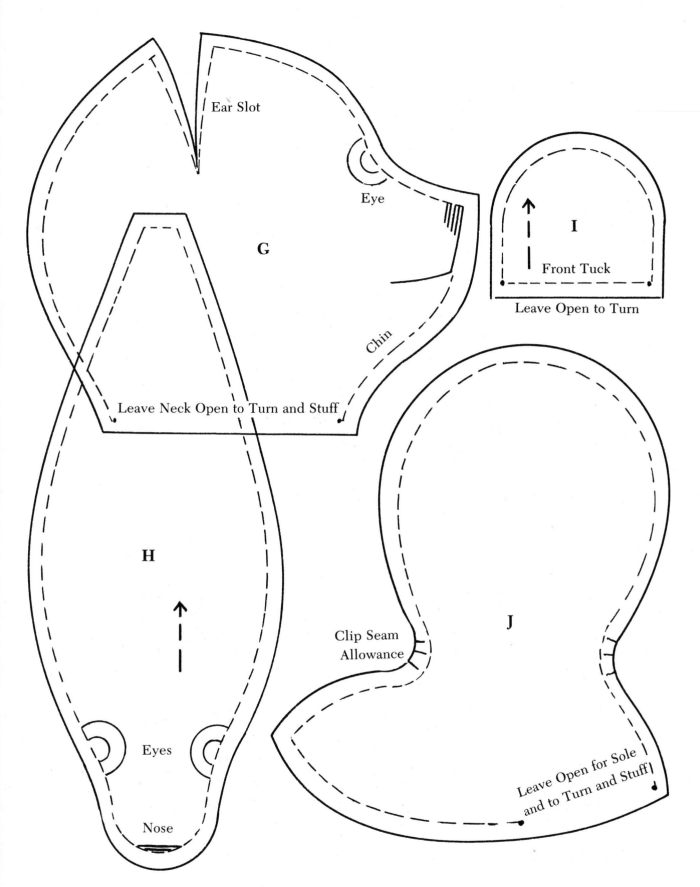

Ear Slot

Eye

**G**

**I**

Front Tuck

Leave Open to Turn

Chin

Leave Neck Open to Turn and Stuff

**H**

Clip Seam
Allowance

**J**

Eyes

Leave Open for Sole
and to Turn and Stuff

Nose

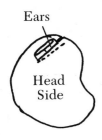

Ears

Head Side

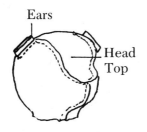

Ears

Head Top

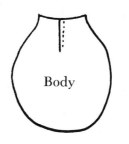

Body

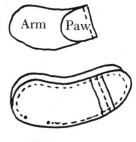

Arm  Paw

**ATTACH EARS**

**JOIN HEAD SIDES TO HEAD TOP, TURN**

**SEW BODY DART**

**SEW ARMS**

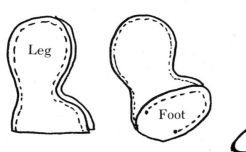

Leg

Foot

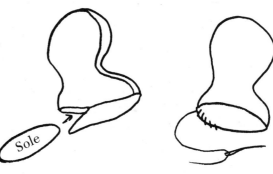

Sole

**SEW LEG AND FOOT**

**INSERT SOLE AND STITCH SHUT**

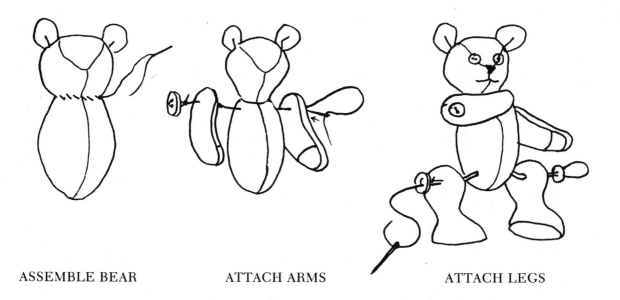

**ASSEMBLE BEAR**

**ATTACH ARMS**

**ATTACH LEGS**

Assembling Flat Foot Bear.

32

**D.** Pin the HEAD TOP to the HEAD SIDES section. Align the nose front to the chin seam. Stitch this seam very carefully to keep the head symmetrical. Turn.

**E.** Pin and stitch the darts in the BODY pieces. Pin the BODY pieces face to face. Seam from one side of the neck all the way around the BODY to the other, leaving the neck hole open. Turn.

**F.** Pin the PAW to the INNER ARM, face to face; stitch. Open flat. Repeat for the other ARM.

**G.** Pin the INNER ARM section to the OUTER ARM. Beginning 2 inches down on the back side, stitch around the arm, ending 1 inch down on the back side. This leaves a 1-inch opening to turn and stuff. Trim seam allowances and turn. Repeat for the other ARM.

**H.** Pin one LEG piece to the other, face to face. Stitch from the toe all the way around the leg to the heel, leaving the bottom open. Trim or clip the seam allowance at the ankle carefully so this seam will not pull when turned. Repeat for the other LEG.

**I.** Pin the FOOT section to the foot hole in the LEG. Beginning at one side, seam around the foot front to the other side, leaving a hole large enough to insert the STIFF SOLE. Turn. Repeat for other FOOT and LEG.

*Note:* If you do not plan to use stiff soles in the bear's feet so he can stand easily, leave the opening in the leg on the back leg seam and stitch the foot in place completely, as shown on Carolyn's Teddy Bear.


## STEP 2: STUFFING THE BEAR

**A.** Push small wads of stuffing into the BODY, fitting the stuffing to fill. The front and back seams will wrinkle unless the body is stuffed very fully and firmly. Poke the stuffing with a tool to adjust the placement.

**B.** Push a ball of stuffing into the NOSE. Continue to fill the HEAD as firmly as the body.

**C.** Poke small wads of stuffing into the ARMS. Stuff fully and firmly. Sew the arms seams closed with tiny hidden stitching.

**D.** Push small wads of stuffing into the LEGS. Stuff very firmly. Push the STIFF SOLE into the stuffed foot, aligning the edges with the foot seam. Add more stuffing, if necessary. Sew the heel seam closed with hidden stitching.


## STEP 3: ASSEMBLING THE BEAR

**A.** Pin the stuffed HEAD to the stuffed BODY. Add more stuffing, if necessary. Hand sew the head to the body using hidden stitching. Don't worry if a stitch shows since the ribbon will cover the neck seam.

**B.** Using a long sharp needle with unbreakable thread, insert the needle from the back into the joint button and back through the other hole in the button. Tie a firm knot in the thread to hold it tightly to the button.

**C.** Insert the needle in the top of the ARM, 1 inch down from the top seam in the center of the OUTER ARM. Push the needle through the top of the arm. The stuffing may be difficult to penetrate so wiggle and turn the needle to work it through. Push the needle through the BODY ¼ inch up from the end of the dart, emerging at the same place on the opposite side. Push the needle into the other ARM from the inside to the outside of the ARM. Thread through the second ARM button. Sew back through the other button. Pull the thread as tightly as needed. Sew two or three knotted stitches under the button to hold the thread end firmly. Clip the thread ends.

**D.** Repeat step B to attach a thread to a LEG button. Push the needle through the top of the leg, down 1 inch from the top seam in the center of the outside leg. Insert the needle in the BODY 1 inch or a little more from the body bottom, emerging at the same spot on the opposite side. Stick the needle into the inside of the other leg, through the leg. Thread on the other button. Sew back through to the first other leg button. Pull the thread tightly to adjust the legs so they move but stay in place. Sew several knots under the button.


## STEP 4: FINISHING THE BEAR

**A.** Using four-hole buttons, sew the bear's eye buttons in place, making an X crossing for the pupil. With embroidery floss, sew a triangular nose and a mouth to achieve the expression you want (see the diagram on page 21).

**B.** Tie the ribbon around the bear's neck and loop the ends in a bow. Trim off excess.

Small teddy bears no more than 4 inches tall can still have most of the special qualities of the larger, authentic bears.

# Small Bears

What is almost 6 inches tall, light as a sparrow, and very serious looking? Right! It's a tiny teddy bear with articulated joints just like the old-timers. Little kids will enjoy a small-scale toy like this because it fits the child's small world. Nostalgia buffs will enjoy it too as an unobtrusive way of retaining a bit of childhood.

## TIPS ON STITCHING

Small bears must be sewn very accurately to attain the intended shape. Set your sewing machine to very fine stitching, perhaps 20 stitches per inch. This will keep the seams from fraying when the seam allowances are trimmed very closely. Stitch over stress points twice if needed.

## PATTERN PIECES

**A.** BODY: cut 1
**B.** ARM: cut 2
**C.** LEG: cut 2
**D.** HEAD SIDE: cut 2, 1 reversed
**E.** HEAD TOP: cut 1
**F.** EAR: cut 4
(see p. 35)

## MATERIALS

BEAR:   6 by 12 inches of upholstery plush (not too heavy), velvet, fleecy knit, or whatever looks right and sews well
EYES:   two ¼-inch plastic post eyes with friction-fit washers

THREAD:   embroidery floss, cotton-wrapped polyester-core sewing thread
TRIM:   10 inches of ¼-inch ribbon
STUFFING:   small wad of fiberfill

## TO MAKE THE BEAR

Note that no seam allowances are shown on the patterns, so when you lay out the pattern pieces on the fabric, leave room to cut a ¼-inch seam allowance all around the pieces. Trace each pattern on heavy paper or cardboard and use it as a template to trace the pieces on the back of the fabric. Use a pencil or tailor's chalk rather than ink marker since the ink may bleed. When you pin the pieces together, match these drawn lines and stitch on them directly. Several pattern pieces are designed to fold so there are as few seams as possible. Cut ¼-inch seam allowance all around each piece. (Trim all seam allowances before turning.)

## STEP 1: SEWING THE BEAR

**A.** Place the EAR sections face to face, then pin and stitch around each ear, leaving the bottom open. Trim the seam allowances to ⅛ inch so the ear will not be too full. Turn the ear.
**B.** Lay the HEAD SIDE pieces face to face, pin and sew the chin seam.
**C.** Open the HEAD SIDE pieces flat. Beginning at the rounded nose end of the HEAD TOP piece, pin the center to the chin seam. Stitch from nose

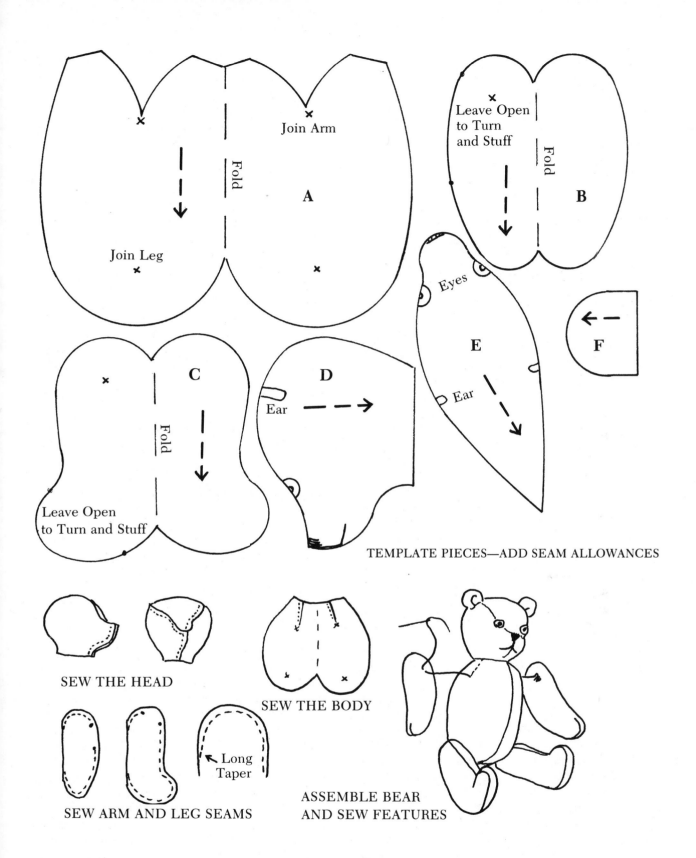

Join Arm

Fold

**A**

Join Leg

Leave Open
to Turn and Stuff

Fold

**B**

Eyes

**E**

Ear

**F**

Leave Open
to Turn and Stuff

Fold

**C**

**D**

Ear

Long
Taper

**TEMPLATE PIECES—ADD SEAM ALLOWANCES**

**SEW THE HEAD**

**SEW THE BODY**

**SEW ARM AND LEG SEAMS**

**ASSEMBLE BEAR
AND SEW FEATURES**

Pattern pieces and assembly drawings for Small Bears.

the Bear Facts

# More About the First Teddy Bear

Everybody loves a winner, so it's no surprise that more than one person claimed to be the inventor of the teddy bear. Nobody knows who made the first toy bear, but we do know who made the first one named "Teddy Bear."

In 1902 President Teddy Roosevelt went hunting in the South. His hunting companions caught a bedraggled adult bear, perhaps singed by a forest fire, and roped him to a tree for Roosevelt to shoot. Sportsman Roosevelt refused. Clifford Berryman, a political cartoonist, coupled this event with a current political incident concerning a border dispute between Mississippi and Louisiana. He portrayed Roosevelt refusing to "Draw . . . the line in Mississippi."

Berryman's first cartoon showing an angry, stubborn bear appeared in the *Washington Post* on November 16, 1902. A subsequent, more familiar, version of the cartoon appeared in the *Evening Star* with a more appealing shivering bear cub. The public loved Berryman's bears, which were reprinted literally millions of times and became the standard symbol of the Roosevelt Republicans.

It was probably the *Evening Star* cartoon that inspired Morris Michtom to create two small toy bears. Michtom, a Russian immigrant, had played with carved wooden toys in his childhood. He, like his countrymen, knew hundreds of folk tales about Russia's most famous bear, Mishka.

Michtom was always on the lookout for new ideas for his novelty and stationery store in Brooklyn. Both he and his wife, Rose, often made small playthings to sell. In the shop window, Michtom displayed the small bears he and Rose made using Berryman's cartoon as a model.

to nape. Then return to the nose and stitch the other side of the head. Trim the seam allowances and turn.

**D.** Insert the EYES at this point if you are using post eyes with washers. Poke a small hole with the tip of the scissors, then insert the eye. Push the washers on the post on the back side.

**E.** Fold the ARM and LEG sections face to face, and pin and stitch the seams, leaving a tiny opening for turning. The openings should be in the center of the seam so you can make carefully tapered seams at the folds. Don't taper these seams too bluntly or an unwanted bump will appear at the end of the seam.

**F.** To turn ARM and LEG pieces, trim the seam allowances and clip at the ankle front of the leg piece if necessary. To help turn these tiny pieces, use blunt scissors ends, a dowel stick, or some other narrow blunt stick. Stuff the pieces firmly and sew the opening closed with tiny concealed hand stitching.

**G.** Fold and stitch the two darts at the top of the BODY section. Fold the entire body face to face, and pin and stitch the body seam, leaving the neck open. Trim seam allowances. Turn and then stuff firmly.

## STEP 2: ASSEMBLING THE BEAR

**A.** Pin the HEAD onto the BODY with the front seams aligned. Be sure both pieces are stuffed firmly enough. Hand sew with a sturdy thread. Tuck a seam in on each piece and sew with concealed stitching to join the head to the body.

**B.** Tuck a small hem in the bottom of each EAR. Fold the ear toward the front. Hand stitch the ear with concealed stitching to the top of the bear's head on the seam line. (It is possible to sew the ear into the head seam when you assemble the head (Step 1, C) but I never can get the ears on evenly, so I recommend hand sewing later.)

**C.** Embroider the nose and mouth with embroidery floss or four strands of sewing thread (see the diagram on page 21). Also embroider claws on the paws and feet if you wish.

**D.** Place the ARMS on the ends of the BODY top darts, with the seams of the arms facing backward. Use a very sturdy double thread to sew into the top of the arm on the inside. Make several stitches as if you were sewing on a button. Sew as deeply as you can to catch some stuffing in your stitches. Then push the needle through the body to join the arm and pull through very tightly. Sew the other ARM with several stitches, as with the first arm. Sew a knot in the thread to finish. Attach the LEGS in the same manner. Tie the ribbon around the bear's neck in a bow.

*Note:* Some bears have arms and legs joined with buttons or beads. To do this, follow and adapt the directions in Step 3, C and D, of the Flat Foot Bear. Another way to make articulated joints is to sew snaps to the bear's arms and legs, then sew the other half of the snap set to the body. Pull the stitch threads tightly to seat the snap firmly so it will hold well and be barely visible.

The first toy bear named "Teddy Bear," created by Morris Michtom, was based on Berryman's cartoon of President Theodore "Teddy" Roosevelt in 1902–3.

They did not have long to wait for public reaction. Five minutes later, a customer walked in to buy one of the bears. Orders for 12 bears came in that historic first day.

Overwhelmed by success, Michtom decided he should ask President Roosevelt's permission to name the bears after him. Michtom made a special bear and mailed it off to Washington. Roosevelt's famous reply arrived quickly. "Dear Mr. Michtom, I don't think my name is likely to be worth much in the toy bear business, but you are welcome to use it."

Before the end of the next year, Michtom established the Ideal Toy and Novelty Company (now Ideal Toy) and manufactured teddy bears by the hundreds. Michtom's son, later head of the company, maintained that nearly all bears produced in the United States between 1903 and 1906 came from Ideal, but since they couldn't patent the name at the time, many companies soon turned out teddy bears.

At the same time, the teddy bear was "invented" by Margarete Steiff and her nephew in Germany. Crippled by polio as a child, Margarete earned her living by making stuffed toys. Her little felt elephants delighted neighborhood children so much that she created other animals—a donkey, a pig, a horse, and a camel.

Descendants of Margarete Steiff describe her invention of the teddy bear as follows. By 1897, her business had grown to include several family members, among them her nephew Richard Steiff. As a student artist, he spent hours observing and sketching bears at the zoo. In 1902 he designed a fluffy mohair bear with movable head and limbs. Margarete doubted the plump bear made from expensive fabric would sell. It did not—until the following year at the Leipzig Toy Fair. An American buyer delighted with the cuddly bear ordered 3000!

Both the Steiff Company and the Ideal Toy Company began to sell hundreds of teddy bears, then millions! Innumerable bear objects followed: coloring and story books, postcards, paper dolls, clothing for bears, mechanical bears, bear decorations on dishes, and more. This fad passed, but teddy bears didn't fade away. Today, millions of teddy bears are sold each year.

# Gare's Bear

Gare's Bear may be enormous, but its lightweight stuffing makes it easy to move.

What does a real bear look like? The best place to see a real live bear is a public zoo or national park. Nearly all the bears in storybooks, TV cartoons, and toy stores are, of course, stylized versions of bears. The teddy bear itself is a combination bear-person. The realistic bear in this project uses the begging zoo bear as a model. The big bear in this project has fur resembling that of a grizzly or Kodiak—mixed-color fibers. He's the perfect size for use as a bolster. Just nestle your head on the furry body like my son Gare does (he's the owner and keeper of this bear). Although large in size, the shredded foam stuffing makes this bear light enough to carry around. The good-quality synthetic fur makes a sturdy, enduring animal. With its uncomplicated pattern, this bear is not at all difficult to make.

## PATTERN PIECES

**A.** BODY FRONT: cut 1, folded (tan fake fur)
**B.** FOOT: cut 2 (tan velveteen for trapunto feet, or fake fur for plain)
**C.** FOOT LINING: cut 2 (cotton broad cloth)
**D.** MUZZLE: cut 1, folded (tan)

**E.** HEAD TOP: cut 1 (brown)
**F.** PAW: cut 2 (tan velveteen or fake fur)
**G.** PAW LINING: cut 2 (cotton broad cloth)
**H.** OUTER ARM (entire piece): cut 2, 1 reversed (brown)
**I.** INNER ARM: cut 2, 1 reversed (brown)
**J.** BODY SIDE: cut 2, 1 reversed (brown)
**K.** EAR: cut 2 (brown), cut 2 (tan)
**L.** HEAD SIDE: cut 2, 1 reversed (brown)
**M.** EYELINER: cut 2 (black fabric)
**N.** INNER LEG: cut 2, 1 reversed (brown)
**O.** NOSE: cut 1 (black fabric)
**P.** TAIL: cut 2 (brown)
(see p. 39)

## MATERIALS

BODY: two yards of 60-inch-wide brown/gray fake fur with a 1-inch pile. (The salt-and-pepper brown and tan furs shown are currently available in fabric stores. However, styles change, so use what you can find.)
FRONT, MUZZLE, and EARS: 24 by 36 inches of tan fake fur with 1-inch pile
PAWS and FEET: 18 by 24 inches of tan velveteen
PAWS and FEET LINING: 18 by 24 inches of cotton broadcloth

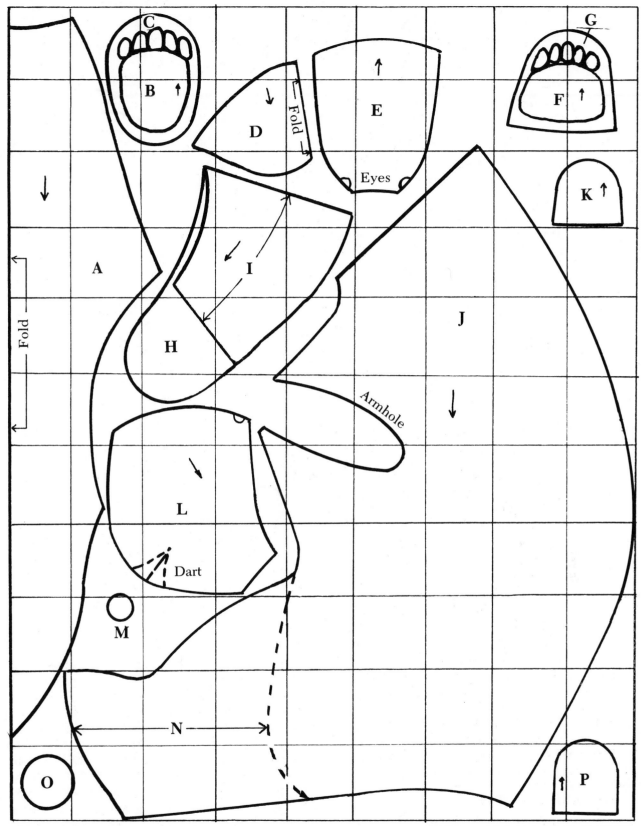

SCALE: EACH SQUARE = 4"

Pattern pieces for Gare's Bear.

⅝" SEAM ALLOWANCE INCLUDED

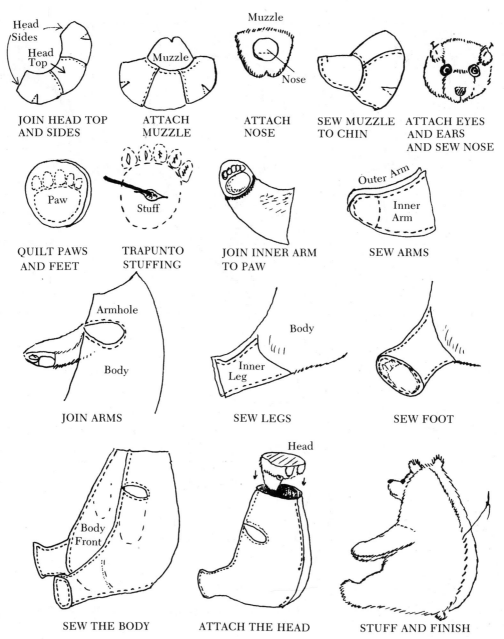

JOIN HEAD TOP AND SIDES    ATTACH MUZZLE    ATTACH NOSE    SEW MUZZLE TO CHIN    ATTACH EYES AND EARS AND SEW NOSE

QUILT PAWS AND FEET    TRAPUNTO STUFFING    JOIN INNER ARM TO PAW    SEW ARMS

JOIN ARMS    SEW LEGS    SEW FOOT

SEW THE BODY    ATTACH THE HEAD    STUFF AND FINISH

Assembling Gare's Bear.

EYES: 1-inch plastic post-and-washer eyes

EYE LINER: two 1½-inch circles of black or dark brown nonfraying fabric, leather, suede, or felt

STUFFING: three to four 1-pound bags of shredded foam, one batt of bonded batting

THREADS: very strong dark brown sewing thread, black embroidery floss

## TO MAKE THE BEAR

Scale up the design to the size you want (see Scaling Up Teddy Bear Patterns). The dimensions given are for a 32-inch-high bear. Draw the pattern on large pieces of kraft paper, newsprint, or wrapping paper, or get short ends of paper rolls from a printer. Placing the pieces will be easier if you make two patterns of the "cut 2" pieces—especially the BODY, ARMS, and HEAD. It may be necessary to piece the BODY FRONT to make the fur run downward.

Lay the fake fur face down and pin the pattern pieces to the back side. Be sure the nap runs in the right direction for each piece. (Follow the arrows on the pattern.) Cut the fur by sliding the tip of the scissors next to the backing fabric at the base of the pile on the face side to avoid cutting the pile. Cut out all pieces. Save the scraps for other projects or stuffing.

## STEP 1: SEWING THE BEAR'S HEAD

*Note:* Use a ¼ to ½ inch seam allowance. Use a long machine stitch so you can pull the fur pile from the seams more easily. Reinforce with a second row of stitching.

**A.** Place the tan EARS on the brown ones, face to face. Pin and stitch. Be sure to tuck the fur out of the seams with your fingers or a needle as you stitch. Trim the seam allowances, if necessary, and turn.

**B.** Pin and stitch the dart in the HEAD SIDE pieces. Trim the dart to reduce bulk in the seam. Pin one HEAD SIDE to the HEAD TOP piece, face to face. Stitch. Repeat for the other side.

**C.** Pin the MUZZLE to the HEAD section, face to face. Ease, if necessary. Stitch and trim.

**D.** Place the NOSE tab face to face on the MUZZLE at right angles to the nose seam end and ¾ inch up (see step 1 in diagram on page 21 for making a fabric nose). Stitch for 2 inches. This leaves a loose flap to be formed into a nose later.

**E.** Fold the HEAD section in half, face to face, aligning edges. Sew the MUZZLE and CHIN seam.

**F.** Insert the plastic post-and-washer EYES at this point. If you find it hard to place the eyes on a floppy head, push a bag of stuffing into the head and a wad in the nose to give the head shape. Position the EYES on the HEAD SIDE pieces next to the HEAD TOP and MUZZLE seam joining. Punch a small eye hole in the head fabric with the tip of the scissors, carefully! Put the EYE post through the EYE LINER, then through the fur. (To change the eye placement if necessary, punch a new hole and insert the eye. Sew up the old hole from the back side.) When you are sure of the placement, force the washer on the eye post firmly.

**G.** Pin the EARS to the HEAD on the HEAD SIDE at the top seams with the light side forward. Machine baste in place.

## STEP 2: SEWING THE BEAR'S PAWS AND FEET

**A.** Trace the PAW and FOOT pattern details on the PAW and FOOT LININGS. Pin the PAW and FOOT LININGS to the back side of the velveteen PAWS and FEET, detail side up. Using a dark brown thread, machine-stitch through both layers, following the pattern detail lines. This "quilts" one layer to the other.

*(Optional)* For a quicker, easier bear, eliminate the trapunto step and make the paws and feet of fake fur, using the lighter color.

**B.** To trapunto-stuff the PAWS, cut short slits in the lining, within the pad and toe stitching. Push small wads of stuffing into the slits to fill out the toe and pad forms. Stuff very tightly. Sew the slits closed by hand.

**C.** Pin the INNER ARM to the PAW, right sides up. Machine appliqué the arm to the paw, shaping the fur to the pad.

*(Optional)* If you eliminated the trapunto step, pin the fur PAW to the INNER ARM and stitch.

**D.** Pin the OUTER ARM to the INNER ARM. Stitch and trim seam allowances. Turn right side out. Repeat for other ARM.

**E.** Insert the ARM into the armhole on the BODY. The front seam on the arm matches the body seam. The paw faces downward. Stitch in place. Repeat for other ARM.

**F.** Pin the INNER LEG to the BODY LEG. Match the corners at the feet. Stitch the upper and lower seams. Trim.

**G.** Fit the FOOT into the foot holes on the LEGS. Pin and stitch in place. Trapunto-stuff the pad and toes firmly. Trim the edges. Repeat for other FOOT.

## STEP 3: SEWING THE BEAR'S BODY

**A.** If the BODY FRONT is cut in two pieces so the fur runs downward, pin the BODY FRONT top to the BODY FRONT bottom, and stitch the joining seam. Pick fur out of the joining to make the joint invisible. Brush the seam with a dog brush.

**B.** Pin the BODY SIDES to the BODY FRONT. Match the neck corners, the angle at the top of the leg, and the back seam to the body front shape. Stitch. Repeat for the other side.

**C.** Sew the TAIL and pin in place at the bottom of the back seam.

**D.** Match the back of one BODY SIDE to the other, face to face. Pin. Stitch the back seam from the tail to the neck, leaving an opening 6 inches up from the tail for 12 inches to turn and stuff.

## STEP 4: JOINING THE BEAR'S HEAD

**A.** Pin the HEAD to the BODY. The head darts and the front body seams align. Ease the longer head seam under the chin to fit the body. The whole head seam is the most difficult. The fabric is unwieldy and the ear seams are very bulky. Trim the ear seams to take away any extra bulk.) Stitch the seam to join the head to the body. Don't be surprised if you break a sewing machine needle or two. Use a new sharp needle.

**B.** Stitch over the ear-joining seam two or three times. If this is too difficult by machine, do it by hand. The ears make such convenient "handles" to drag the bear around that they need reinforcement. Trim any seam allowances.

**C.** Turn the bear right side out.

## STEP 5: STUFFING THE BEAR

*Note:* Work in an easy-to-clean room; the shredded foam sticks to everything!

**A.** Use bonded batting for the head stuffing. This prevents the head stuffing from shifting downward. First push a ball of batting into the nose, then hold this in place with a larger ball of batting for the head. This should fill the head firmly to the neck seam. Using long hand stitches, sew the batting to the neck seam. (This is not absolutely necessary, but allows you to stuff the bear loosely so he flops naturally.)

**B.** Push rolls of batting into the paws and feet to the fullness you wish.

**C.** Turn the bear on his front. Open one of the shredded foam bags and pin the top edges to the fabric opening in the bear's back. Knead and shake the bag to transfer the shredded foam to the bear. Try to contain the foam as much as possible.

**D.** When you've shaken the first bag into the bear, stick your arm into the stuffing and push it into the leg, arm, and head corners to make room for the next bag. Attach the second bag and transfer the stuffing.

**E.** For the third bag, you will need to push the stuffing in by the handful. Stuff the bear to a pleasing fullness, but not too full, or he will look blown up like a balloon.When the bear is full, pin the back seam.

**F.** Brush the foam bits off the bear and out of his fur with a dog brush. (Sweep the foam with a hand broom into a wastebasket. Finish collecting the tiny bits with a vacuum cleaner.)

**G.** Use a sturdy long needle with strong double thread to sew the back seam. Tuck in the edges and blind stitch by hand to close.

## STEP 6: FINISHING THE BEAR

**A.** Fold the sides of the NOSE tab under, then roll the nose tab into shape. Hand stitch the nose in place, shaping it as you sew. See the diagram on page 21.

**B.** Using two double strands of black embroidery floss, insert the needle under the NOSE. Embroider down the middle of the nose and the mouth, going over the stitches to make a thick line.

**C.** If the bear looks too shaggy, use sharp scissors or hair trimmers to trim away the hair over the bear's eyes. He will look gentler immediately. Trim the hair over the nose, around the muzzle front, and along the mouth. Clip little by little to create the shape and look you want. Clip carefully since it can't grow back.

**D.** Sew embroidery floss claws, going over the ends of the toes from fur to pad.

Bean Bag Bears, stuffed not with beans but with dried lentils, feel heavy, soft, and almost alive in your hand. Toss the bears through cutout holes in a cardboard or wooden gameboard.

# Bean Bag Bears

The charm of Bean Bag Bears comes from their shifting stuffing. Different stuffings create different effects. Most of the bears in this book are stuffed with polyester fiberfill because it is lightweight, resilient, nonshifting, washable, inexpensive, and easy to obtain. In spite of all these wonderful qualities, it is not heavy and shifting like dried beans, peas, popcorn, rice, or lentils. These heavier stuffings allow for posing bears in various floppy positions, or tossing the bears in a game.

These velvet bears, designed as a series of circles, are filled with dried lentils, but could contain any dried grain or legume. In this small size, they would be easier to make in a tightly-woven cotton than in the velvet shown, but the velvet looks and feels so nice. The bears each measure 9 inches tall.

The game board shown has no rules in particular. Make up your own. For example, give 10 points for tossing your bear through the tree hole, 10 points for the cave, and 5 points off for going in the dog house.

## TEMPLATE PIECES

**A.** BODY BACK: cut 1, folded
**B.** BODY FRONT: cut 2, 1 reversed
**C.** EAR: cut 4
*(see p. 44)*

## MATERIALS

EACH BEAR: 10 by 16 inches of printed velvet or other fabric
STUFFING: about 12 ounces of lentils or other dried grain or legumes
EYES: buttons, embroidered eyes, or movable eyes
THREAD: embroidery floss for mouth
GAME BOARD: 20 by 24 inches matt board, cardboard, plywood, or Masonite
TOOLS: matt knife, or drill and sabre saw to cut holes
COLOR: felt tip markers, crayons, or paint for picture

## TO MAKE THE BEAR

Trace around templates adding ¼ inch seam allowances. Cut out the pattern pieces. Use the trace line as stitching line.

### STEP 1: MAKING THE BEAN BAG

**A.** Pin the EAR pieces together face to face and sew around the top. Leave the bottom open. Turn right side out. Fold a small tuck in the ear front and pin.
**B.** Pin the BODY FRONTS together and stitch the front seam. If you plan to machine embroider EYES, do it at this point.

43

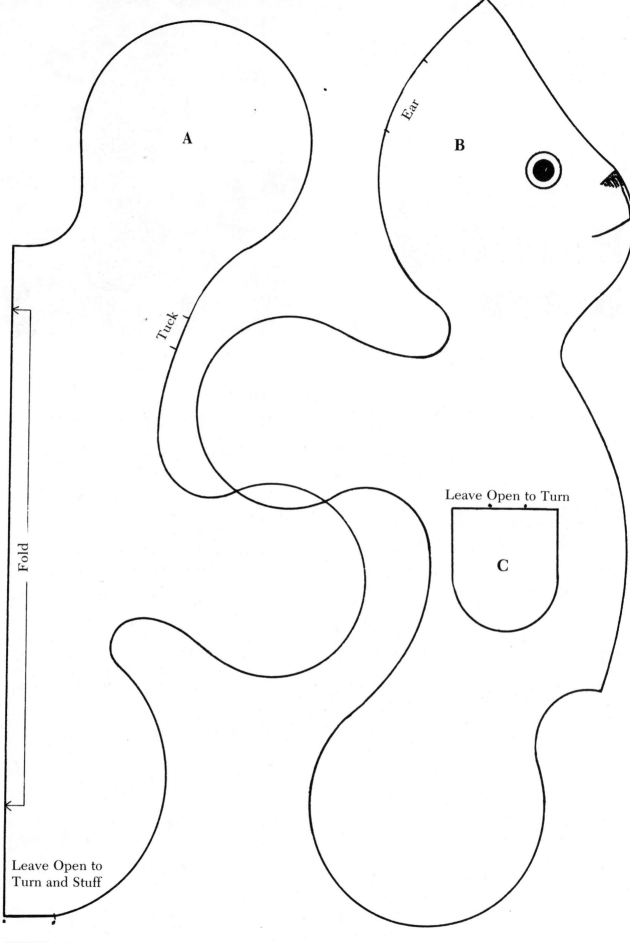

A

B

Ear

Tuck

Fold

Leave Open to Turn

C

Leave Open to
Turn and Stuff

TEMPLATES—ADD ¼″ SEAM ALLOWANCE

Pattern pieces for Bean Bag Bears.

**C.** Open the front. Pin the EARS in place on top of the HEAD. Stitch in place.

**D.** Fold a small tuck, as shown on the pattern, on both sides of the BODY BACK piece at the

top of the LEGS. This forms the bear's seat. Pin or baste in place.

**E.** Pin the BODY BACK and BODY FRONT together, matching the circle shapes. Stitch around the entire body, except for a 1½-inch opening on top of the HEAD for turning and stuffing. Clip the seam allowances on all inside corners so the seams will not pull when turned.

**F.** Turn the bear right side out. Open the top of a bag of lentils. Push the opening into the bear's hole. Carefully pour the bear almost full of lentils.

**G.** To finish, close the hole by tucking in a small hem and blind stitching or overcasting the seam shut. Sew on the bear's button eyes. Embroider the nose and mouth (see the diagram on page 21).

**STEP 2: MAKING THE GAME BOARD**

**A.** Cut a piece of heavy matt board, cardboard, plywood, or Masonite 20 by 24 inches. Scale up the drawing for the game (or design your own) and trace onto the board.

**B.** Cut out three holes 5 inches across, according to the plan. To cut holes in the boards, drill a series of holes within the circle. Insert the sabre saw blade. Cut out the hole. Sand it smooth.

**C.** Color or paint the design on the board. Or let the children who will play the game color it within black lines drawn from the pattern..

**D.** Have fun playing Bean Bag Bears.

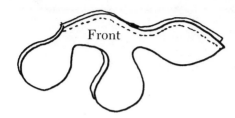

SEW FRONT SEAM

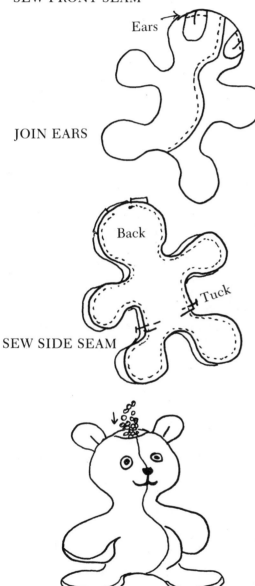

JOIN EARS

SEW SIDE SEAM

TURN AND STUFF

Assembling Bean Bag Bears.

GAME BOARD SCALE   ½ = 4″

# Bear Rug

Bear rugs sprawl invitingly, enjoyed here by a barely visible cat. This sheared opossum fur rug comes from a recycled fur coat.

The first version of this bear rug was made 25 years ago from my sister's old mouton coat. In those days, my son Rand draped the bear rug over himself then burst out from behind the sofa, hoping to scare his sister Claudia. This version uses my mother's fine old sheared opossum coat that protected her from Chicago's winter winds. Of course, a bear rug can be made from any fur or fake fur fabric available, but there's a nostalgic charm about recycling an old favorite.

Directions given for this project emphasize using an old fur coat, which limits the size and shape of the bear rug. Bypass these limitations if you have a larger piece of fabric or a long fur coat, and make the rug the size and shape you want. Quilted lining gives the rug added softness, and the stuffed head provides a pillow. The overall bear measures about 48 inches square.

## PATTERN PIECES

**A.** BODY: cut 1, folded (fur)
**B.** LINING: cut from completed bear rug top (quilted cotton)
**C.** MOUTH: cut 2 (red velveteen)
**D.** CHIN: cut 1 (fur)
**E.** TEETH: cut 4 (white leather)
**F.** MUZZLE: cut 1, folded (fur)
**G.** TAIL: cut 1 (fur)
**H.** EAR: cut 4 (fur)
(see p. 47)

## MATERIALS

BODY:  one old fur coat three-quarter to full length, or 1⅓ yards of 48- to 60-inch-wide fake fur fabric
LINING:  two yards of quilted cotton fabric
MOUTH:  8 by 8 inches of brown or red velveteen
TEETH:  10 by 12 inches of white leather, suede cloth, or similar fabric
EYE LINERS:  two 1½-inch circles of dark brown fake fur, leather, or felt
EYES:  1-inch plastic post-and-washer eyes
NOSE:  3 by 4 inches of black leather or wool fabric
STUFFING:  ½ pound of fiberfill or shredded foam
STUFFING BAG:  ½ yard of cheesecloth or similar fabric
TOOLS:  razor blade/seam ripper, chalk, spring clothes pins

### TO MAKE THE BEAR

Scale up the pattern for the bear on newsprint or wrapping paper. A ¼-inch seam allowance is included.

### STEP 1: PREPARING THE FUR COAT

**A.** Use a seam ripper or a single-edge razor blade to cut the lining stitching. If the lining is in very

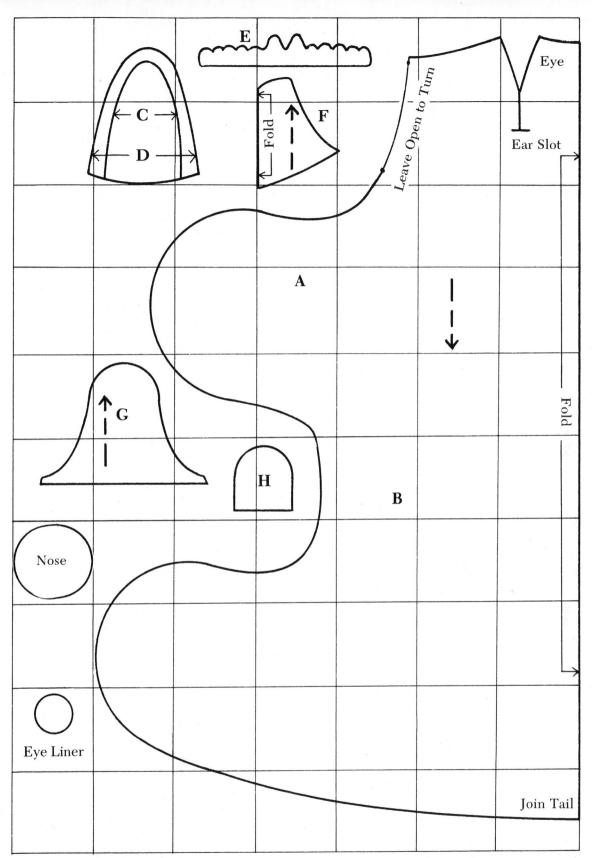

E

C

D

Fold    F

Leave Open to Turn

Eye

Ear Slot

A

Fold

G

H

B

Nose

Eye Liner

Join Tail

SCALE: EACH SQUARE = 4″
¼″ SEAM ALLOWANCE IS INCLUDED

Pattern pieces for Bear Rug.

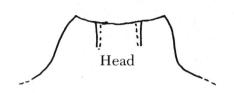
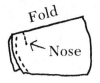

Head

Fold

Nose

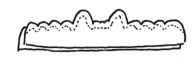

FOLD HEAD SEAMS AND SEW

SEW MUZZLE
TO NOSE

SEW TEETH

Mouth

Mouth

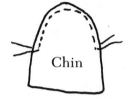

Chin

SEW TEETH TO MOUTH

EASE END OF CHIN

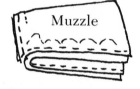

Muzzle

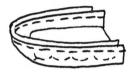

SEW TEETH TO MUZZLE AND CHIN

STUFF TEETH AND TOPSTITCH

JOIN MUZZLE
TO HEAD

SEW CHIN TO MUZZLE

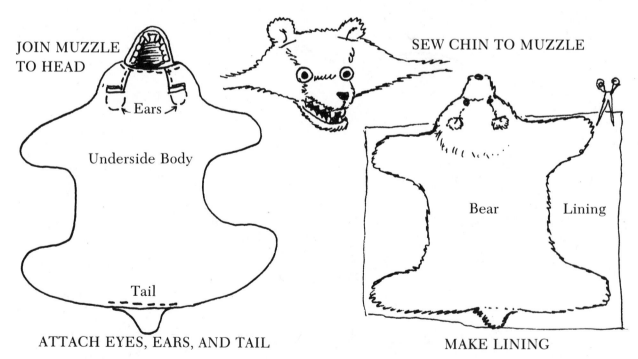

Ears

Underside Body

Tail

Bear

Lining

ATTACH EYES, EARS, AND TAIL

MAKE LINING

Assembling Bear Rug.

good shape, it can be used to line the bear rug. To reuse, remove it carefully. Remove the lining and any padding sewn into the coat.

**B.** Shake the coat over a wastebasket to loosen any debris that has sifted into the lining and edges.

**C.** Using a razor blade, make any cuts on the fur from the back or leather side to avoid cutting the hairs. Cut off the collar; cut the shoulder seam; and remove the sleeves. Set these aside.

**D.** The fan-shaped fur piece remaining will now lie fairly flat. Spread the fur on a flat working surface, face down, and fit the paper pattern onto it. Since every coat is a different size and shape, you will need to make adjustments to fit the pattern on it. If the pattern is too long, make a fold across the body. If the front paws fall over the slash pockets, add an inch to the length so you can seam up the pockets. When you have achieved the best fit possible, draw around the BODY pattern with chalk or tailor's chalk on the leather side.

**E.** Carefully slice along this line with a sharp, single-edge razor blade to cut out the rug. Fit the MUZZLE, CHIN, TAIL, and EARS patterns on the remaining coat front, making sure the fur runs in the right direction and markings match. Oddly, on the bear shown, the pile on the coat ran up. Since this was not a very pronounced nap nor long length of fur, I cut the rug as described.

**F.** Cut out the TEETH from the white fabric, and the MOUTH from the brown or red. Do not cut the lining yet.

## STEP 2: SEWING THE FUR

*Note:* Examine the leather backing of a fur coat and you will see tiny machine-sewn seams all over. Tiny pieces of the right color and length of fur are patchworked into the full-sized pelts for the coat. (It is this labor that adds to the cost of a well-made coat.) You can sew similar seams on your sewing machine.

The following suggestions will help in sewing fur:

1. If the needle sticks, wax it occasionally or use a leather needle with a blade-shaped point.
2. Back the leather with paper so it will not stick on the throat plate of the machine. Tear off the paper after stitching.
3. Ease the pressure on tne presser foot so it will not stick on the top side of the leather.

4. Leather is fragile and will tear unless handled with care. Don't sew stitches too close together since this may perforate the leather, causing it to tear.
5. Use your hands to guide the leather carefully through the sewing machine, assisting the forward movement as needed.

Few of these extra steps may be necessary since most leather backings are not very thick and not difficult to sew.

## STEP 3: MAKING THE BEAR

**A.** Place the EAR sections face to face and machine stitch the curved seams. Use spring clothes pins to clip pieces together since leather is hard to pin. Leave the bottom open to turn. Set the machine for a wide zigzag, medium-length stitch and "overcast" stitch the edges to make the seam. Stitch a tuck in the front of each EAR. Trim the tuck seam allowance and turn.

**B.** Fold the HEAD seams with edges aligned and stitch.

**C.** Fold the MUZZLE face to face and stitch the NOSE seam.

**D.** Place two TEETH sections face to face. Pin and stitch the entire row of teeth with a short-length straight stitch. Trim the seam allowances carefully, clipping to the seam line on inside corners so the turned piece does not wrinkle. Repeat for the other row of TEETH.

**E.** Align the INSIDE EDGE OF THE LOWER TEETH to the lower MOUTH piece. Pin in place and straight stitch. Be sure the molars are no longer than ¼ inch. Repeat for the INSIDE EDGE OF THE UPPER TEETH and the upper MOUTH piece.

**F.** Stitch a gathering thread in the front curve of the CHIN. Pull this thread so the chin fits the MOUTH. Sew the chin to the OUTSIDE EDGE OF THE LOWER TEETH.

**G.** Align the MUZZLE and OUTSIDE EDGE OF THE UPPER TEETH. Hold with clothes pins and straight stitch.

**H.** Turn the TEETH. Stuff the canines (front teeth) tightly using a stuffing tool (scissors tip or dowel rod). Lay a ½-inch roll of stuffing the length of the teeth inside the teeth. Using a straight stitch, hand sew through the TEETH at the gum line, running the needle under the stuffing to hold it in place and shape the teeth. Repeat for both sets of TEETH.

*I.* Fit the MUZZLE into the HEAD and zigzag stitch this seam.

*J.* To sew the CHIN to the MUZZLE pin and sew the upper MOUTH to the lower MOUTH at the back edge.

## STEP 4: MAKING THE EYES, NOSE, AND TAIL

*A.* Make a 1½-inch slit at right angles to the HEAD seams at the top end, for the EARS. Insert the ears into the slit and hand or machine sew them in place.

*B.* Trim the EYE LINERS to look right for the eyes. Cut a small hole in the center.

*C.* Slit a ¼-inch hole near the HEAD seams just above the muzzle seam, for the EYES. Insert the eye post through the eye liner and into the head. Force the washer securely on the post to hold the eye in place.

*D.* Hand sew the NOSE top seam to the top of the bear's nose. Fold the sides under and roll the nose under toward the seam. Sew this rolled nose in place. (See the diagram on page 21.)

*E.* Sew the TAIL to the bottom edge of the BEAR BODY, matching the fur markings.

## STEP 5: STUFFING THE BEAR

*A.* Roll a 3-inch wad of stuffing about 6 inches long and fit into the NOSE. This should fit loosely so the roof of the mouth does not bulge. The lower mouth has no stuffing except the teeth.

*B.* Roll the rest of the stuffing, or as needed, into a ball. Lay the ball on ½ yard of cheesecloth. Fold the cheesecloth edges over to form a bundle and hand baste closed. Hand stitch this stuffing bundle to the MUZZLE seam allowance inside the HEAD at a few points.

## STEP 6: LINING THE BEAR

*A.* Lay the bear on the lining, back to back (fur side up and lining face down). Smooth the bear as flat as possible. Cut out the lining around the bear, being sure not to cut off the fur from the edges. This bear will probably fit best sideways on the lining fabric, which eliminates piecing the legs.

*B.* Align the lining face to face with the fur bear, using spring clothespins to hold the pieces together. Stitch from the right shoulder around the paws to the left shoulder, using overcast zigzag stitching. Trim any necessary seam allowances and clip any necessary corners.

*C.* Turn the bear right side out. Spread the bear flat to see if he looks right. Make any adjustments at this point. Add stuffing to the head or muzzle as needed through the neck opening.

*D.* Align the raw edges of the lining at the neck with the bottom edge of the chin and the remaining shoulder seams. Turn a hem under on the lining and hand sew this seam closed.

# Riding Bear

The Riding Bear, popular in Victorian nurseries, delights contemporary children as well.

Another version of the bear appeared in nurseries around the turn of the century—the riding bear. A child could mount this realistic-looking animal and be pulled along. Like most nineteenth-century toys, these bears had firm to hard bodies for long wear and enduring shape.

The large bear shown here stands 22 inches high, including the base, and contains a sturdy framework that can support an adult. This framework can be made to be used as a wooden toy, with no covering except paint or varnish and a padded saddle. These directions appear also.

The bear's framework is covered by fur fabric with seams partly sewn on the machine. This covering stretches over padding fitted onto the wooden shape and is stapled and sewn in place. The axles and wheels carry out the antique theme and are not difficult to make with the proper hand tools. These wheels don't operate as well as swivel casters, however, since they can't turn corners.

## PATTERN PIECES

**A.**  WHEEL: cut 4 (plywood)
**B.**  BODY: cut 2 (plywood)
**C.**  BASE: cut 1 (9″ × 20″, plywood)
**D.**  TOP AND BOTTOM BRACES: cut 2 (2″ board)
**E.**  BRACES: cut 9 (2″ board)
**F.**  NOSE: cut 1 (plywood)
**G.**  NOSE SUPPORT: cut 4 (plywood)
**H.**  EAR (for all-wood bear): cut 2 (plywood)
**I.**  BACK LEG: cut 2, 1 reversed (fur)
**J.**  BODY: cut 2, 1 reversed (fur)
**K.**  FRONT LEG: cut 2, 1 reversed

For a simpler version of the Riding Bear, bypass the upholstery. Fill in openings, add ears and eyes, then paint or varnish to finish.

**L.** TAIL: cut 2 (fur)
**M.** EAR: cut 4 (fur)
**N.** NOSE: cut 1 (black fabric)
**O.** CHIN: cut 1 (fur)
**P.** MUZZLE: cut 1 (fur)
(see p. 53)

## MATERIALS

### Wood

BEAR AND BASE:  24-by-48-inch piece of ½-
to ¾-inch-thick plywood or particle board
AXLES:  two 12-inch sections of 1-inch wooden
dowel
PINS:  four 2-inch-long pieces of ¼-inch wooden
dowel
TOP AND BOTTOM BRACES:  two 3¾-inch
sections by 1-by-10-inch board or plywood
BRACES:  nine 3¾-inch sections of 1-by-2-inch
board or lumber (more for the all-wood version)
BEARING:  four 1-inch conduit clamps
PAINT:  undercoat, spray enamel; top coat, red-
orange
SCREWS:  four 2-inch wood screws, 8 ¾-inch
wood screws
NAILS:  box of 2-inch finishing nails (or screws)
WASHERS:  four 3-inch washers with 1-inch
hole in center

### Fabric

BODY:  1½ yards of woven black fur fabric
SADDLE:  23 by 20 inches of corduroy, velvet,
or similar fabric
SADDLE LINING:  16 by 20 inches of red lining
TRIM AND CINCH BELT:  36 inches of woven
1¼-inch wide ribbon, 60 inches of 1-inch-
wide printed tape (in three equal pieces)
NOSE:  2-inch circle of black wool, velveteen,
or felt
PADDING:  large bat of cotton-polyester uphol-
stry batting (or if this is not available, bonded
polyester batting)
AXEL PADS:  four 1-by-2-inch felt pads
THREADS:  matching cotton-wrapped polyester
sewing thread, black embroidery floss
SPECIAL TOOLS:  saw, staple gun, 1 package
of ½-inch staples, hammer, screwdriver,
yardstick and measure, drill and bits, paint
brush, sandpaper, pencil, large paper for pattern, snaps

## TO MAKE THE BEAR

Scale up the pattern pieces about 4 times larger
so the wooden bear measures 18 by 27. Cut out
all the wooden pieces, using a circular, table, or
rip saw for the straight cuts, and a sabre saw for
the shapes.

Cut out all fur pieces according to the scaled-
up pattern. Be sure to reverse the "cut 2" pattern
piece as indicated. Seam allowances of ½ inch
are included.

## STEP 1: MAKING THE WOODEN BEAR

**A.** Glue and nail the NOSE SUPPORT sections
onto the NOSE. Let the glue dry.
**B.** To mark positions for added pieces, lay one
BODY piece flat. Place the TOP BRACE upright
at the top of the body, aligned with the top edge.
Mark along the edges on the BODY. Lay the
NOSE SECTION on the BODY HEAD end.
Draw lines for placement. Position the BOTTOM
BRACE on the bear's BODY belly; mark. Remove
pieces.
**C.** To assemble, start nails within the marks on
the BODY: two for the TOP BRACE, two within
the NOSE, and two more within the BOTTOM
BRACE. Drive the nails through until they begin
to surface on the opposite side. (Use scrap wood
under the body section to avoid marking the floor
or other surface.)
**D.** Lay the second BODY piece flat. Set the TOP
and BOTTOM BRACES and NOSE sections on
the second BODY piece, aligned as on the first,
and mark. Spread glue on the tops of these
BRACES and NOSE. Position the first BODY
piece on top of the upright BRACES and NOSE.
Nail the first BODY piece to the BRACES and
NOSE.
**E.** Space 1-by-2-inch BRACES every few inches
along the top, back, and under the neck. Butter
the end of a BRACE with glue, place it on the
body, and nail in place on the top side. Repeat
for all the BRACES.
**F.** Turn the bear over. Spread glue on the ends
of all the BRACES. Position the second BODY
on the TOP and BOTTOM BRACE ends and
NOSE as marked. Nail the BODY in place.
**G.** (Optional) If you plan to make a wooden bear
with no fabric, add enough braces to fill the bear's
body solidly, shaping them to fit or filling the
cracks between them with Plastic Wood. Sand the

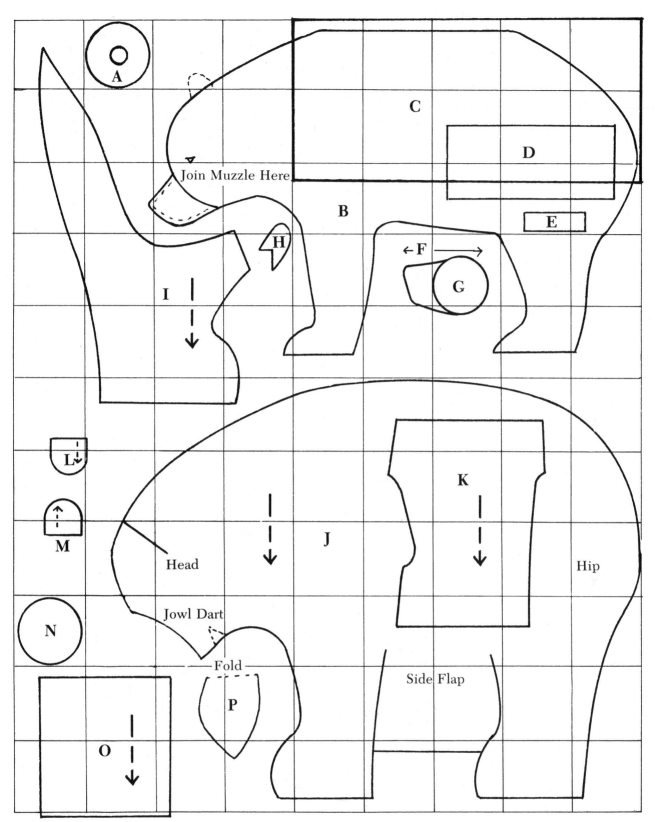

A

C

D

B

Join Muzzle Here

H

I

F

G

E

L

M

Head

J

K

Hip

N

Jowl Dart

Fold

P

O

Side Flap

SCALE: EACH SQUARE = 4″
½″ SEAM ALLOWANCE INCLUDED

Pattern pieces for Riding Bear.

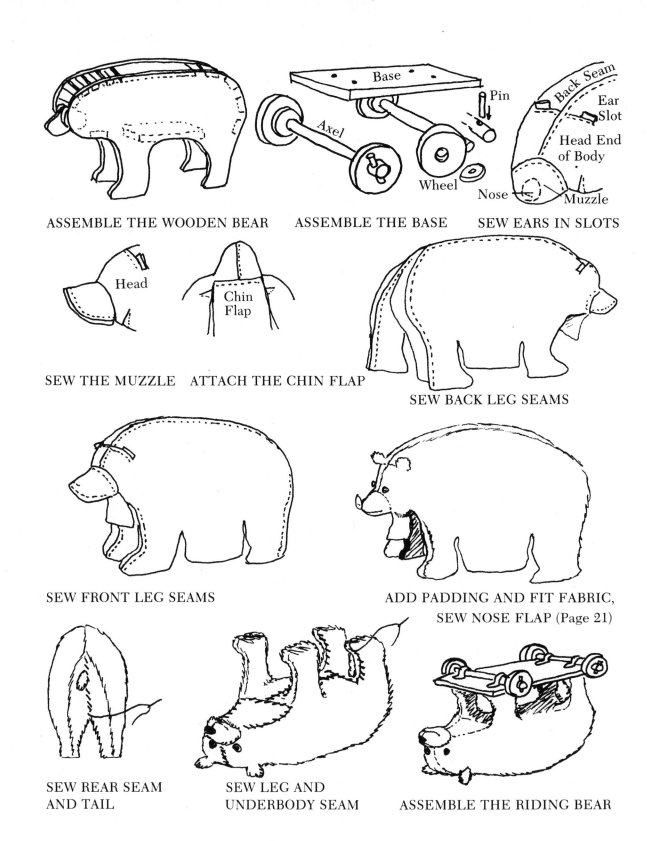

ASSEMBLE THE WOODEN BEAR     ASSEMBLE THE BASE     SEW EARS IN SLOTS

Base

Pin

Axel

Wheel

Back Seam

Ear Slot

Head End of Body

Nose     Muzzle

Head

Chin Flap

SEW THE MUZZLE     ATTACH THE CHIN FLAP

SEW BACK LEG SEAMS

SEW FRONT LEG SEAMS

ADD PADDING AND FIT FABRIC,
SEW NOSE FLAP (Page 21)

SEW REAR SEAM
AND TAIL

SEW LEG AND
UNDERBODY SEAM

ASSEMBLE THE RIDING BEAR

Assembling Riding Bear.

body smooth with a power sander (a drill attachment will do). Cut out wooden ears, then glue and nail them in place. Sand all edges smooth.

## STEP 2: MAKING THE BASE

**A.** Sand the edges and surface of the BASE well. Place the wooden bear on the base accurately and mark around the FEET. Drill one hole within each foot mark toward the heel end.

**B.** Lay the bear on its back. Align the foot marks with the FEET. Continue the drill holes into the FEET.

**C.** Drill a ¼-inch hole near each end of the 1-inch AXLE centered between ¼ and ½ inch from the end. Leave room for the wheels to clear the BASE.

**D.** Slide a washer on the AXLE. Pound the WHEEL on the AXLE just past the ¼-inch hole.

**E.** Sandpaper the end of the ¼-inch dowel enough so it will begin to enter the AXLE hole. Pound it into the hole so it extends evenly on each side. This holds the WHEEL on. Repeat steps C, D, and E for each AXLE and WHEEL. (Don't forget the washers!)

**F.** Paint one or more coats of undercoat or varnish on the BASE and WHEELS. Sand after each coat to achieve a smooth finish. Spray paint the top coat with several light coats rather than a heavy coat that might (will!) run.

## STEP 3: SEWING THE FABRIC BEAR

**A.** Stretch scrap fabric over any holes between braces to contain padding (except on the under-body, where this is not necessary). Staple in place.

**B.** Pin the EAR pieces face to face and stitch. Trim the seam allowances and turn. Place the TAIL pieces face to face, pin and stitch, leaving the end open. Trim and turn.

**C.** Pin the BODY pieces face to face from the MUZZLE to the TAIL; stitch the back seam. Fold, pin, and stitch the JOWL DARTS.

**D.** Slit the dart at the top of the HEAD and insert the EARS. Pin and stitch them in place. Reinforce this seam with double stitching to anchor the EARS firmly.

**E.** Position the MUZZLE at the HEAD end of the BODY. Pin and stitch in place, Fold the MUZZLE flat, face to face, and sew the nose seam. Top stitch the NOSE PIECE in place (see Step 1 in the diagram on page 21).

**F.** Match the MUZZLE bottom seam and the CHIN FLAP top edge. Pin and stitch. Pin the CHIN FLAP to one side of the NECK BODY and stitch.

**G.** Insert the EYES. Place them ¼ inch up from the MUZZLE (to the edge of the eye) and 1½ inches from the center HEAD seam.

**H.** Align the BACK LEG with the BACK LEG BODY, face to face. Pin and stitch from top to heel. Repeat for the other side.

**I.** Sew the FRONT LEG to the FRONT LEG BODY section, stitching the front seam only from the shoulder to the end of the toes. Repeat for other side.

**J.** Check to see that all seams are sewn securely with a very sturdy thread. Go over any seam that you think needs reinforcement. This is as much as can be sewn by machine; the rest of the seams are sewn by hand.

## STEP 4: PADDING THE BEAR

*Note:* Because of the sturdy framework, this bear is heavy. To work, place the bear on a low table, or on the floor; this will allow you to roll the bear over freely.

**A.** Using upholstery padding, lay a section over the bear's BACK covering down each body side. Pad the top enough for comfort. Be sure the bear's back is covered from TAIL to NOSE. Wrap the NOSE with padding. Staple the padding in place on the underside in a few places.

**B.** Fit the fur on the framework over the padding. Smooth the fur on the body from NOSE to TAIL so there are few wrinkles on the back seam. This seam runs down the exact middle of the bear's back. Staple the fur MUZZLE onto the wooden nose.

**C.** Staple/tack the FEET to the framework with one staple each, to be removed.

*Note:* "Staple/tack" means to drive the staple in only part way so it can be removed easily later.

**D.** Stuff extra padding under the body padding to "sculpt" the shape of bear you want. Stuff the HIPS fully. Staple/tack the bottom edge of the SIDE FLAP to the BOTTOM BODY BRACE. Repeat for the other side, but hand sew the under body seam, then remove visible staples.

**E.** Beginning at the top of the rear seam on the BACK LEGS, hand stitch the seam closed, tucking in the edges. Pull the fabric tightly to eliminate wrinkles. Blind stitch the seam. Insert the TAIL 2½ inches down this seam. Sew the tail firmly in place.

**F.** Pin the front edge of the BACK LEG to the front top edge of the BODY BACK LEG. Pin the two edges of the continuation of the rear seam together. Remove the front pins and stitch the continuation of the rear seam. Repeat for the other BACK LEG.

**G.** Turn the bear on his back. Re-pin the BACK LEG front edge to the front edge of the BODY BACK LEG. Stuff the rear firmly. Staple the end of the rear seam to the BOTTOM BRACE on the underbody.

**H.** Stuff the outside of the leg to the shape you want. Hand sew the front seam of the BACK LEG, turning the hem in and blind stitching it closed. Remove the foot staple. Stuff the foot to a wider shape. Staple the foot edges to the bottom of the foot framework. Trim away any extra fabric over the screw hole. Repeat for the other leg.

**I.** Stuff extra padding into the HEAD to create the head shape. Don't add too much stuffing. Hand stitch the CHIN FLAP to the side of the neck. Stitch the neck seam to the top of the leg, tucking in any needed padding. Staple the end of the CHIN FLAP to the BOTTOM BRACE.

**J.** Shape the NOSE and hand sew it in place over the staple, tucking in the raw edges. (See steps 2–4 in the diagram on page 21.)

**K.** Pin the back edge of the FRONT LEG to the BODY FRONT LEG. Hand sew the seam. Add padding to shape the leg and additional padding to make the foot. Staple the foot edges to the bottom of the foot framework, clipping extra fabric away from the screw hole. Repeat for the other FRONT LEG.

**L.** Sew the FRONT LEG pieces together on the bear's chest. Remove the side staple/tacks. Pull one side flap over the bear's BOTTOM BRACE and staple in place. Pull the other side flap over the edge of the first and hand stitch or staple in place.

**M.** Embroider the bear's mouth.

## STEP 5: MAKING THE SADDLE

**A.** To make the pieced SADDLE, cut ten 4-inch squares, two 4-by-16-inch strips, and one 7-by-16-inch strip. Cut the woven design ribbon in half.

**B.** Arrange the 10 squares into two units. In each square, run the wale of the corduroy at right an-

gles to the next piece, giving a checkerboard look. Make ½-inch seams so the finished squares will measure 3 inches. Sew the abutting seams of each square to form two strips of squares each 16 inches long.

**C.** Lay the pieced strips on the 4-by-16-inch strips, face to face. Pin and seam each pieced strip to a plain strip.

**D.** Pin one pieced strip to the 7-by-16-inch section, face to face. Stitch. Pin the other pieced section to the other side of the 7-by-16-inch section and stitch. The complete top should measure 16 by 20 inches, the same as the lining.

**E.** Lay the woven design ribbon ½ inch from the edge on the plain strip. Top stitch in place on the edge of the ribbon nearest the edge of the strip. Repeat on other side.

**F.** Lay the SADDLE LINING on the pieced top, face to face. Stitch a ½-inch seam all around on the corduroy side so you will be able to see the ribbon stitching. Sew ⅛ inch from the ribbon stitching. Leave a 4-inch opening to turn. Clip the seam allowances at the corners. Turn and press.

**G.** Cut the printed ribbon in half. Tuck the printed ribbon end under the woven ribbon. Top stitch the printed ribbon ½ inch from the edge of the saddle, running from one woven ribbon to the other. Top stitch both sides of the printed ribbon. This stitching helps to "quilt" the saddle flat. Top stitch the second seam of the woven ribbon. Repeat on other side.

**H.** Attach the cinch belt ribbon at one side with machine stitching and sew a set of snaps on the other side.

**I.** If you plan to pull the bear, screw a large screw eye in the front edge of the base and attach a strong cord.

## STEP 6: ASSEMBLING THE BEAR

**A.** Turn the bear upside down. Place the BASE on the feet, aligning the screw holes. Screw each foot to the base with the 2-inch screw.

**B.** Lay the AXLES in place near the ends of the BASE (for stability). Position the conduit clamps. Mark, remove the axles and drill the screw hole ½ inch into the wood.

**C.** Lay felt pads 1 inch wide and 3 inches long, with holes cut out for the screws, over the screw holes and under the clamps. Lay the AXLES on the pads between the screw holes. Reposition the clamps and screw in place using the ¾-inch screws.

Knit this soft bear in acrylic yarn for a wash-and-wear bear, or in novelty yarns for a more elegant teddy.

# Knitted Bear

If you can knit a simple mitten or a baby bootie, you can knit this bear. Even though the directions look lengthy, the bear takes only a short time to knit. (Refer to a basic knitting book for general instructions on knitting.) This bear is knitted in one piece continuously on four needles. If you want a solid-colored (sweaterless and hatless) bear, choose the color you like and skip the instructions for changing colors.

Use a fat yarn and knit tightly so the white stuffing does not show through. The bear's nose and mouth are embroidered and the eyes are glued on over embroidered circles. If you use a dark body color, choose eyes with enough contrast to show up well. Use washable yarns and stuffing and the bear will maintain his knitted-in shape, even though lightly stuffed, through many washings. Embroider the eyes if you plan to wash the bear or give it to a small child.

## MATERIALS

BODY:   2 ounces 4-ply brown yarn
SWEATER:   ½ ounce or less of off-white, red, orange, fuchsia, purple, and black
EYES:   glue or sew on movable eyes, or embroidered yarn eyes
NEEDLES:   four size 1 double-pointed needles or the size you need to make tight knitting, one blunt-end tapestry or yarn needle, one size 3 crochet hook, two stitch holders (or safety pin or string)

STUFFING:   about 8 ounces of polyester fiber-fill

## TO MAKE THE BEAR

*Note:* Instructions are marked by abbreviations for color (B = brown, W = off-white, O = orange, R = red, F = fuschia, PP = purple, Bl = black). The number at the end of the row tells you how many stitches in the row.

## STEP 1: KNITTING THE HEAD

Using B, cast on 32 sts, 10 B on each of two needles, and 12 B on the third. Join, being careful not to twist sts.

*ROWS 1 to 7:*   K B for 7 rows (the head is knitted solid brown). (32)
*ROW 8:*   K 7 B, add 1, K 2, add 1, K 23. (34)
*ROW 9:*   K 34.
*ROW 10:*   K 8, add 1, K 2, add 1, K 24. (36)
*ROW 11:*   K 36.
*ROW 12:*   K 9, add 1, K 2, add 1, K 25. (38)
*ROW 13:*   K 38.
*ROW 14:*   K 10, add 1, K 2, add 1, K 26. (40)
*ROW 15:*   K 40.
*ROW 16:*   K 9, K 2 tog, K 2, K 2 tog, K 25. (38)
*ROW 17:*   K 8, K 2 tog, K 2, K 2 tog, K 24. (36)
*ROW 18:*   K 7, K 2 tog, K 2, K 2 tog, K 23. (34)
*ROW 19:*   K 6, K 2 tog, K 2, K 2 tog, K 22. (32)
*ROWS 20 and 21:*   K 32.

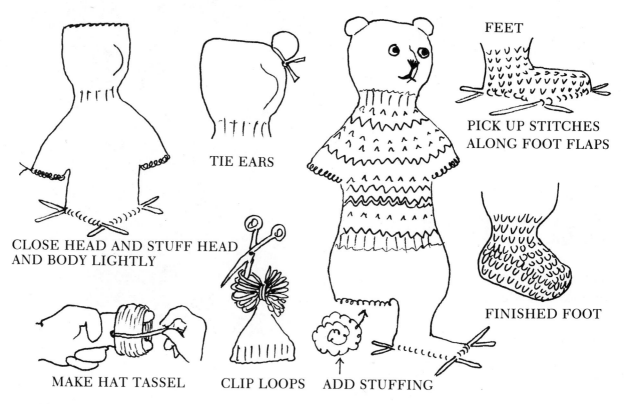

FEET

PICK UP STITCHES ALONG FOOT FLAPS

TIE EARS

CLOSE HEAD AND STUFF HEAD AND BODY LIGHTLY

FINISHED FOOT

MAKE HAT TASSEL    CLIP LOOPS    ADD STUFFING

Assembling Knitted Bear.

## STEP 2: KNITTING THE SWEATER AND BODY

*ROWS 1 to 3:*  Change to W yarn, K 1, P 1 for 3 rows to make ribbing (32 sts per row).

*ROW 4:*  (All W) K 1, add 1, K 14, add 1, K 2, add 1, K 14, add 1, K 1. (36)

*ROW 5:*  (Alternating R and W) K 1 W, add 1 W, K 1 R and 1 W for 16 sts, add 1 R, K 1 W, K 1 R, add 1 W, K 1 R and K 1 W for 16 sts, add 1 R, K 1 W. (40)

*ROW 6:*  K 40 W.

*ROW 7:*  K 40 R.

*ROW 8:*  (O and W) K 1 O and K 1 W for 40 sts.

*ROW 9:*  (All O) K 2, add 1, K 16, add 1, K 4, add 1, K 16, add 1, K 2. (44)

*ROW 10:*  K 44 F.

*ROW 11:*  (F and PP) K 1 F, K 1 PP, K 1 F, add 1 PP, K 1 F and K 1 PP for 16 sts, add 1 F, K 1 F and 1 PP for 6 sts, add 1 F, K 1 F and K 1 PP for 16 sts, add 1 F, K 1 PP, K 1 F, K 1 PP. (48)

*ROW 12:*  (PP and W) K 1 W, K 1 PP, K 1 W, K 1 PP, add 1 W, K 1 PP and K 1 W for 16 sts, add 1 PP, K 1 W and K 1 PP for 8 sts, add 1 W, K 1 PP and K 1 W for 16 sts, add 1 PP, K 1 W, K 1 PP, K 1 W, K 1 PP. (52)

*ROW 13:*  (All PP) K 5, add 1, K 16, add 1, K 10, add 1, K 16, add 1, K 5. (56)

*ROW 14:*  K 56 W.

*ROW 15:*  K 56 R.

*ROW 16:*  (All O) K 6, add 1, K 16, add 1, K 12, add 1, K 16, add 1, K 6. (60)

*ROW 17:*  (O and W) K 1 W and K 1 O for 60 sts.

*ROW 18:*  (All W) K 60 W.

*ROW 19:*  Beginning of W row cast off 7 sts onto stitch holder; cast on 2 PP, K 16 PP across back, cast off next 14 W sts onto stitch holder, cast on 4 PP, K 16 PP across the front; cast off 7 more sts onto first stitch holder for arms; cast on 3 PP. (40 sts on needles, 14 on each armhole stitch holder)

*ROW 20:*  (PP and W) K 1 PP and K 1 W for 40 sts.

*ROW 21:*  (All F) K 40 F.

*ROW 22:*  (O and F) K 1 O, K 1 F, add 1 O, K 1 F and K 1 O for 16 sts, add 1 F, K 1 O and K 1 F for 4 sts, add 1 O, K 1 F and K 1 O for 16 sts, add 1 F, K 1 O, K 1 F. (44)

*ROW 23:*  K 44 O.

*ROW 24:*  (R and W) K 1 R, K 1 W, K 1 R, add 1 W, K 1 R and K 1 W for 16 sts, add 1 R, K 1

W and K 1 R for 6 sts, add 1 W, K 1 R and K 1 W for 16 sts, add 1 R, K 1 W, K 1 R, K 1 W. (48)

*ROW 25:* (All PP) K 48.

*ROW 26:* (R and W) K 1 W and K 1 R for 48 sts.

*ROWS 27 to 29:* K 1, P 1 in W for 3 rows. (48)

*ROW 30:* Change to B for the rest of the body. K 48.

*ROW 31:* K 5, add 1, K 14, add 1, K 10, add 1, K 14, add 1, K 5. (52)

*ROW 32 TO 40:* K 52 sts per row.

*ROW 41:* K 2, K 2 tog, K 18, K 2 tog, K 4, K 2 tog, K 18, K 2 tog, K 2. (48)

*ROW 42:* K 48.

## STEP 3: STUFFING THE BEAR

At this point the head and body are knitted. Turn the piece inside out and crochet the top of the head closed. To do this, flatten the head front to back, and crochet sets of 2 stitches together across the top. This gives 16 crochet stitches. Chain these stitches into each other to cast off the crochet and tie the last stitch. Turn the body to the right side and push a small ball of stuffing in each corner of the head. Tie brown yarn tightly around each corner to form the ears. Tie a double knot and thread the ends into a yarn needle; sew the ends into the bear head. Stuff the bear head. Experiment to find just the right firmness that does not stretch the knitting and show the stuffing. You may wish to use old nylon stockings for stuffing since the color more closely matches the bear. Stuff the body loosely if you wish at this point, or wait to stuff it from the armholes at step 4.

## STEP 4: KNITTING THE LEGS

*ROW 1:* Cast on 12 B sts on stitch holder. K 8 B sts on one needle, K next 8 sts on second needle, K 8 B sts on third needle. Cast on 12 more sts on stitch holder (24 sts on stitch holder; 24 st on needles).

*ROW 2:* K 8, K 2 tog, K 4, K 2 tog, K 8. (22)

*ROW 3:* K 22.

*ROW 4:* K 2, K 2 tog, K 14, K 2 tog, K 2. (20)

*ROW 5:* K 20.

*ROW 6:* K 2, K 2 tog, K 12, K 2 tog, K 2. (18)

*ROW 7 to 9:* K 18.

*ROW 10:* To form the top of the foot, and to center it forward, K 3, then K 6 on Needle A, slide remaining 12 sts including first 3 stitches onto needles B and C (6 sts on each needle; 2 of these needles of 6 sts B and C are re-

the Bear Facts

# Famous Bears

Mishka, the famous Russian bear of folklore and legend, has been the symbol of Russia for hundreds of years. Russians are said to identify with the great, gruff bear's endurance and comical lumbering gait, among other characteristics. Recently, Mishka drew worldwide attention as a rotund little stuffed mascot-toy wearing the circled symbol belt to promote the 1980 Olympics in Moscow. (This belted bear is now considered a collector's item.) In Russia, Mishka appears in stories, drawings, and cartoons.

Americans have several favorite bears. Yogi and his pals were created by Hanna Barbera for television cartoons. His name is a pun on baseball catcher Yogi Berra's. Fozzie Bear is one of Jim Henson's famous creations seen on television and in motion pictures. Wearing a hat, playing the piano, and looking confused, he's an adorable bear. What's most remarkable about him is that

For generations, dancing brown bears have been entertaining children and offering a cup for tips.

he *can* wear a hat, accomplished by the dome between his ears that other bears do not have.

Smokey the Bear was created to assist the National Forestry Department. No cute little bear, Smokey wears a ranger hat and a stern expression as he asks for everyone's help to combat forest fires. Bruno, a large brown bear, played Gentle Ben on TV's *Grizzly Adams* series.

Aloysius Bear became famous in the United States and Britain overnight when Evelyn Waugh's novel *Brideshead Revisited* was skillfully adapted for television by John Mortimer. Aloysius has a long, narrow muzzle, widely spaced ears, and fully articulated joints typical of bears of the 1930s period of the story.

The British are great animal lovers and have taken to teddy bears since their invention. (Hoping to claim the teddy bear's invention, some loyal Britishers suggested that the teddy bear was actually named after Prince Edward when he admired a koala at the zoo.) Andy Panda, a television

Russians have a love/hate relationship with bears. This fierce but funny animal appears in their folklore as Mishka, and is their national symbol.

served for later). Using needle A and the fourth needle, turn knitting over and P 6 sts. Repeat K row and P row for 6 rows to form top of foot tab.

*ROW 11:* On needle A, K 6, pick up 4 sts on side of tab. K 6 on needle B, K 6 on needle C, and pick up 4 sts on side of tab. (26) Balance the sts on the needles with the center at the foot front.

*ROWS 12 to 16:* K 26 sts each row.

*ROW 17:* Needle A K 2, K 2 tog, K 4. (7) Needle B K 1, K 2 tog, K 4, K 2 tog, K 1. (8) Needle C K 4, K 2 tog, K 2. (7)

*ROW 18:* Needle A K 1, K 2 tog, K 4. (6) Needle B K 1, K 2 tog, K 2, K 2 tog, K 1. (6) Needle C K 4, K 2 tog, K 1. (6)

*ROW 19:* Needle A K 2 tog, K 4. (5) Needle B K 2 tog, K 2, K 2 tog. (4) Needle C K 4, K 2 tog. (5)

Stuff the leg. To close the foot, put the last 12 stitches on the stitch holder. Turn wrong side out. Fold foot flat front to back and crochet 2 stitches together for 6 stitches to close the foot. For the other leg, repeat the directions for step 4, knitting the leg, except make the foot face in the same direction as the other. Stuff the body from the armholes.

## STEP 5: KNITTING THE ARMS

On 2 needles, pick up the 14 sts on one arm from the stitch holder. Pick up 4 sts under the arm.

*ROW 1:* K 18 PP.

*ROW 2:* K 1 W and K 1 PP for 18 sts.

*ROWS 3 to 4:* K 18 F.

*ROW 5:* K 1 F and K 1 R for 18 sts.

*ROW 6:* K 1 W and K 1 R for 18 sts.

*ROW 7:* K 18 W.

*ROW 8:* K 18 R.

*ROW 9:* K 18 PP.

*ROW 10:* K 1 W and K 1 PP for 18 sts.

*ROWS 11 TO 13:* (All W) K 1, P 1 for ribbing. (18)

*ROWS 14 to 20:* K 18 sts B each row. Stuff the arm.

*ROW 21:* K 2 tog for entire row. (9)

*ROW 22:* K 2 tog for 8 sts, K 1. (5)

To close the paw, cut yarn off at 8 inches. Thread the end into a stitch holder. Run the needle through the remaining 5 stitches, removing them from the needle. Turn the hand wrong side out. Pull the yarn tight and sew the opening closed. For the other arm, repeat step 5.

## STEP 6: FINISHING THE BEAR

**A.** Thread the yarn needle with B1 yarn. Embroider the nose and mouth (see the diagram on page 21).
**B.** Glue or sew eyes in place.

## STEP 7: KNITTING THE HAT

Using W, cast on 32 sts onto 3 needles, 10, 10, 12. Join, being careful not to twist sts.

*ROWS 1 to 3:* K 1 W, P 1 W for 32 sts.
*ROW 4:* K 32 W.
*ROW 5:* K 32 R.
*ROW 6:* (All PP) K 2 tog, K 14, K 2 tog, K 14. (30)
*ROW 7:* K 1 O, K 1 W for 30 sts.
*ROW 8:* (All F) K 2 tog, K 13, K 2 tog, K 13. (28)
*ROW 9:* K 28 R.
*ROW 10:* (All O) K 2 tog, K 12, K 2 tog, K 12. (26)
*ROW 11:* (All PP) K 2 tog, K 11, K 2 tog, K 11. (24)
*ROW 12:* K 1 R and K 1 W for 24 sts.
*ROW 13:* (All R) K 2 tog, K 4, K 2 tog, K 4, K 2 tog, K 4. (20)
*ROW 14:* K 2 tog for 20 sts. (10)

To finish the hat, cut the yarn off 8 inches long. Thread the yarn on the yarn needle. Run the needle through the remaining 10 stitches, removing stitches from needle. To make a tassel, cut 1 piece of string 8 inches long. Wrap W yarn loosely around two fingers 16 times. Insert the string between your two fingers above and below the yarn. Tie a single knot. Slide the yarn off your fingers. Tie the string tightly with a double knot. Clip the 32 loops to form the tassel. Turn the hat wrong side out. Push the tassel strings through the top. Pull the red yarn end tightly to gather the top. Tie the red yarn and the string ends in a tight double knot. Clip the ends.

cartoon character, owns Teddy Bear, who cheerfully gets into mischief. Andy has been rescuing Teddy for 30 years now on British tellys.

Rupert, a long-time top favorite British bear created by Mary Tourtel, has appeared in comic strips in the *Daily Express* since 1920. When the artist's eyesight failed in 1935, a search for a replacement found Alfred Bestall, who illustrated Rupert for the next 30 years. Now a team of artists carries on the tradition. Rupert's cheery face appears on all kinds of products.

Other countries enjoy bears too. Australians have long loved a character called Billy Bluegum, a koala. Norman Lindsey created Billy in a sketch for a Sidney newspaper in 1904. (These were great years for teddy bears to be invented!) Lindsey's drawings had a sophisticated style and satirical wit ideal for political cartoons as well as for children's stories.

Japan, Spain, Germany, and Switzerland all have favorite bears. And many French children won't go to bed without their "nou-nous."

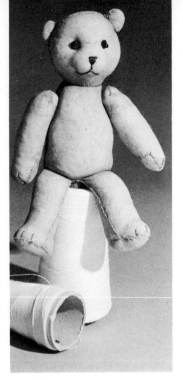

(*Left*) Natural cotton stuffing, chosen for its textured appearance, shows through this teddy made from a nylon stocking.

(*Right*) If the bear is too bare, make a small fur coat for him.

# Stocking Bear

Stocking dolls are long-time favorites of mothers and children. Mothers like them because they are easy to make. Children like them because they are soft, floppy toys that take a lot of squashing. Recently, stocking dolls have grown sophisticated. They've graduated from familiar work socks in sturdy gray cotton with the red-tipped toes, to sheer nylons. Knitted nylon stocking fabric can be sculptured into shape much like clay by stitching the fabric over a polyester stuffing. The bear shown here is made from nylon stocking fabric but stuffed with an unbleached natural cotton upholstery stuffing. This stuffing gives a little texture and color to the stocking fabric so it won't look so fleshlike. Even so, the finished bear looked so bare that I made him his own fur coat.

## TIPS ON SOCKS

Choose either a nylon stocking or a heavier sock without color knitted into the toe. Search the stores to find bear-colored socks with at least a 10-inch cuff. Or, if you just happen to have a stray sock at home, make the bear any color you wish. Choose any size; the bigger the sock, the bigger the bear; and the more the stuffing, the fatter the bear.

## MATERIALS

BODY: one stocking (nylon in the example shown) or sock

EYES: two ¼-inch beads or buttons, or embroider eyes for a baby's toy
THREAD: brown embroidery floss and brown sewing thread
STUFFING: polyester fiberfill, cotton, or scraps, such as old nylons, other socks, or soft fabric scraps

## TO MAKE THE BEAR

For a nylon stocking bear, cut a piece 12 inches long, unstretched, with no runs. Cut another piece 4 inches long, and cut this piece in half, lengthwise, for the arms. Cut another piece 2 inches long and cut this piece into four equal pieces for ears and feet bottoms. For regular socks, cut off the cuff 4 inches (more or less, depending on how large the sock is) from the inside turn at the ankle.

## STEP 1: MAKING THE HEAD

**A.** Sew across the top of the 12-inch piece to close the stocking in a curve. If you use a nylon with a sheer toe, or a regular sock, the toe will form the head top.
*Note:* The bear shown is sewn by hand since sheer nylon knit is difficult to sew by machine. To sew by machine, back with paper and stretch the seams as you sew. A narrow zigzag or overcast stitch may work. Remove the paper backing when you are finished.

**B.** Roll a round, firm ball of stuffing about the size of a tennis ball and push this into the HEAD. Stuffing will compress about 2½ times its bulk. Roll a second firm ball about 1 inch across and push into place on the front of the face for the NOSE.

**C.** For the EYES, thread a long sharp needle with brown embroidery floss. Tie the eye bead or button onto the end. Push the needle into the HEAD where the eye will appear. Push the needle behind the NOSE ball to come out at the other eye. Pull on the thread to pull the eye into its socket, and sew a knot to keep the thread taut. Sew the other EYE in place.

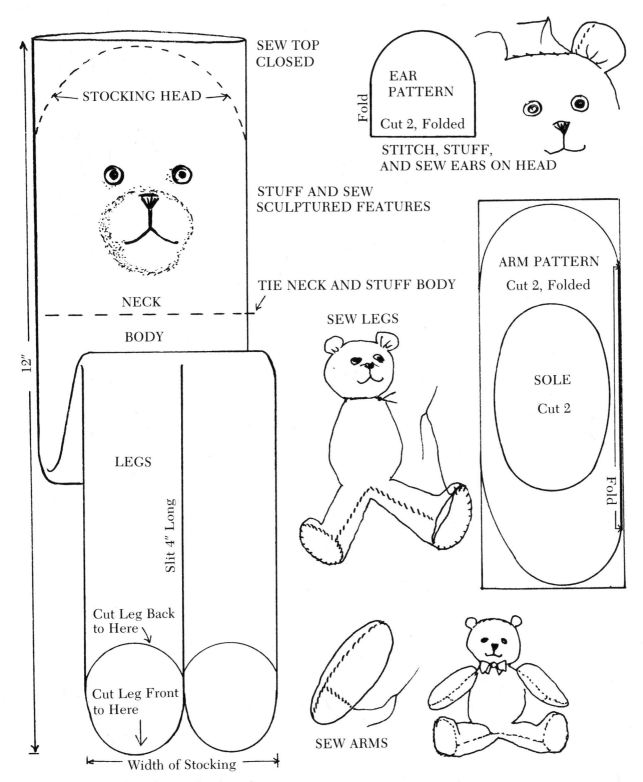

NOTE: *Width and stretch of stockings vary. Approximate pattern given.*

Assembling Stocking Bear.

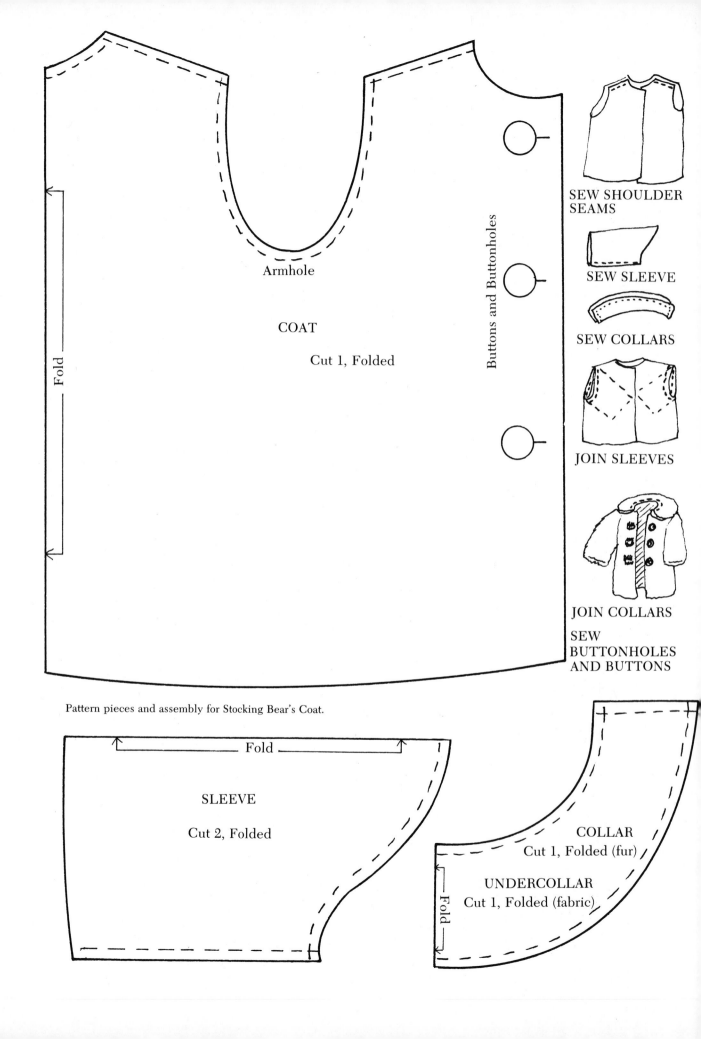

Armhole

COAT

Cut 1, Folded

Fold

Buttons and Buttonholes

SEW SHOULDER
SEAMS

SEW SLEEVE

SEW COLLARS

JOIN SLEEVES

JOIN COLLARS

SEW
BUTTONHOLES
AND BUTTONS

Pattern pieces and assembly for Stocking Bear's Coat.

Fold

SLEEVE

Cut 2, Folded

COLLAR
Cut 1, Folded (fur)

UNDERCOLLAR
Cut 1, Folded (fabric)

Fold

*Note:* To sew a knot, stick the needle tip in the fabric to catch a small bit (⅛ inch). Keep the thread tight with your other hand while you do this. Pull the thread to a small loop. With the tip of the needle, wind this loop once or twice around the needle tip. This means you will be drawing the thread through the loop twice. Then pull the needle and thread tightly while still holding the thread near the fabric. This will draw into a tight knot.

**D.** For the NOSE and MOUTH, thread the needle with embroidery floss and insert the needle in the tip of the nose. Sew a knot. Insert the needle and come up at the base of the nose. Sew a triangular-shaped nose, then stitch across the top. Now push the needle through the nose stuffing ball and come out at the corner of the mouth. Push the needle in at the top of the mouth and come out at the other corner of the mouth. Push the needle under the thread at the top of the mouth and insert the needle at the base of the nose so it comes out under the nose at one side. Pull tightly to shape the mouth like the other side. When you have the shape you wish, sew a knot that can be tucked under the nose stitching.

**E.** Use two of the small pieces for the EARS. Fold each double and sew a curved seam the shape of an ear, leaving the bottom open. For hand sewing, do not cut the thread. Turn the ear, then stuff firmly with a small ball of stuffing. Sew the ear in place on the bear's HEAD. Repeat for the other EAR.

## STEP 2: MAKING THE BEAR'S BODY

**A.** Roll a large wad of stuffing slightly larger than you want the BODY (stuffing compresses a lot, as mentioned before). Push this into place. Tie a thread or string around the bear's NECK for shaping. You can add a ribbon later to cover the thread.

## STEP 3: MAKING THE LEGS

**A.** For a stocking with a heel, cut LEGS about 3½ or 4 inches long from the ankle (depending on the stocking). The heel provides a rump for the bear to sit on. For a nylon or tube sock, cut the legs 3 to 4 inches long and the bear will stand but will have no rump.

**B.** Hand sew the crotch seam closed with sewing thread. Trim the bottom of the legs ¾ inch shorter

on the back side, with a longer curve on the front.

**C.** Stuff the LEGS with rolled tubes of stuffing, leaving the top end lightly stuffed so it will be flexible.

**D.** Cut two ovals 1 by 1¼ inches (or larger) from the remaining 2 small pieces for soles of the FEET. Stuff the front of the feet and pin the soles in place. Trim off any excess fabric. Sew the soles of the feet in place with sewing thread.

## STEP 4: MAKING THE ARMS

**A.** Fold each 4-inch piece of fabric lengthwise. Trim to make the ARM shape. Sew this seam with ordinary thread almost to the end. Stuff to shape firmly, then stitch closed.

**B.** With a sturdy thread, sew the ARMS to the body at one point so they can move.

## STEP 5: FINISHING THE BEAR

**A.** With embroidery floss, sew claws on all PAWS.

**B.** Create a paw patch by overcast stitching around the paw seam and across the wrist.

**C.** Tie a ribbon on the bear.

*Note:* If your bear looks too bare, make him a coat, or other clothing. This coat pattern does not have hems, so use felt or fake fur.

## COAT PATTERN PIECES

COAT (1), SLEEVE (1), COLLAR (1), UNDER COLLAR (1)

## MATERIALS

COAT:   12-by-12-inch piece of felt or fur
THREAD:   brown sewing thread
BUTTONS:   three shank buttons

## TO MAKE THE COAT

**A.** Cut out pattern pieces.
**B.** Sew the COAT shoulder seams.
**C.** Sew the SLEEVE seams.
**D.** Sew the upper and under COLLARS together and turn.
**E.** Pin the SLEEVE in place and stitch.
**F.** Sew the COLLAR in place and trim very close to the seam.
**G.** Sew the buttonholes by machine.
**H.** Sew on the buttons.

An updated pattern for our oldest son Rand's well-loved 1940s bear (shown lower left) appears in three versions. Each has different features and body fabrics for a varied effect.

# Rand's Bear

The threadbare bear shown lower left in the photograph was my son Rand's favorite when he was a small boy. The bear shows imaginative changes from the earlier articulated-joint bears. His simplified 1940s design makes him much easier to construct. The arms are flexible because they are sewn into the side seam, prestuffed. The legs move easily since there is no stuffing in the hip joint. He sits well on his rump, which is created by making the body back longer than the front and seaming it for shape.

The following pattern simulates Rand's 1940s bear (whose manufacturer's tag has long ago disappeared) with additional changes: the head is not articulated; the size is a little larger—17 inches tall; a seam replaces a dart; and his nose is different. The original nose was chewed off and replaced several times.

## CHOOSING THE FABRIC

The fabric you choose to make the bear will greatly affect his finished form. The firmly woven, flat-finished calico makes a slender bear. The napped, fleecy knitted fabric stretches to make a softer, fatter bear (top, left). The fake fur fabric with a ½-inch pile makes a bulkier, bigger bear (bottom, right). All three bears are made from exactly the same pattern. Different eyes are used to complete the different effects possible with one pattern, and, of course, the bear at the bottom left is smaller. In addition, choose any number of other fabrics for other effects.

## PATTERN PIECES

**A.** FACE TOP: cut 1 (fur)
**B.** HEAD BACK: cut 1 (fur)
**C.** LEG BACK: cut 2, 1 reversed (fur)
**D.** FACE SIDE: cut 2, 1 reversed (fur)
*(see p. 68)*

**A.** BODY FRONT (attach to B): cut 2, 1 reversed (fur)
**B.** BODY FRONT (attach to A): cut 2, 1 reversed (fur)
**C.** EAR: cut 2 (contrasting fur)
*(see p. 69)*

**A.** MUZZLE: cut 1 (contrasting fur)
**B.** BODY BACK: cut 2, 1 reversed (fur)
**C.** INNER ARM: cut 2, 1 reversed (fur)
**D.** OUTER ARM (entire piece): cut 2, 1 reversed (fur)
**E.** PAW: cut 2 (contrasting fur)
*(see p. 70)*

## MATERIALS

BEAR BODY:   15 by 34 inches of fake fur, fleece, muslin, corduroy, or other fabric
PAWS, EARS, and MUZZLE:   6 by 10 inches of contrasting but related fabric
EYES:   ½-inch movable sew-on or glue-on eyes,

plastic post-and-washer eyes, handmade ceramic button eyes, hand- or machine-embroidered eyes, or whatever looks good on your bear

THREAD: black embroidery floss for the mouth and nose, cotton wrapped polyester core sewing thread to match the fabric, for stitching the bear

NOSE: plastic shank-and-washer noses are available

BOW: 24 inches of 1- to 1½-inch-wide ribbon

STUFFING: 1 pound fiberfill

## STEP 1: MAKING THE HEAD, ARMS, AND EARS

**A.** Pin the EAR pieces face to face and stitch together. Trim the seam allowances and turn.

**B.** Pin the PAW face to face with INNER ARM. Stitch the seam. Open this piece flat and lay it face to face with the OUTER ARM. Stitch around the edges, leaving the end open for stuffing.

**C.** Pin the FACE SIDE face to face with the FACE TOP and stitch. Repeat for the other face side.

**D.** Pin the MUZZLE to the FACE section, carefully matching the seams. Stitch and trim seam allowances.

**E.** Fold and pin the chin seam. Stitch carefully, tapering the end smoothly for a well-rounded nose.

**F.** Do the EYES and NOSE now if you plan to appliqué or machine-embroider them, or if you use the plastic eyes with a shank and force-fit washer. Place them close to the nose, on or near the head seam.

**G.** Pin a ½-inch tuck (more or less) in the front side of the EAR with the fold in the center. The ear is attached on a curve and will wrinkle if there is no tuck or gathering. Pin the EARS to the FACE with the tuck on the front. Place the edge of the EAR at the FACE seam, raw edges aligned.

## STEP 2: MAKING THE BODY

**A.** Fold and stitch the ANKLE dart in the BODY FRONT, tapering the ends carefully. This shapes the foot. Pin and stitch the seams at the feet on the BODY FRONT and LEG BACK pieces to make the TOE and HEEL.

**B.** Pin the BODY FRONTS face to face and seam from the neck to the crotch. Trim the seam allowances.

**C.** Pin the LEG BACKS to the BODY BACKS, face to face. Stitch and trim.

**D.** Pin the BODY BACKS face to face and stitch the seam, leaving a 4-inch opening for stuffing and turning.

**E.** Turn the arms and stuff them firmly, but leave 1 inch of each top end unstuffed. Fold the ARMS so the side seams match, and pin. This makes the arms curve forward with the paw down.

**F.** Pin the ARMS onto the BODY FRONT, aligning the raw edges so the top of the arm comes exactly at the point of the shoulder on the seam line. Baste in place.

## STEP 3: SEWING THE HEAD TO THE BODY

**A.** Run a gathering thread on the front of the FACE. Pull this thread so the head and body seams align.

**B.** Pin the front of the FACE to the BODY FRONT, face to face. Pin the HEAD BACK to the BODY BACK. Stitch each in place.

**C.** Pin the BODY BACK to the BODY FRONT, aligning the seams at the neck, feet, and crotch. Sew around the entire BODY. Before turning, clip any seam allowances that might bind at the neck and crotch in particular.

## STEP 4: STUFFING THE BEAR

**A.** Turn the bear right side out. The arms are already stuffed and this makes turning a bit difficult. Turn the feet first, pushing in with your thumb to fill out the seams well, then pull the feet through the hole. Pull the arms through, and then the head.

**B.** Use polyester fiberfill, or a similar soft stuffing. Insert the stuffing in small soft puffs for more careful placement. Push balls into the feet first to make them firm. Stuff the legs firmly, bit by bit. If the stuffing gets lumpy, roll the legs between your hands. Stuff almost to the top of the leg.

**C.** Stuff the top of the head. Use a dowel stick to help reach distant places, if need be. Roll a large, firm ball and stuff the nose to a full shape. Continue to fill the head.

**D.** Place a large, firm roll in the body across the top of the legs, leaving a small space at the top of the legs unstuffed so they will bend. Continue to stuff the body with large soft pieces to avoid lumps.

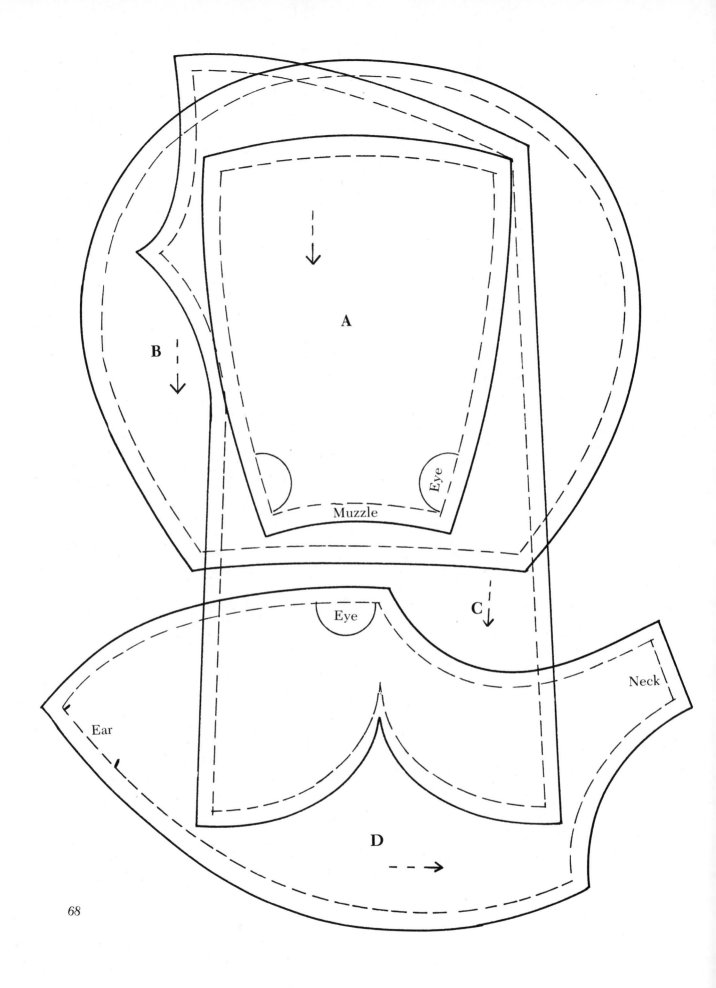

A

B

Eye

Muzzle

C

Eye

Neck

Ear

D

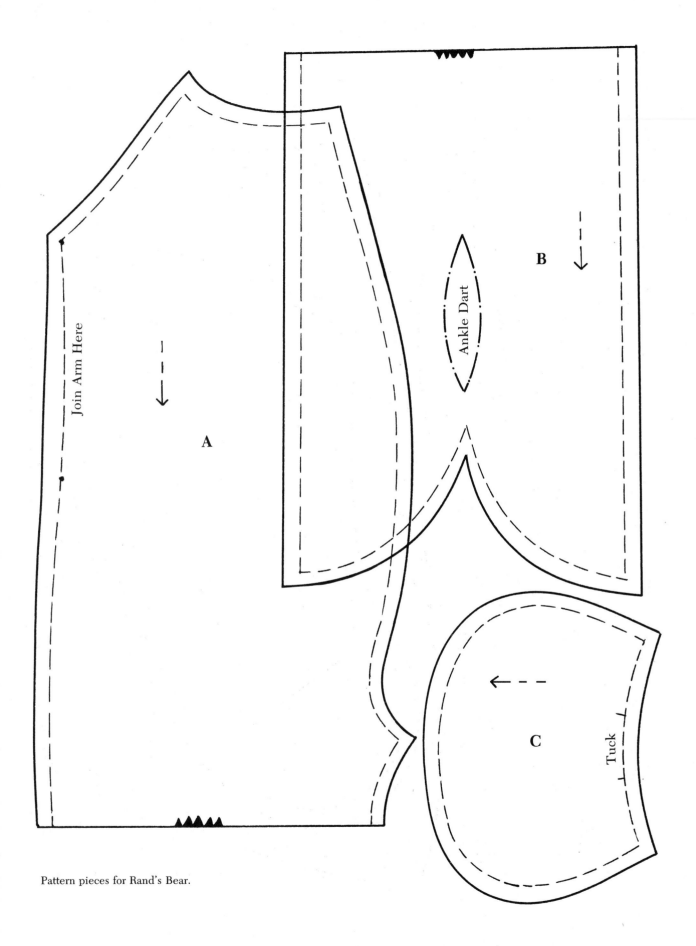

Join Arm Here

A

B

Ankle Dart

C

Tuck

Pattern pieces for Rand's Bear.

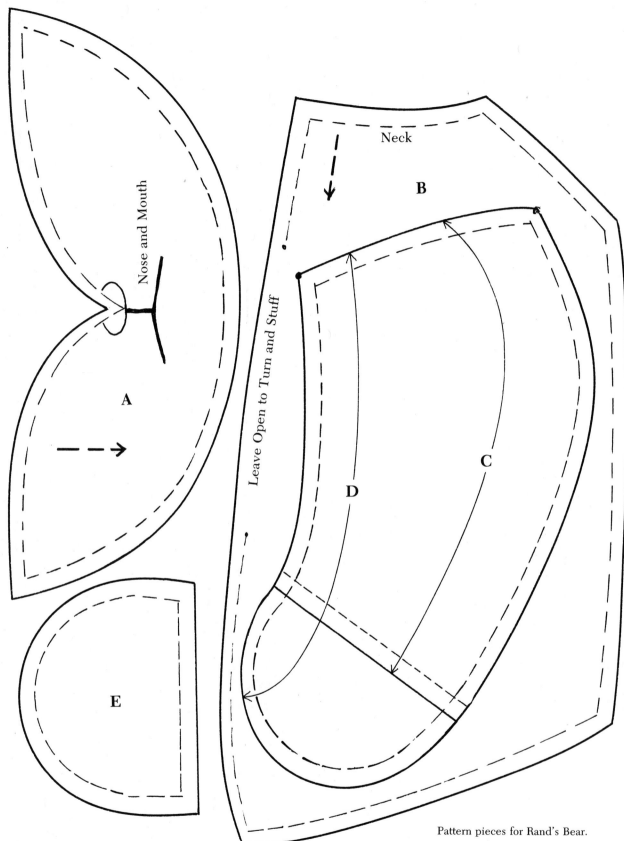

Nose and Mouth

A

Neck

B

Leave Open to Turn and Stuff

C

D

E

Pattern pieces for Rand's Bear.

**E.** After you have stuffed the bear to a pleasing plumpness, pin the opening closed and hand sew this seam with blind stitching or overcasting.

## STEP 5: FINISHING THE BEAR

**A.** Embroider a triangular-shaped NOSE and MOUTH with embroidery floss (see the diagram on page 21). Sew or glue on the eyes, if they are not already in place.

**B.** Tie the BOW in place. Don't worry if the bow looks tacky or is missing the next time you see the bear. That's a sign of a well-loved teddy.

Assembling Rand's Bear.

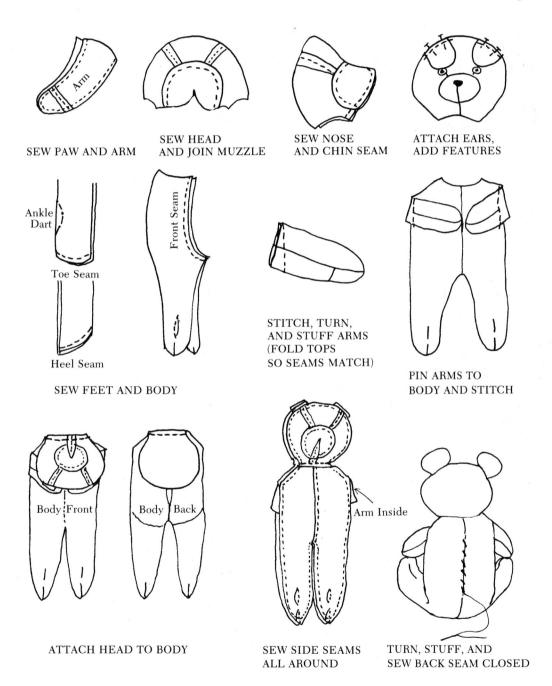

SEW PAW AND ARM

SEW HEAD AND JOIN MUZZLE

SEW NOSE AND CHIN SEAM

ATTACH EARS, ADD FEATURES

Ankle Dart

Toe Seam

Heel Seam

Front Seam

STITCH, TURN, AND STUFF ARMS (FOLD TOPS SO SEAMS MATCH)

PIN ARMS TO BODY AND STITCH

SEW FEET AND BODY

Body Front

Body Back

Arm Inside

ATTACH HEAD TO BODY

SEW SIDE SEAMS ALL AROUND

TURN, STUFF, AND SEW BACK SEAM CLOSED

When the hook is released, not a Jack—but a bear—jumps out of this wooden box decorated with wrapping paper and tape.

# Jack-in-the-Box Bear

Young children love little surprises. That's the eternal appeal of the same Jack jumping out of the box every time. These old-time favorite toys are activated by a coil spring inside the fabric toy figure compressed by the box lid. When the hook is released from the hasp, up leaps Jack.

Easy. Now to find a spring. After a fruitless search for a source, I consulted my dad, a remarkable inventor. After a lengthy discussion on how to make a spring by coiling tempered wire in a spiral around a tube, he suggested that I make the whole thing out of compressible foam rubber instead. It works fine! To be authentic, you may still wish to use a spring, if you can find one or have one made. However, this 11-inch bear-Jack, with his soft foam body, makes a huggable toy and leaps out of the box nicely. For the box, find a 5-inch metal box with a hinged lid, or construct a plywood box.

## PATTERN PIECES

A.  BODY: cut 1, folded (cotton)
B.  HEAD TOP: cut 1 (fur)
C.  EAR: cut 4 (fur)
D.  FOOT (entire piece): cut 2, folded (fur)
E.  PAW: cut 2, folded (fur)
F.  ARM: cut 2, folded (cotton)
G.  HEAD SIDE: cut 2, 1 reversed (fur)
     (see p. 73)

## MATERIALS

BEAR:   12 by 15 inches of brown fake fur fabric
BODY:   12 by 18 inches of gold printed cotton fabric
RUFFLES:   1 yard of 1¼-inch-wide soft yellow ribbon cut in three pieces: one 18 inches and two 9 inches
EYES:   plastic post-and-washer eyes
NOSE:   plastic post-and-washer nose
THREAD:   gold embroidery floss, thread to match
STUFFING:   10-inch tube of polyurethane foam, 3 inches in diameter
BOX:   SIDES, two 5 by 4½, FRONT and BACK, two 5½ by 4½, TOP and BOTTOM, two 5½ by 5½ inches of ¼-inch plywood or Masonite
FITTINGS:   one small brass hook and hasp, two small hinges (these fittings come with screws; if you use a metal box, buy small bolts with nuts of the same sizes)
NAILS:   1¼-inch finishing nails
TRIM:   roll of plastic decorative tape, paint, or decorator paper
SPECIAL TOOLS:   hammer, saw, screwdriver, pliers for bolts, drill and bit, masking tape

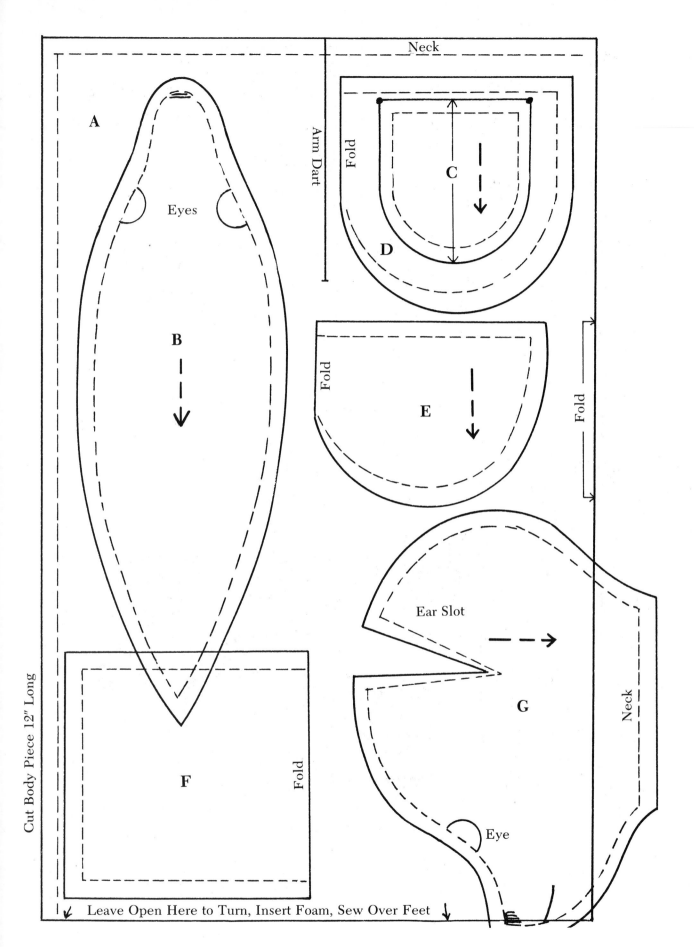

Pattern pieces for Jack-in-the-Box Bear.

SEW EARS
TO THE HEAD

SEW HEAD TOP
TO SIDES

MAKE THE
RUFFLES

SEW PAW
TO SLEEVE

Head Top

Head Side

Curve Ends

Sleeve

Paw

STITCH ARM AND TURN

JOIN ARMS TO BODY

ATTACH NECK RUFFLE

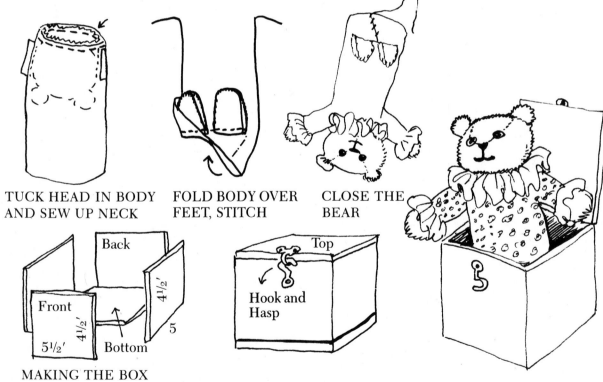

TUCK HEAD IN BODY
AND SEW UP NECK

FOLD BODY OVER
FEET, STITCH

CLOSE THE
BEAR

MAKING THE BOX

Back

Front

4½'

4½'

5½'

5

Bottom

Top

Hook and
Hasp

Assembling Jack-in-the-Box Bear.

74

## STEP 1: MAKING THE BOX

*Note:* To saw the wood, a table or circular saw works best for straight line cutting, but other saws will do.

**A.** Use masking tape to tape the BOX SIDES (5 inches wide by 4½ inches high) to the BOX FRONT. Using the finishing nails, nail the FRONT to the SIDE edges.

**B.** Flip the box over, tape the BOX BACK (5½ inches wide by 4½ inches high) to the BOX SIDES and nail in place.

**C.** Tape the BOX BOTTOM (5½ inches square) onto the BOX SIDES and nail in place. Remove all masking tape.

**D.** Decorate the box and lid. To do this, paint the box and lid or glue on decorative papers, such as shelf paper, wallpaper, or wrapping paper. If you plan to paper the inside of the box, you may wish to do this before assembly. When the box is decorated, carefully tape over all the edges with the decorative plastic tape.

**E.** Place the lid on the box and position the hinges. Drill holes and screw the hinges in place.

*Note:* If you use a metal box, bolt the hinges in place. Make the hole for the bolt with a nail, pounding on a wooden reinforcement inside so as not to dent the metal. Insert the nut through the fitting, washer, and holes, then hold the nut with pliers while turning the bolt.

**F.** Close the lid and position the hasp. If the hasp does not fit correctly, remodel it with pliers and tin snips. Screw or bolt the hasp in place. Position the hook. Fit the end in the hasp and make a hole at the other end of the hook. Use washers and a lock nut on the hook so it will rotate freely. If possible, find a hook with a tiny tab to release the hook more easily.

## STEP 2: MAKING THE STUFFING

**A.** If possible, use a round polyurethane tube 3 inches in diameter and 10 inches long.

**B.** If not, begin with a piece of foam measuring more than 3 inches wide, 3 inches deep and 10 inches long. Use an electric carving knife to whittle the tube shape. It doesn't have to be perfect since it's inside the bear. Lacking an electric carving knife, use a bread knife or sharp scissors to carve the shape.

## STEP 3: MAKING THE BEAR

**A.** Place the pairs of EAR pieces face to face and sew together. Trim the seam allowances and turn.

**B.** Pin the EARS in the EAR SLOTS. Fold the dart over the end of each ear, with the ear angled slightly upward, and stitch. Leave a small seam allowance at the end.

**C.** Place the HEAD SIDE pieces face to face and stitch the CHIN seam.

**D.** Pin the HEAD TOP to the HEAD SIDES at the nose seam, and stitch. Trim the seam allowances and turn. Insert post-and-washer eyes and nose.

**E.** Run a gathering thread along one side of the three ruffle pieces with curved stitching at the ends.

**F.** Pull the gathering thread of the 9-inch piece to fit the ARM. Baste the ruffle to the ARM. Pin the PAW to the ARM over the ruffle, and stitch.

**G.** Fold the PAW and ARM lengthwise with the ruffle tucked in, matching the wrist seams. Sew the ARM seam tapered at the PAW end, with the top open. Trim the seam allowances and turn. Repeat F and G for the other ARM.

**H.** Insert the unstuffed arms in the BODY ARM dart. Sew the ARMS into this seam.

**I.** Run a gathering thread in the top of the BODY. Pull this to fit the bear's HEAD NECK seam. Pull the 18-inch NECK ruffle thread to fit the BODY NECK. Pin the ruffle to the BODY and baste in place.

**J.** Fold the BODY face to face and sew the back seam.

**K.** Insert the HEAD in the BODY, matching the back HEAD seam and the back body seam. Sew the head to the body by machine or hand, whichever is easier.

**L.** Fold the FEET face to face and stitch. Leave the straight edge open. Trim the seam allowances and turn.

**M.** Pin the FEET to the BODY FRONT up 1½ inches from the edge as shown in the diagram. Fold the body up over the top raw edges of the feet and sew them into this seam.

**N.** Stuff the bear's head. Insert the foam tube. Fold the body ends together and hand stitch neatly closed, tucking in any raw seams.

**O.** Sew the bear's mouth and nose if needed. Put the bear in the box.

75

# Dressed Bears

Many a teddy bear has donned exotic outfits to act out fantasy roles for his owner. Alas, what's true for people is true for bears—the skinny ones look snappier in their fancy outfits. The dressed bears shown have been additionally anthropomorphized, that is, made more human in shape to look better in human clothes

The clothing for these bears (except for the clown bear) is sewn as part of the bear's body. The bear is designed to be made in units entirely by machine, except for one closing seam.

## PATTERN PIECES

WESTERN BEAR: HEAD BACK (1), HEAD SIDE (2), HEAD TOP (1), MUZZLE (1), EAR (4), BODY TOP (2), BODY BOTTOM (2), ARM (2), PAW (4), FOOT TOP (2), FOOT SOLE (2), SHIRT COLLAR (4)

CHEERLEADER BEAR: HEAD BACK (1), HEAD SIDE (2), HEAD TOP (1), MUZZLE (1), EAR (4), BODY TOP (2), LETTER (1), ARM (2), PAW (4), FOOT TOP (2), PANTIES (2), LEG (2), FOOT SOLE (2), SKIRT (1), SKIRT LINING (1), EYELASHES (2)

POSH BEAR: HEAD BACK (1), HEAD SIDE (2), HEAD TOP (1), MUZZLE (1), EAR (4), BODY TOP (2), ARM (2), PAW (4), BODY BOTTOM (2), FOOT TOP (2), FOOT SOLE (2), SHIRT COLLAR (4), SHIRT COLLAR INTERFACING (2), JACKET FRONT (2),

Western Bear, shown with sewn-on clothing, wears blue denim jeans, a plaid shirt, and a string tie.

The honey-colored Cheerleader Bear has a red and white outfit, but can wear any school colors you choose.

JACKET BACK (1), JACKET COLLAR (2),
JACKET SLEEVE (2), TIE (1), BOW (1),
SHOULDER PAD (2), LAPEL INTERFAC-
ING (2), JACKET COLLAR INTERFACING
(1), CUMMERBUND (2)

CLOWN BEAR: HEAD BACK (1), HEAD SIDE
(2), HEAD TOP (1), MUZZLE (1), EAR (4),
BODY TOP (2), BODY BOTTOM (2), ARM
(2), PAW (4), FOOT TOP (2), FOOT SOLE
(2), CLOWN SUIT BODY (2, Pieced Pattern),
CLOWN SUIT SLEEVE (2), HAT (3)

A.  HEAD BACK: cut 1
B.  HEAD TOP: cut 1
C.  EAR: cut 4
D.  HEAD SIDE: cut 2, 1 reversed
E.  EYELASHES: (cut 2)
SEE MATERIALS FOR FABRIC
   *(see p. 79)*
A.  FOOT SOLE: cut 2
B.  MUZZLE: cut 1
C.  PAW: cut 4
D.  FOOT TOP: cut 2
SEE MATERIALS FOR FABRIC
   *(see p. 80)*
A.  PANTIES: cut 2, folded
B.  BODY BOTTOM: cut 2, folded
C.  LEG: cut 2, folded
D.  ARM: cut 2, folded
E.  BODY TOP: cut 2, folded
F.  SHIRT COLLAR: cut 4, 2 reversed
SEE MATERIALS FOR FABRIC
   *(see p. 81)*
A.  SKIRT: cut 1 (red), folded
B.  SKIRT LINING: cut 1 (white), folded
C.  LETTER: cut 1
D.  CLOWN SUIT SLEEVE: cut 2 (1 red, 1 green),
   folded
E.  CLOWN HAT: cut 3 (1 in each color)
SEE MATERIALS FOR FABRICS
   *(see p. 82)*
A.  CLOWN SUIT BODY (attach to *B*): cut 2
   (1 green, 1 red), folded
B.  CLOWN SUIT BODY (attach to *A*): cut 2
   (1 green, 1 red), folded
SEE MATERIALS FOR FABRICS
   *(see p. 83)*
A.  JACKET FRONT: cut 2, 1 reversed
B.  LAPEL INTERFACING: cut 2, 1 reversed
C.  SHOULDER PAD: cut 2, 1 reversed
D.  SHIRT COLLAR: cut 4, 2 reversed
E.  SHIRT COLLAR INTERFACING: cut 2,
   1 reversed
F.  JACKET COLLAR: cut 2, folded

Posh Bear, dressed in shiny holiday fabrics trimmed with pearl buttons, looks down his long polar bear nose.

G.  JACKET COLLAR INTERFACING: cut 1,
   folded
SEE MATERIALS FOR FABRICS
   *(see p. 84)*
A.  JACKET SLEEVE: cut 2, folded
B.  JACKET BACK: cut 1, folded
C.  BOW: cut 1
D.  TIE: cut 1
E.  CUMMERBUND: cut 2, folded
SEE MATERIALS FOR FABRICS
   *(see p. 85)*

## MATERIALS

### Western Bear

BEAR HEAD, FOOT TOPS, AND FOOT
   SOLES:  15 by 18 inches of dark brown fake
   fur
MUZZLE, PAWS, AND EARS:  9 by 12 inches
   of medium brown, shorter-pile fake fur or
   velvet

Clown Bear balances his hat rakishly on one ear, since he lacks an egg-shaped human head.

BODY BOTTOM (PANTS):  9 by 18 inches of blue jeans fabric, preferably used (cut the pattern to take advantage of a sewn side seam on old jeans)

BODY TOP (SHIRT):  12 by 15 inches of red and grey small plaid fabric, nine tiny buttons, one ¼-inch bead, 4 inches of leather thong

EYES AND NOSE:  three 15mm (⅝ inch) plastic posts and washers

THREAD:  brown and white polyester/cotton sewing threads, black embroidery floss for mouth

**Cheerleader Bear**

BEAR HEAD, LEGS, AND FOOT TOPS:  15 by 15 inches of honey-colored fake fur

PAWS, MUZZLE, 2 EARS, FOOT SOLES:  9 by 12 inches of brown fake fur

SKIRT, SKIRT LINING, AND BODY TOP (SWEATER):  12 by 20 inches of white knitted fleece

SKIRT, PANTIES, AND LETTER:  8 by 19 inches of red fabric

EYES:  two 15 mm (⅝ inch) plastic posts and washers

EYELASHES:  1 by 2 inches of brown suede or felt

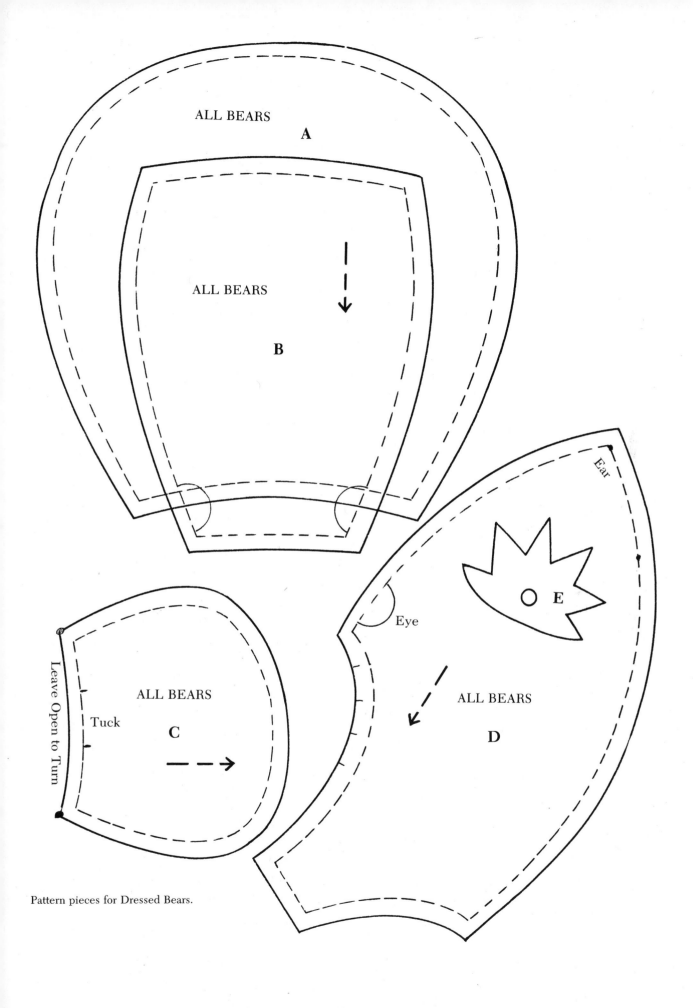

ALL BEARS

A

ALL BEARS

B

Ear

Eye

E

Leave Open to Turn

ALL BEARS

Tuck

C

ALL BEARS

D

Pattern pieces for Dressed Bears.

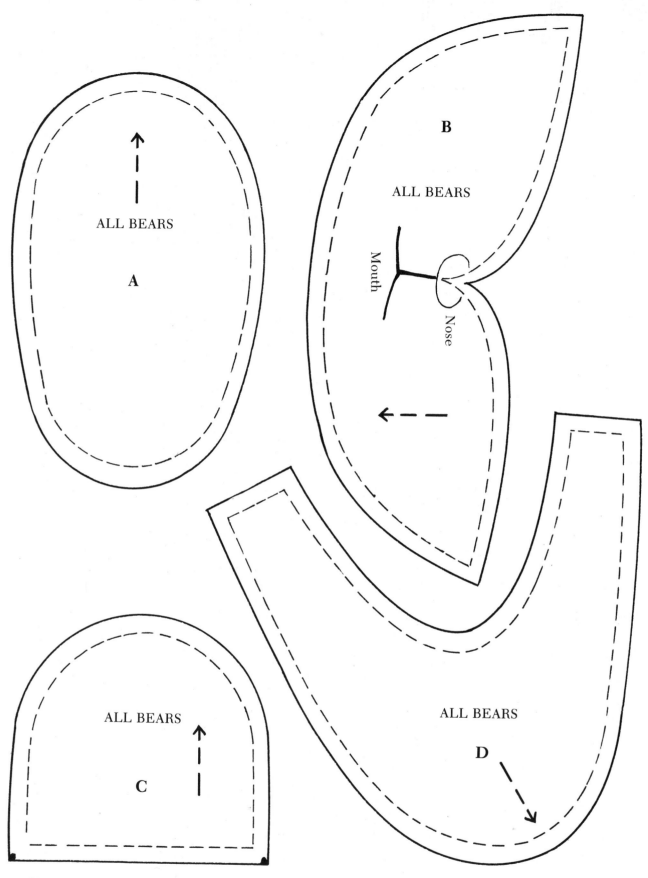

ALL BEARS

A

B

ALL BEARS

Mouth

Nose

ALL BEARS

C

ALL BEARS

D

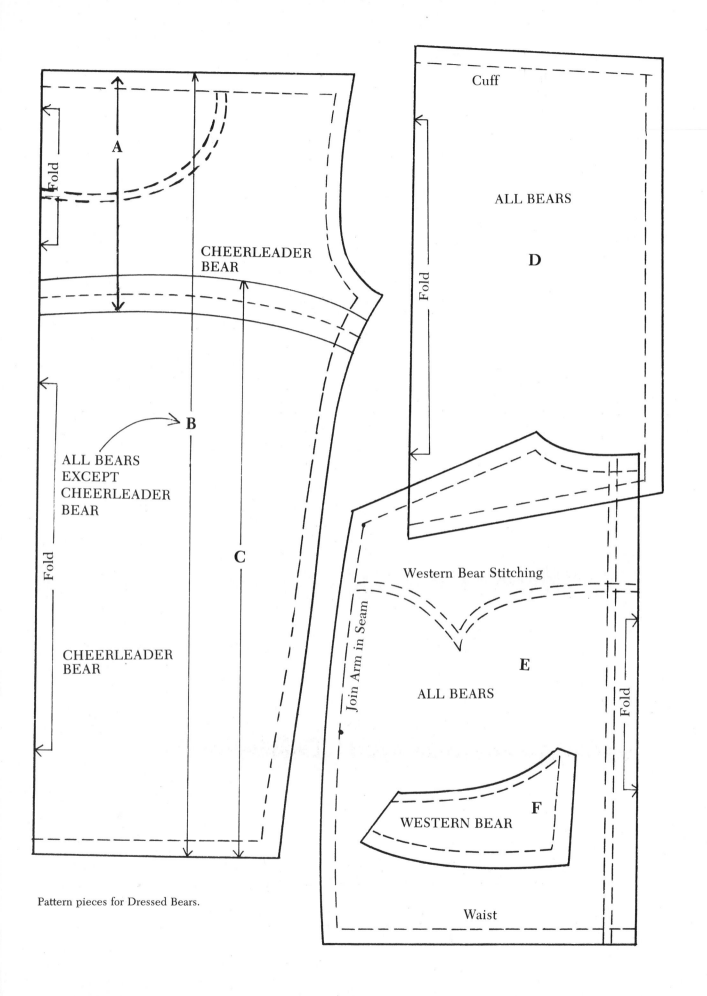

Pattern pieces for Dressed Bears.

**A**

**B**

**C**

**D**

**E**

**F**

Fold

CHEERLEADER BEAR

ALL BEARS EXCEPT CHEERLEADER BEAR

Fold

CHEERLEADER BEAR

Cuff

ALL BEARS

Fold

Western Bear Stitching

Join Arm in Seam

ALL BEARS

Fold

WESTERN BEAR

Waist

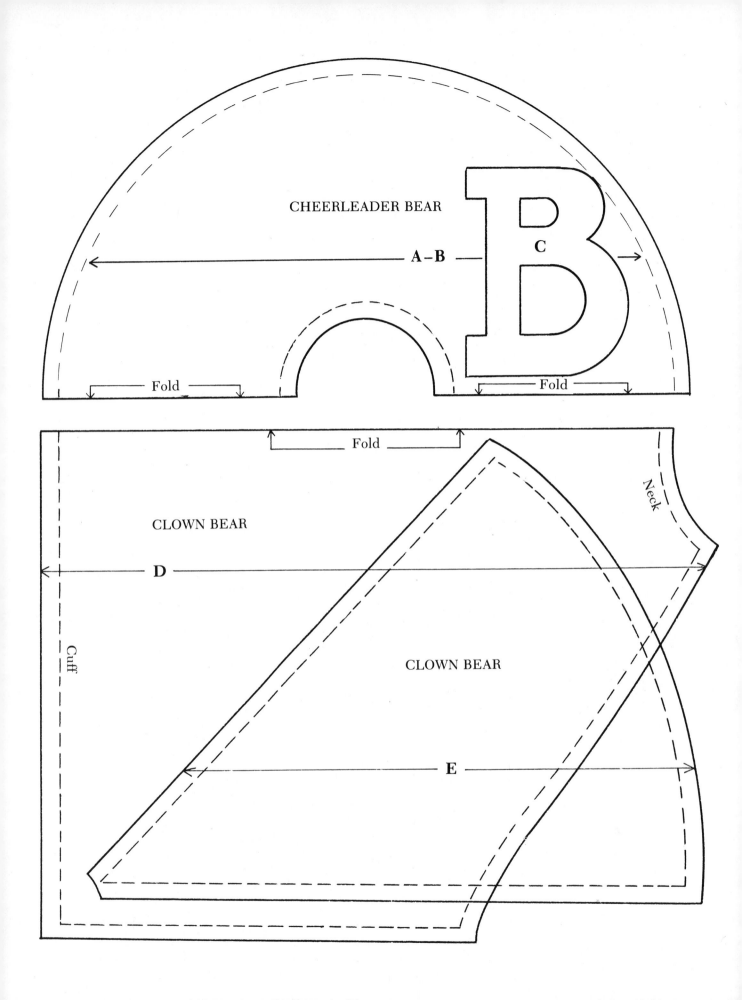

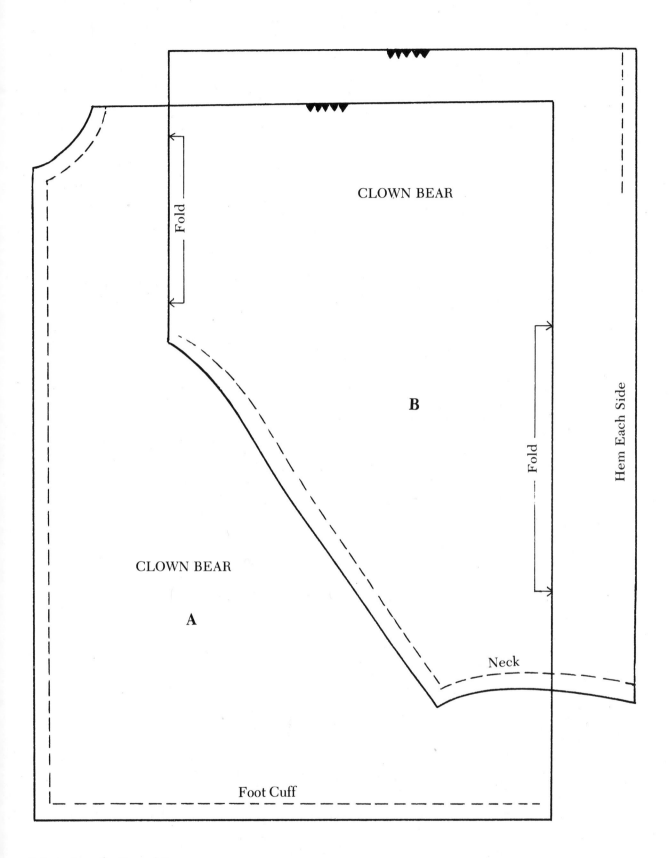

CLOWN BEAR

Fold

B

Hem Each Side

Fold

CLOWN BEAR

A

Neck

Foot Cuff

Pattern pieces for Dressed Bears.

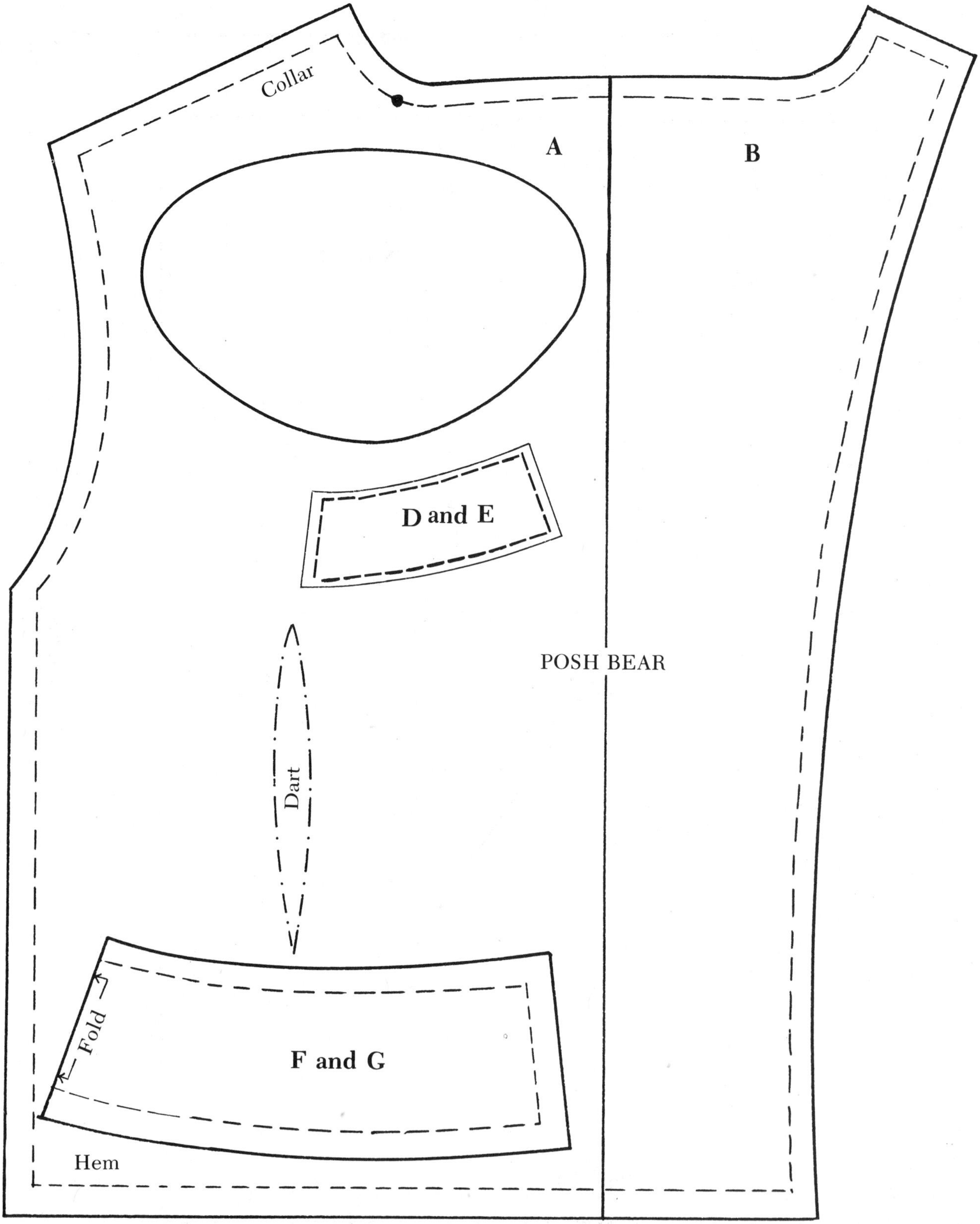
Collar
A
B
D and E
POSH BEAR
Dart
Fold
F and G
Hem

Pattern pieces for Dressed Bears.

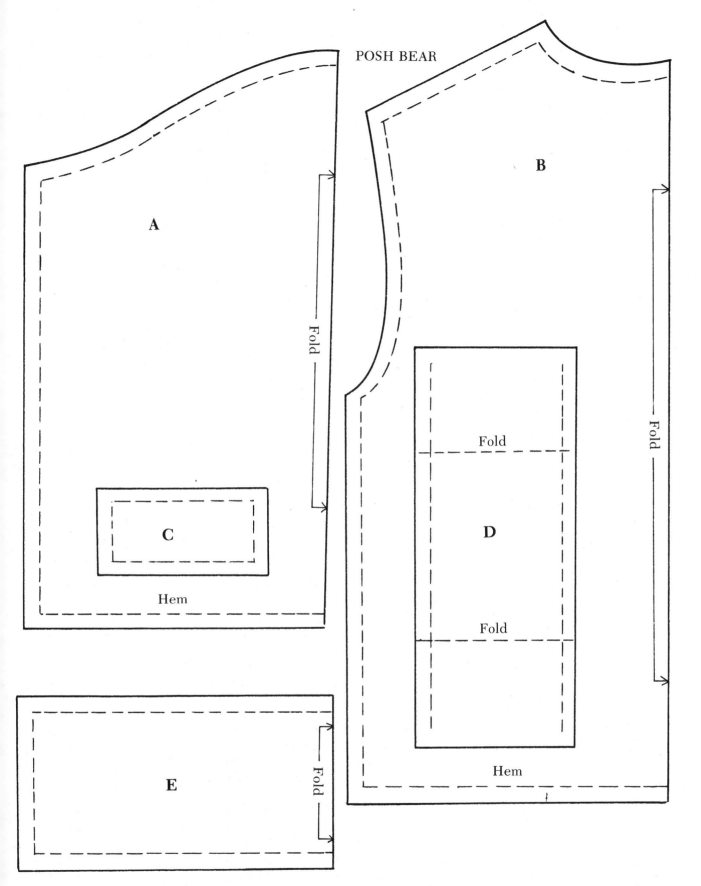

POSH BEAR

A

Fold

C

Hem

B

Fold

D

Fold

Fold

Hem

E

Fold

85

NOSE: 15 mm (⅝ inch) plastic post and washer
THREAD: black embroidery floss for mouth, red machine embroidery thread for letter
PAPER: typing or newspaper for backing

**Posh Bear**

BEAR HEAD, PAWS, AND FOOT TOPS: 15 by 27 inches of off-white fake fur
FOOT SOLES: 5 by 6 inches of honey-colored fake fur
BODY TOP (PANTS): 9 by 18 inches of silver-coated fabric
BODY BOTTOM (SHIRT): 12 by 15 inches of white shirting
RUFFLES: 32 inches of ¾-inch-wide ruffled eyelet
CUMMERBUND: 3 by 14 inches of gold lamé fabric
JACKET: 18 by 21 inches of metallic brocade fabric
TIE: 3 by 5 inches of silver metallic fabric
LAPEL AND COLLARS INTERFACING AND SHOULDER PADS: 6 by 8 inches of interfacing
EYES AND NOSE: three 15 mm (⅝ inch) plastic posts and washers
THREAD: black embroidery floss for mouth
NOTIONS: 4 inch bias tape, four pearl buttons

**Clown Bear**

BODY TOP AND BOTTOM, ARMS, FOOT SOLES, AND FOOT TOPS: 18 by 36 inches of brown fake fur
PAWS, MUZZLE, EARS: 9 by 12 inches of lighter brown, shorter-pile fake fur or velvet
CLOWN SUIT: 22 by 27 inches of red print cotton fabric, 22 by 27 inches of green print cotton fabric
RUFFLES: 22½ by 24 inches of off-white cotton fabric cut into 3 strips each 4½ inches wide. Use one 24 inches long and four cut to 11 inches long.
EYES: two 15 mm (⅝ inch) plastic posts and washers
TRIM: one package of red rick rack, pompoms
NOTIONS: 18 inches round elastic, 24 inches bias tape, 24-inch cord or bias tape, folded and stitched

## MAKING THE BEARS

Cut out all pattern pieces for each bear, making sure the pile or fabric grain runs in the right direction.

## STEP 1: MAKING THE HEAD (ALL BEARS)

**A.** Pin the EAR pieces face to face. Stitch around the ear, leaving the bottom open. Trim the seam allowances and turn. Pin a ½-inch tuck in the front ear section. Pin the ears on the HEAD SIDE section and machine baste in place. Cheerleader bear has 2 honey and 2 brown ear pieces.
**B.** Pin the HEAD SIDE to the HEAD TOP. Stitch from the muzzle to the top of the head. Repeat for the other side. Trim the seam allowances and open flat.
**C.** Fit the MUZZLE to the HEAD section. Pin and stitch across the top of the muzzle. Trim the seam allowance.
**D.** Fold the HEAD section flat, face to face, aligning the sides of the MUZZLE. Stitch the chin seam, tapering it smoothly at the nose end. Trim and open.
**E.** Insert the plastic post-and-washer eyes on the head seam line.
*Note:* For the Cheerleader Bear's EYELASHES, insert the eye post through the eyelash then through the head fabric. Push the washer firmly on the back.
**F.** Insert the plastic nose. (Do not sew the mouth until the bear is stuffed, unless it is machine embroidered.)
*Note:* For the Posh Bear, place the eyes higher on the head for the long-nosed polar bear look.

## STEP 2: WESTERN BEAR: MAKING THE BODY TOP

**A.** With contrasting thread, sew the SHIRT detailing on the BODY TOP front and ARM cuffs. Sew the tiny buttons on the shirt and cuffs by machine (set to narrow zigzag, the shortest stitch length).
**B.** Place the COLLAR sections face to face and seam. Trim the seam allowances and clip across the collar point closely to diminish fabric bulk when turned. Turn the collar sections and top stitch with contrasting thread. Pin and machine baste the COLLAR sections on the BODY TOP front at the neck. There is no collar on the back.
**C.** Pin the PAWS face to face, and stitch one side of the paws for 1 inch; open flat.
**D.** Pin the PAWS on the ARM and stitch across the wrist seam. Repeat steps C and D for the other ARM.
**E.** Fold the ARM flat lengthwise and continue stitching the PAW seam all the way to the top of

ALL BEARS: BODY TOPS

MAKE THE HEAD

BODY TOPS: WESTERN, POSH, CHEERLEADER

SEW ARMS AND PAWS

JOIN ARMS TO BODY

SEW HEAD FRONT TO BODY FRONT AND HEAD BACK TO BODY BACK

JOIN TOPS

ALL BEARS: BODY BOTTOMS

SEW CROTCH SEAMS

SEW LEG SEAMS

SEW FEET

ATTACH SOLES

CHEERLEADER BEAR

STITCH TOP TO BOTTOM

SEW THE SKIRT TO THE LINING

SEW CHEERLEADER'S LEGS

Assembling Dressed Bears.

the ARM, leaving the top open. Trim and turn.
**F.** Stuff the ARMS nearly to the top. Pin them on the BODY TOP front, side edges aligned, and machine baste in place.
**G.** Pin the HEAD FRONT to the BODY TOP front at the neck. Ease the HEAD seam if necessary. Stitch and trim; open flat.

**H.** Pin the HEAD BACK to the BODY TOP back at the neck. Stitch and trim; open flat.
**I.** Position the BODY TOP front on the BODY TOP back with the ARMS and EARS tucked carefully inside. Stitch around the entire TOP, leaving the bottom open. Clip the seam allowance at the neck to avoid pulls. Turn.

87

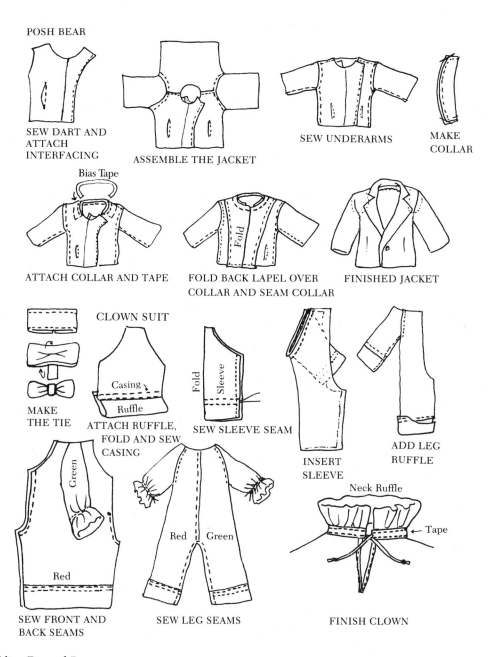

POSH BEAR

SEW DART AND ATTACH INTERFACING

ASSEMBLE THE JACKET

SEW UNDERARMS

MAKE COLLAR

Bias Tape

ATTACH COLLAR AND TAPE

FOLD BACK LAPEL OVER COLLAR AND SEAM COLLAR

Fold

FINISHED JACKET

CLOWN SUIT

MAKE THE TIE

Casing

Ruffle

ATTACH RUFFLE, FOLD AND SEW CASING

Fold

Sleeve

SEW SLEEVE SEAM

INSERT SLEEVE

ADD LEG RUFFLE

Green

Red

SEW FRONT AND BACK SEAMS

Red  Green

SEW LEG SEAMS

Neck Ruffle

Tape

FINISH CLOWN

Assembling Dressed Bears.

## STEP 3: WESTERN BEAR: MAKING THE BODY BOTTOM

**A.** Stitch the machine detailing on the PANTS front and back. Align the crotch seams face to face and stitch. Trim the seam allowances and clip at the curve.

**B.** Align the LEG seams face to face. Stitch and trim.

**C.** Fold the FOOT TOP face to face and sew the heel seam. Align the FOOT TOP with the PANTS cuff, face to face. Tuck the FOOT TOP into the LEG for this seam. Sew around the entire cuff. Repeat for the other LEG.

**D.** Fit the FOOT SOLE onto the FOOT TOP. Pin and stitch around the entire foot. Trim the seam allowances and turn the BODY BOTTOM right side out. Repeat for other foot.

**E.** Pin the BODY TOP and the BODY BOTTOM

together, face to face, matching side seams. Beginning ½ inch on the BODY back, stitch across the body front to the other side, ending ½ inch into the BODY back. This leaves a 5-inch opening for stuffing on the back.

*F.* Stuff the bear carefully from head to toe and firmly enough so the bear stands without wrinkled legs. (This may not be possible with some fabrics.) Hand sew the back waist seam closed.

*G.* Hand embroider the mouth. Trim fur away from the features, if needed.

*H.* Hand sew the large bead to the collar. Thread the thong through the bead and knot both ends.

## STEP 2: CHEERLEADER BEAR: MAKING THE BODY TOP

*A.* Pin the LETTER on the BODY TOP front. (I chose "B" for Bear; choose any letter you like.) Pin a piece of medium-weight paper on the back of the sweater front, behind the letter, to stabilize the fabric. Machine baste the letter in place with small straight stitches. Zigzag stitch over the baste line with solid satin stitching to outline the letter. Remove the paper backing.

*B.* Follow the Western Bear Body Top instructions, Step 2, from C to I.

## STEP 3: CHEERLEADER BEAR: MAKING THE BODY BOTTOM

*A.* Align the RED SKIRT with the WHITE SKIRT LINING face to face. Stitch around the entire outside edge of the skirt hem. Trim a narrow seam allowance. Turn right side out. Press flat. Pin and machine baste the waist edges together.

*B.* Match the LEG top with the PANTIES leg edge. Stitch. Trim and open flat. Repeat for the other LEG.

*C.* Pin the PANTIES and LEG crotch seams together, face to face. Stitch. Clip the seam allowances at the curve to avoid pulls.

*D.* Follow Western Bear Body Bottom instructions, step 3, C and D.

*E.* Insert SKIRT as follows: Pin the SKIRT to the PANTIES top edge, red side up. Stitch around the entire skirt waist. (If the completed skirt sticks out too straight, place it in neat folds and tie a ribbon over them until the folds stay in place when the ribbon is removed.)

*F.* To complete the bear, follow Western Bear Body Bottom instructions, step 3 E to G.

## STEP 2: POSH BEAR: MAKING THE BEAR TOP

*A.* Cut four 4-inch pieces of eyelet ruffle and pin them on the BODY TOP front vertically. Top stitch them in place with matching thread.

*B.* Pin the top of the CUMMERBUND to the BODY TOP front face to face 1 inch up from the waist, and stitch in place. Fold down, aligning the BODY TOP and CUMMERBUND bottom edges. Repeat for BODY TOP back.

*C.* Place the shirt COLLAR sections together, face to face, add the collar interfacing, and seam. Trim the seam allowances and clip across the collar corner to diminish fabric bulk when turned. Turn the collar sections and top stitch. Pin and machine baste the collar sections onto the BODY TOP front neck.

*D.* Place the PAWS face to face and pin. Stitch down the top side for 1 inch; open flat.

*E.* Pin a 6-inch piece of ruffle to the ARM cuff. Stitch. Pin the PAWS on the shirt sleeve ruffle and ARM, then stitch across the wrist seam. Repeat steps C, D, and E for the other ARM.

*F.* Follow the Western Bear Body Top instructions, step 2, from E to I.

## STEP 3: POSH BEAR: MAKING THE BODY BOTTOM

*A.* Align the PANTS crotch seams face to face and stitch. Trim the seam allowances and clip at the curve.

*B.* Follow the Western Bear Body Bottom instructions, step 3, from B to G.

## STEP 4: POSH BEAR: MAKING THE JACKET

*A.* Fold and stitch the JACKET darts. Pin the INTERFACING to the LAPEL face to face. Stitch a ⅛-inch seam. Turn and fold the interfacing to the back of the lapel. Top stitch the seam edge.

*B.* Place the JACKET FRONTS on the JACKET BACK, aligning the shoulder seams. Stitch. Press the seam open.

*C.* Fit the SLEEVE top onto the JACKET, pinning at the shoulder seam. Stitch. Trim the seam allowances and clip the curves. Repeat for the other SLEEVE.

**D.** Fold the JACKET at the shoulder seams, face to face, with the sides and sleeves aligned. Stitch the sleeve and side seam. Trim at the shoulder seam. Turn right side out.

**E.** Lay the JACKET COLLAR sections face to face, pin on the interfacing, and seam. Trim the seam allowances and clip across the corners. Turn the collar and press flat.

**F.** Pin the COLLAR to the JACKET, aligning the center of the collar with the middle of the jacket back. Baste in place. Sew bias tape over this seam.

**G.** Fold the LAPEL facing to the lapel, face to face, overlapping the end of the collar and aligning the neck edges. Do this for each side. Stitch the seam. Trim the seam allowance, clipping the seam on the curve so it will lie smoothly. Turn the LAPELS.

**H.** Turn and press the JACKET hem and the SLEEVE hems. Stitch by hand. Top stitch all around the JACKET, across the hem, up the LAPELS, and around the COLLAR.

**I.** Machine stitch the buttonhole. Hand sew a pearl button on the jacket front and on the shirt front.

**J.** Fold the TIE pieces with the ends into the center. Seam the edges and turn. Tuck raw edges under and wrap the BOW around the TIE. Sew the BOW TIE to the bear's shirt collar.

**K.** Place shoulder pads inside the jacket and hand stitch to the seam allowance.

## STEP 2: CLOWN BEAR: MAKING THE BODY TOP

**A.** Follow the Western Bear Body Top instructions, step 2, from C to I.

## STEP 3: CLOWN BEAR: MAKING THE BODY BOTTOM

**A.** Pin the BODY BOTTOM sides together at the crotch. Stitch and clip the crotch seam joint.

**B.** Follow the Western Bear Body Bottom instructions, step 3, from B to G.

## STEP 4: CLOWN BEAR: MAKING THE CLOWN SUIT

**A.** Pin one edge of the 11-by-4½-inch ARM ruffle to the SLEEVE, face to face. Stitch in place; open flat. Press the seam to the ruffle side.

**B.** Press a small hem in the other edge of the ruffle. Fold the ruffle back to back with itself and stitch the hem to the sleeve on or near the seam line. To make the casing, stitch another line on the ruffle, ⅜ inch below and parallel with the first, all the way around. Thread round elastic through the casing. Pull to fit the bear's ARM and pin.

**C.** Fold the SLEEVE flat lengthwise, face to face. Stitch the SLEEVE seam, making sure to catch the ends of the elastic in the stitching. Tie the elastic ends that protrude. Clip the seam allowance. Repeat for the other SLEEVE.

**D.** Match the red SLEEVE to the green SUIT and stitch the SLEEVE in place. Repeat for the other SLEEVE, mating the green SLEEVE with the red side of the suit.

**E.** Apply the 11-by-4½-inch leg ruffles in the same manner as the arm ruffles, A and B.

**F.** Align the CLOWN SUIT front and back seams. Stitch the front seam from neck to crotch. Stitch the back seam from the crotch up for 3 inches. Turn a narrow double hem on the edges of the back opening and stitch.

**G.** Fold the 24-by-4½-inch neck ruffle lengthwise, face to face. Seam across each end; turn and press flat. Run long gathering stitches on the bottom edge. Gather to fit the CLOWN SUIT neck. Pin and stitch in place.

**H.** Sew bias tape over the neck seam, folding the tape ends under. Sew the other edge of the bias tape on the CLOWN'S SUIT to make a casing. Thread a cord through the casing.

**I.** Fold the CLOWN SUIT so the leg seams align. Beginning at the ruffle, stitch the leg seam, making sure to catch the leg elastic in the seam. Trim the seam allowances and tie the elastic ends. Turn.

**J.** Sew pompoms on the front seam. Fit the suit on the bear and pull the neck cord to fit. Tie in a bow.

## STEP 5: CLOWN BEAR: MAKING THE HAT

**A.** Place two sections of the HAT face to face and stitch. Align the third hat section with the first two edges and stitch. Press the seams flat.

**B.** Fold a ½-inch double hem in the bottom of the hat and pin. Pin rick rack to the outside hem of the hat and stitch the rick rack and the hem in place. Pin a second row of trim next to the first and stitch in place. Sew a pompom on top.

There's room inside this stuffed koala puppet for a large or a small hand.

# Koala Puppet

You know, and I know, and all Australians know that koalas are not bears. But let's just ignore biological classification and go on visual evidence. Koalas look so huggable that we'll invite them into this teddy bear collection. This koala puppet looks and sits like any stuffed bear, but there's space inside for a little or large hand to manipulate his head and arms in a lifelike way.

Short- and long-pile honey-colored fake furs are used for the koala. Polyester fiberfill stuffs most of the body. Any scrap fabric will do for lining. The puppet is a bit more complicated to construct than some stuffed toys because of lining, but it is not difficult to make.

## PATTERN PIECES

**A.** BODY FRONT: cut 1 (short-pile fur), folded
**B.** BODY SIDE (attach to C): cut 2, 1 reversed (short-pile fur)
**C.** BODY SIDE (attach to B): cut 2, 1 reversed (short-pile fur)
**D.** BODY LINING (entire pattern): cut 1 (cotton fabric), folded
**E.** NOSE: cut 2 (black fabric)
*(see p. 92)*

**A.** HEAD SIDE: cut 2, 1 reversed (short-pile fur)
**B.** HEAD TOP: cut 1, (short-pile fur)
**C.** FOOT: cut 2 (short-pile fur)
**D.** EAR: cut 2 (long-pile fur), cut 2 (short-pile fur)
**E.** HEAD LINING: cut 2 (cotton fabric)
*(see p. 93)*

## MATERIALS

BODY:    20 by 26 inches of short-pile honey-colored fake fur
EARS:    4 by 8 inches of long-pile honey-colored fake fur
NOSE:    4 by 6 inches of black suede, leather, or fake fur
LINING:    18 by 20 inches of cotton scrap fabric
EYES:    ⅞-inch plastic post-and-washer eyes
MOUTH:    black embroidery floss
STUFFING:    less than ½ pound of fiberfill

## TO MAKE THE BEAR

Cut out all pattern pieces, with the fur pile going in the right direction.

## STEP 1: MAKING THE KOALA'S HEAD

**A.** Pin the long-pile EAR fronts to the short pile EAR backs, face to face. Stitch. Be careful to keep the pile out of the seam since it will be difficult to pull out later. Trim the seam allowances and turn.

**B.** Pin a tuck in the EAR fronts. Pin the EAR to the EAR SLOT front on the HEAD SIDE, aligning raw edges. Fold the EAR SLOT to cover the EAR and align with the front. Be sure to leave a small seam allowance at the top. Stitch. Repeat for the other EAR.

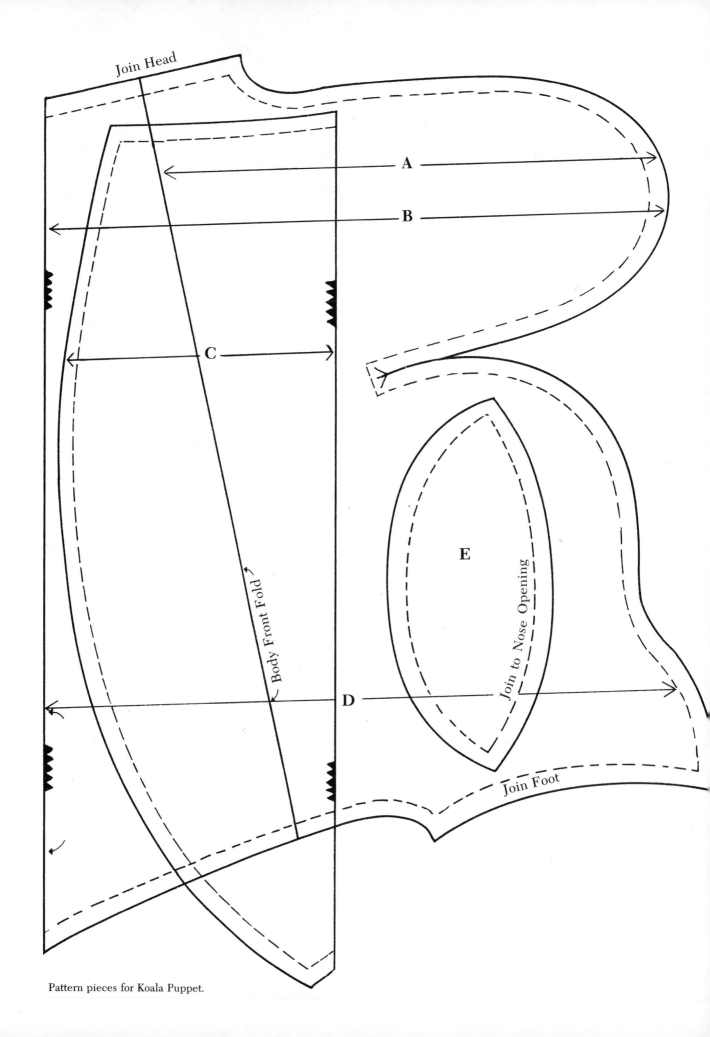

Join Head

A

B

C

Body Front Fold

D

E

Join to Nose Opening

Join Foot

Pattern pieces for Koala Puppet.

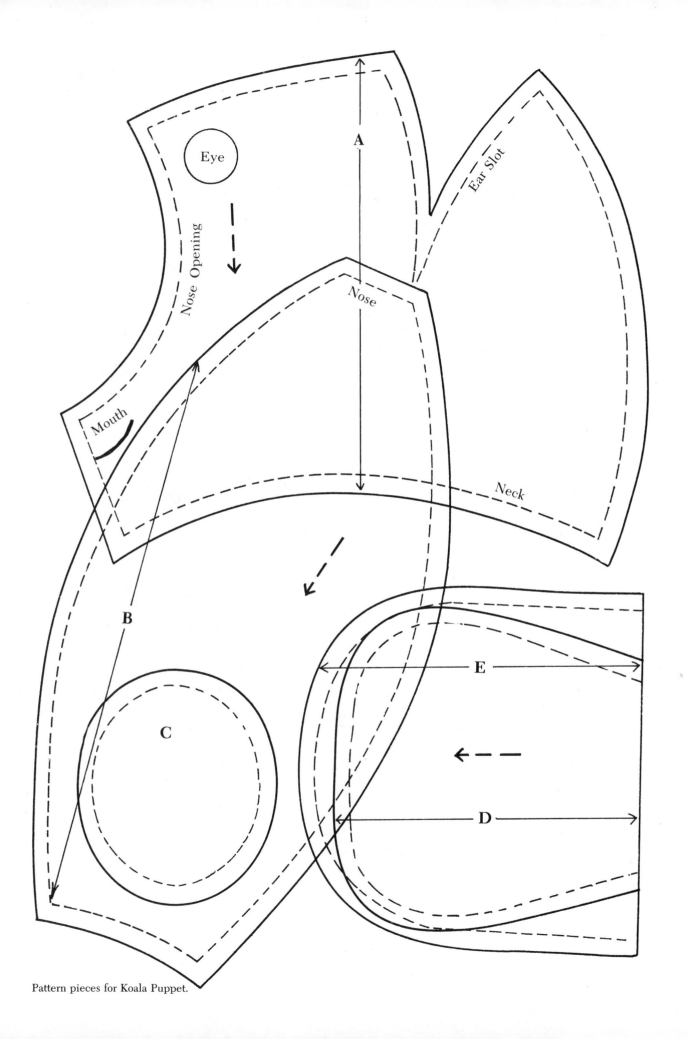

Pattern pieces for Koala Puppet.

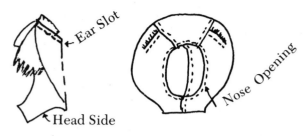
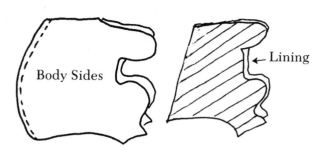

SEW EARS AND HEAD AND ATTACH NOSE

SEW BODY SIDE PIECES TOGETHER AND
LINING (FOLDED) FOR BODY SIDES

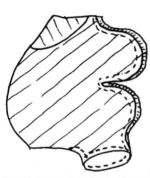

SEW LINING TO BODY

TURN AND PIN

SEW HEAD LINING TO
BODY FRONT AND HEM

SEW FRONT TO BACK

SEW LEG SEAM AND FOOT

ADD STUFFING

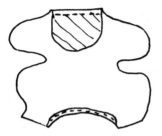

INSERT HEAD, SEW
NECK SEAM, AND TUCK
HEAD LINING IN HEAD

FINISH KOALA

TO MAKE A TEDDY BEAR:
Cut Ears Smaller
Place Eyes Higher
Use Nose for Muzzle
Add Paws
Change Color

Assembling Koala Puppet.

94

*C.* Pin the HEAD SIDE to the HEAD TOP. Tuck the fur in and stitch. Repeat for the other side.

*D.* Place the HEAD SIDES face to face and stitch the chin seam.

*E.* Place the NOSE pieces face to face, pin, and stitch the front seam. Trim the seam allowance and turn.

*F.* Position the NOSE in the nose opening on the head. Align the chin and nose seams. Stitch in place. Turn the head right side out. If you plan to use plastic post-and-washer eyes, insert them at this point on the HEAD SIDES.

## STEP 2: MAKING THE KOALA'S BODY

*A.* Place the BODY SIDES face to face, pin and stitch the back seam.

*B.* Pin the HEAD LINING to the BODY LINING, face to face, and stitch.

*C.* Open the BODY and the BODY LINING flat and match the bottom edges, face to face, easing the BODY as needed. Pin and stitch across the bottom edge only. Trim the seam allowance.

*D.* Turn the BODY LINING so it aligns with the BODY, back to back (right sides out), matching the arm and leg edges. Pin in place.

*E.* Pin the HEAD LINING face to back on the BODY FRONT. Stitch.

*F.* Pin the BODY FRONT to the BODY SIDES, aligning the arms and legs. (The lining is sewn into this seam.) Stitch the side seams only. Clip the seam allowances at the sharp elbow corner.

*G.* Pin the LEG seams on the BODY SIDES and BODY FRONTS, face to face, and stitch. (Sew the lining into this seam.)

*H.* Position the FOOT in the foot hole. Pin and stitch. Sew the lining into this seam.

*I.* Turn a narrow hem in the BODY FRONT bottom and hand stitch.

## STEP 3: FINISHING THE KOALA

*A.* Stuff the LEGS and the bottom edge. Do not stuff the body completely yet.

*Note:* It is possible to stuff the body fully at this point and sew the lining at the neck seams. This makes the body hard to turn, but is efficient.

*B.* Push the HEAD into the BODY. The head is right side out, the body not yet turned. Align the center back seam of the HEAD with the back seam of the BODY. (Do not stitch the lining into this seam unless the body is fully stuffed.) Pin the HEAD to the BODY and stitch.

*C.* Turn the koala. This will take some tugging because of the stuffing already in place. Stuff the head nearly full. Carefully push wads of stuffing between the lining and body at the neck opening to complete stuffing the body.

*D.* When the koala is completely stuffed to your liking, hand sew the HEAD LININGS together. This may not be necessary since you can just push them into the head.

*E.* Hand embroider the koala's mouth in place.

*Note:* To make a bear puppet companion, make these changes: choose a darker body fabric with a matching or lighter muzzle; make the feet and paws lighter; place the eyes higher on the head and closer together; embroider the nose and mouth on the NOSE section as if it were a muzzle.

Turn the switch on the Teddy Bear Night Light to illuminate the wooden dancing bear.

# Teddy Bear Night Light

Who keeps people safe at night? This teddy bear stands guard and the only shadow on the wall is his—cast by the small bulb. By day, the bear holds his dancing pose with a painted smile.

People used to think that electricity leaked out of the sockets on the wall. It's still wise to have a healthy regard for electricity and to perform any work on electrical parts according to safety codes. Beyond this concern, this little lamp is easier than it looks. Of course, it will be sturdier sawed out of hard wood, but for quicker, easier working, use ordinary plywood and pine board. The completed lamp measures about 11 inches tall.

## PATTERN PIECES

**A.** BEAR: cut 1 (¾″ plywood)
**B.** BACK: cut 1 (¼″ plywood)
*(see p. 97)*

**A.** ROOF: cut 1 (¾″ plywood)
**B.** TENT TOP: cut 1 (¼″ plywood)
**C.** TENT FRONT: cut 1 (¼″ plywood)
**D.** BASE: cut 1 (¾″ plywood)
**E.** SIDE: cut 2 (¼″ plywood)
*(see p. 98)*

## MATERIALS

BEAR, BASE, and ROOF:  5 by 13 inches of ¾-inch-thick plywood or particle board (or 1-inch-thick board of hard or soft wood)

SIDES, BACK, TENT TOP, and FRONT:  7 by 10 inches of ¼-inch-thick plywood
LAMP FEET:  four 1-inch-tall wooden beads
SOCKET:  one small socket to fit a night light bulb
BULB:  one night light bulb to fit the socket
SWITCH:  one-way ordinary (not heavy-duty) switch with a turn knob
CORD:  ordinary cord with plug attached (it may be cheapest to buy a ready-made extension cord and cut off the socket end)
SCREWS:  2-inch wood screw, four 1⅜-inch screws
SUPPLIES:  1½-inch finishing nails, wood glue, electrical tape, carbon paper, pencil, ruler
SPECIAL TOOLS:  coping, band, or jig saw; straight saw; common ¼-inch drill with two auger bits for making larger holes, a 1-inch auger bit for the socket, and a ½-inch auger bit for the switch, or sizes as needed (these bits can be purchased in sets of four sizes, from ⅜ to 1 inch); ¼-inch-wide chisel; hammer; screwdriver; wood files or sandpaper; Plastic Wood; counter punch; wire cutters
PAINT:  wood undercoat paint, artist's acrylic paint (golden brown, purple, green, red-orange, light yellow, buff, red, white, sky blue, and dark brown)

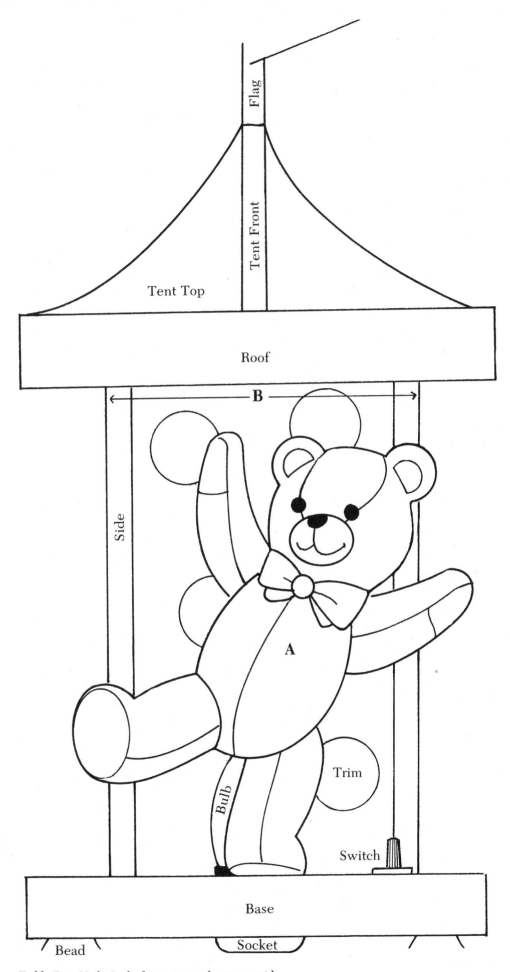

Flag

Tent Front

Tent Top

Roof

B

Side

A

Trim

Bulb

Switch

Base

Bead

Socket

Teddy Bear Night Light front view and pattern guide.

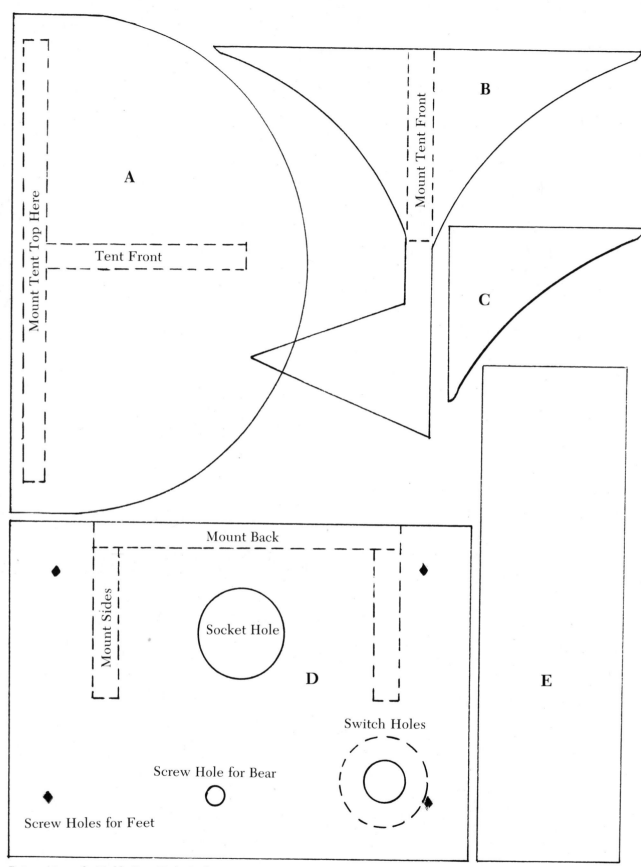

Pattern pieces for Teddy Bear Night Light.

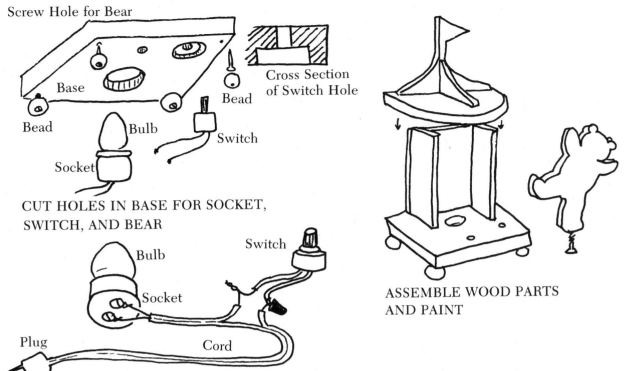

Screw Hole for Bear

Base

Bead

Bead

Socket

Bulb

Switch

Cross Section of Switch Hole

**CUT HOLES IN BASE FOR SOCKET, SWITCH, AND BEAR**

Bulb

Switch

Socket

Plug

Cord

**WIRE THE LAMP**

**ASSEMBLE WOOD PARTS AND PAINT**

Assembling Teddy Bear Night Light.

## STEP 1: WOODWORKING

**A.** Put the carbon paper under the pattern and trace the TEDDY BEAR on one end of the ¾-inch-thick board. Trace the ROOF in the center. Trace the BASE on the other end.

**B.** Using a straight saw, cut out the BASE. To cut out the BEAR and ROOF, use a scroll-type saw, such as a hand coping saw with a wide throat and a narrow blade for intricate cutting (stroke downward to cut), a jig saw, or band saw. Sandpaper or file the edges smooth.

**C.** Measure and trace the SIDES, BACK, TENT TOP (including flag), and TENT FRONT on the ¼-inch plywood. Place the SIDES and BACK pieces adjacent to each other, but add the width of the saw blade if it is fairly wide. Saw out the SIDES and BACK with a straight saw. Use a scroll saw (one of the three above) to cut out the TENT TOP and FLAG, and TENT FRONT. Sand or file these pieces smooth on the edges.

**D.** Mark the holes in the base for the SOCKET, the SWITCH, and the BEAR. Drill the socket hole with the proper-sized auger bit to fit the socket, going all the way through the base. Use scrap lumber under the base to drill into. Mark the holes for the bead FEET on the under side and drill ¼-inch deep holes.

**E.** From the underside of the BASE, drill the

SWITCH hole halfway through with the 1-inch auger bit. Change to the ½-inch auger bit and continue the hole through the base. Fit the switch in the hole. Its knob and threaded sleeve should protrude up enough so the knurled round nut can screw on the sleeve to hold the switch in place. If the ½-inch hole is not big enough, file it larger until the sleeve will fit. If the sleeve still does not come through far enough, chisel out more wood from the 1-inch hole until the switch fits and the threads catch in the nut. You may need to chisel away a little for the wires, too. Keep fitting and sanding or chiseling until the switch fits smoothly in place.

**F.** Drill a small hole the diameter of the 2-inch screw for the BEAR. Hold the bear in position over the screw and continue drilling the hole into the bear's leg for a short distance. Screw the BEAR in place, but not too tightly.

**G.** When the SOCKET, the SWITCH, and the BEAR all fit well in their places, disassemble and set these parts aside.

## STEP 2: ASSEMBLING THE BEAR NIGHT LIGHT

**A.** Start two finishing nails ⅛ inch from the edge on each side of the BACK. Spread glue on the back edges of the SIDE. Position the BACK on

the Bear Facts

# Real Bears

Admiration for the bear did not begin in 1902 with the teddy bear, nor did it begin hundreds of years earlier with Russia's Mishka. It began 110,000 years ago with the Neanderthal people, who placed bear skulls in a shrinelike cave. The Cult of The Bear lasted until 40,000 B.C. They worshiped a large brown bear that resembled America's Kodiak, but it is now extinct.

Bears, classified as carnivorous mammals, nevertheless eat omnivorously, changing their diet with nature's bounty: ants, berries, fish, honey, small animals, even tourists' handouts or campers' caches. Lewis and Clark complained of marauding bears in their camps.

Bears' long, coarse hair and loose skin make them look bigger than they really are. The common American black bear, "clown of the woods," weighs about 400 pounds. He appears almost human with his amusing antics—standing on his head, falling over, dancing, and sitting on his haunches begging for food.

Humans and bears share several characteristics. Both are mammals. Both are plantigrades, meaning they walk on the flat soles of their feet. Unlike most mammals, the bear can stand erect and rotate his arms outward, allowing him to hug (for better or worse). His flat-footed walk makes the bear appear clumsy, but, for a short burst, a black bear can run at a speed of 32 miles per hour.

Bear cubs are born small (10 ounces) and helpless, and they stay with their mothers for an extended childhood while she teaches them to hunt. The cubs are born in winter while the solitary female hibernates in her snug den.

Grizzly bears, most feared by man, are classified as Ursus horribilis (horrible bear) somewhat erronously, since these private animals do not generally attack humans unless provoked. They grow

the back edge of the SIDE and drive the finishing nails into this edge. Repeat for the other SIDE. Countersink the nail ⅛ inch.

*Note:* Countersink all nails with the counter punch or a large, sharp-pointed nail. Later, fill the holes with Plastic Wood, let this dry to hardness, then sand smooth to hide the nail holes.

*B.* Position the SIDES and BACK on the ROOF and draw around the edges. Start four or five finishing nails into the ROOF within these lines. Nail until the tips of the nails come through. Spread glue on the top edges of the SIDES and BACK. Position the ROOF on the top of the SIDES and BACK and nail in place. Countersink the nails. Fill the holes. Sand the piece smooth.

*Note:* You may find it easier to paint all pieces at this point and finish assembly afterward.

*C.* Screw the bead FEET to the underside of the base. Glue the TENT TOP to the BASE. Let this joint dry well.

*D.* Glue the TENT FRONT to the TENT TOP. Tape to hold the pieces if they will not stay together. Remove the tape when dry and glue the TENT TOP and FRONT to the ROOF. Let the glue dry well.

## STEP 3: PAINTING THE BEAR NIGHT LIGHT

*A.* To hold the bear for painting, insert a screw through cardboard or some other temporary base, then insert the anchored screw into the bear.

*B.* Apply a smooth coat of undercoat paint to the bear and the lamp. Allow this to dry completely. Sand smooth. Undercoat contains some filler, so if this coat is not smooth enough, apply another coat and sand.

*C.* Paint the BEAR golden brown, except for the ribbon. Paint the FLAG purple. Paint the BASE a soft bright green. Paint the ROOF red-orange. None of these colors touch, so the paints won't run into each other. Allow the colors to dry and then give them a second coat if necessary.

*D.* When the first colors are dry, paint the TENT SIDE and BACK light yellow. Paint the MUZZLE, PAWS, and EARS on the bear buff. Paint the RIBBON red. Paint the FLAGPOLE and TENT edges white. Allow these colors to dry and give them a second coat if necessary.

*E.* Paint the TENT SIDE front edges sky blue. Paint the outline and detailing on the BEAR dark brown. Paint polka dots or other designs inside the tent. Or use colored 1-inch round labels to stick on the tent.

## STEP 4: WIRING THE BEAR NIGHT LIGHT

**A.** Insert the socket from the top side into its hole. On the cord, cut the insulation away 1 inch from each end of the cord wires. Attach the cord wires to the socket terminals according to the diagram on the packaging. Screw the base of the socket in place. If the socket does not fit firmly in the hole, wrap it with electrical tape to fit.

**B.** Cut *one half* of the cord wire a short distance from the socket. Peel back the insulation from both ends of this wire for 1 inch.

**C.** Insert the switch in the switch hole. Screw on the knurled nut to hold the switch in place. Wire the switch wires to the cord ends. Wrap the joinings well with electrical tape. Wrap wires neatly on the base of the lamp to tuck them in place.

**D.** Insert the bulb in the socket. Push the plug in a wall socket to test the light. Turn the light switch off.

**E.** Remove the bear screw from the BEAR and insert it in the hole in the BASE from the bottom. Hold the BEAR in place and turn the screw as far as it will go to tighten the bear on the base.

**F.** He's done! Turn on the light.

to weigh as much as 1,000 pounds and are characterized by a massive muscular shoulder hump (seen on early teddy bears) used for driving the front legs. The grizzly has a huge head, small ears, and a "dished" face. Hunted and driven back by encroaching civilization, only about 1,000 of the beautiful and awesome animals remain in western North America.

Polar bears differ from the others. These enormous bears can grow to 9 feet long and weigh a maximum of 1,600 pounds. Their dense white fur is made up of hollow, transparent hair shafts for warmth and camouflage against the white Arctic background. They have a sleek structure with a small head, long neck, and slender body, which makes them powerful, agile swimmers. Unlike other bears, their foot pads are covered with fur and act as snow shoes on snow and ice.

The Kodiak is a type of brown bear native to Kodiak Island near Alaska and British Columbia. Brown bears, like black bears, vary in color, from honey and cinnamon to black; cubs of the same litter may differ in fur color.

The brown bear of Europe and Asia appears in many children's stories as Bruin, the late Middle

Polar bears, with their reflective white coats and fur-covered feet, are ideally suited to snowy climates and terrain. Photograph by Kimberly Vigiletti.

English word for brown. Tamed brown bears can dance to music and perform other tricks that have delighted European children over the years.

There are two "nonbears" often used as models for teddy bears. First is the koala, a small Australian animal. This adorable, slow-moving tree dweller is a marsupial, a furry mammal with a pouch for its young.

Another bear that's not a bear is China's panda. Most pandas resemble their relative, the raccoon. The giant panda looks like an elegantly designed bear in beautiful black and white. Both the koala and the panda have been embraced by bear lovers and included as teddy bears, despite scientific classification.

Bears have not always been treated kindly by humans. Many years ago bear baiting, a cruel sport long since outlawed, was popular in England. The European cave bear is now extinct, killed off by hunters, and American bear populations have been greatly reduced by hunting and by expanding human populations.

Brown and black bears, like this one, who also live at the Detroit Zoo, beg visitors for peanuts but may be too lazy to reach for one. "In the mouth, please." Photograph by Kimberly Vigiletti.

The Detroit Zoological Park polar bears, like all polar bears, are sleek and powerful . Polar bears are among the largest of bears.

Scale up this fur fabric-covered wooden Bear Chair to the size you like.

Lines drawn on the framework show that the chair could be finished in wood alone, with ears added and features painted on.

# Bear Chair

"Come sit on my lap," invites this furry bear chair. The 24-inch-tall chair is designed for small children, but the pattern could be scaled up easily to fit anyone. Three chairs in graduated sizes would give Goldilocks her traditional choice, or fit three children. You can either upholster the chair or finish it in wood alone. Wooden bear chairs could have a clear varnish finish or be colorfully painted, with a little pillow added for softness.

Making this project requires some woodworking skill, basic sewing skills, and strong, clever fingers for handling the upholstery. The original chair took one evening to saw and one day to make, working full tilt. You'll enjoy it more at a slower pace.

A fur fabric with a knitted back works best for this bear. This material, like many upholstery fabrics, has been sprayed on the back with a "rubberized" permanent coating to stabilize the fabric. It stretches to allow for the snug, flexible fit of good upholstery, and yet sews easily. If you choose a nonstretch woven fabric such as velvet or denim you will need to be a bit more accurate in cutting, and more careful in sewing and fitting to avoid wrinkles in the wrong places. But don't worry, you can always shove in more padding to flatten a wrinkle.

## PATTERN PIECES

A. LEG: cut 2 (wood)
B. SEAT: cut 1 (wood)
C. BACK: cut 1 (wood)
D. EAR: cut 2 (gold), cut 2 (brown)
E. OUTSIDE ARM (entire piece): cut 2, 1 reversed (brown)

F. INSIDE ARM (minus paw): cut 2, 1
  reversed (brown)
G. PAW: cut 2 (gold)
H. LEG/SIDE (entire piece): cut 4,
  2 reversed (brown)
I. UNDERSEAT (entire piece): cut 1 (brown)
J. BODY (entire piece): cut 2 (brown)
K. TUMMY: cut 1 (gold)
L. EYES: cut 2 (black)
M. NOSE: cut 1 (black)
N. MUZZLE: cut 1 (gold)
O. RIBBON: cut 1 (4 × 8″ red)
  *(see p. 105)*

## MATERIALS

CHAIR: one piece of 24-by-36-inch plywood or
  particle board, ½, ⅝ or ¾ inch thick
SCREWS: ten 2- to 3-inch wood screws (longer
  and larger gauge for thicker wood)
BODY FABRIC, EAR BACKS, and UNDER-
  SEAT: 36 by 48 inches of brown fake fur
  fabric
TUMMY, MUZZLE, EAR FRONTS, and
  PAWS: 8 by 20 inches of gold fake fur
NOSE and EYES: 2 by 6 inches of black velvet
RIBBON: 4 by 8 inches of red wool or satin
PADDING: partial batt of bonded polyester fiberfill, or combination of cotton/polyester
  upholstery stuffing
THREAD: gold machine embroidery thread or
  two strands of ordinary sewing thread, black
  machine embroidery thread, pink machine
  embroidery thread, very strong sewing thread
  for bear's body
TOOLS and SUPPLIES: large sheets of tracing
  paper for the pattern (newsprint will do),
  yardstick, pencil, sabre saw, ratchet screwdriver (plain will do), drill and drill bits to
  match screw size, staple gun and ⅜- to ½-inch
  staples, strong upholstery needle, sharp scissors, plastic-headed pins, sandpaper, undercoat, and semigloss paint in four colors for
  the wooden bear chair

## TO MAKE THE BEAR CHAIR

Scale up the pattern to full size, or the size you prefer, using a grid system. Draw the pattern directly on the wood, if you wish. Draw the pattern for the fabric on wrapping paper, tracing paper, or newsprint. Cut out all the fabric pattern pieces, making sure the fur pile runs downward, except for the ears.

## STEP 1: MAKING THE WOODEN CHAIR

**A.** Saw out the BACK, LEGS, and SEAT. For a wooden chair, include the EARS. For an upholstered chair, remove them.

**B.** Mark the lines and screw holes for the seat joining on the INSIDE LEG according to the pattern.

**C.** The bear shown fits children aged 1 to 6 years. To determine a different height seat, measure the user from heel to knee back and mark this point on the INSIDE LEG at the front.. To establish the seat placement, lay one side LEG flat, and place the BACK and SEAT upright on this piece at the proper angle. The SEAT back should tilt ½ inch lower at the back for comfort. The BACK of the chair should angle back about 2½ inches from base to top, but to ensure stability should not protrude beyond the bear's leg at the back. When you have established the proper angles for your size chair, draw pencil lines on the inside leg along the edges of the seat and back pieces for a guide to assembly. Mark both legs exactly the same. Also, mark the joining of the seat to the back.

**D.** Drill holes in the BACK piece within the two lines drawn for the seat. Hold the SEAT in place with removable finishing nails, tape, or clamps on the marked lines and drill the BACK holes into the SEAT edge. Screw the SEAT and BACK together.

**E.** Drill two holes for the SEAT and two for the BACK on each LEG piece. Drill both at once if you are using a drill press. For a less accurate hand drill, measure each piece.

**F.** Place the BACK and SEAT section on its side. Position the side LEG accurately on top with the marks and edges aligned. Clamp, tape, or tack to hold. Drill the LEG holes into the edges of the SEAT and BACK. Screw the LEG in place. Repeat for the second LEG, making sure it aligns perfectly with the first so the chair won't wobble.

**G.** To make the wooden chair with no upholstery, sand the edges and surface smooth. Paint the bear with undercoat. Sand. Mark the features lightly. Paint the MUZZLE, EARS, and TUMMY with gold paint, overlapping the lines. When this coat is dry, mask the shapes with masking tape, then paint the red ribbon color over the edges. Mask the red, then brush or spray paint the entire bear brown. Remove the masking tape and hand paint the black details, EYES, NOSE and outline, if you wish. For a varnished bear chair, paint on the features, then cover with several coats of varnish.

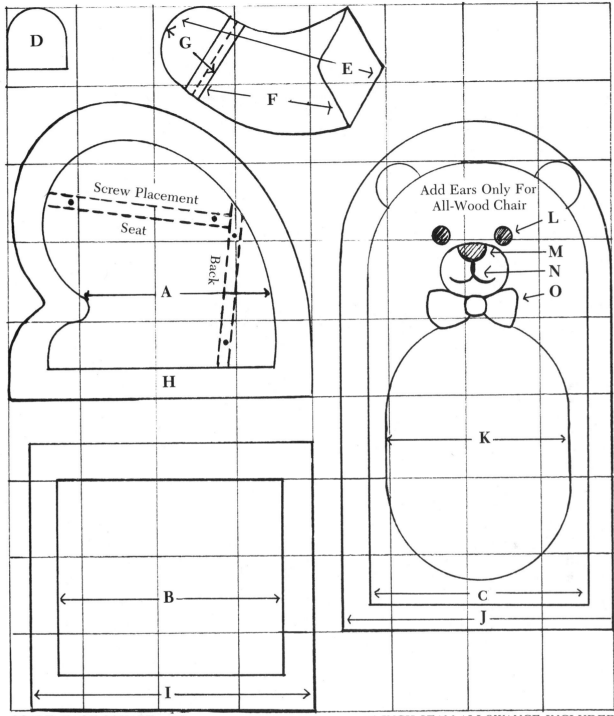

SCALE: EACH SQUARE = 4″

½ INCH SEAM ALLOWANCE INCLUDED

Pattern pieces for Teddy Bear Chair.

## STEP 2: ADDING FABRIC PIECES

**A.** Use ½-inch seam allowances. Place the EAR pieces face to face and sew together. Pick the fur out of the seam. Sew a large tuck in the front of each EAR. Trim the seam allowances and the tuck narrowly to decrease the bulk of the seams.

**B.** Place the PAW face to face on the INSIDE ARM section and stitch. Lay the OUTSIDE and INSIDE ARMS face to face, pin and seam together, leaving the top open. Clip the seam allowance at the inner elbow. Repeat for the other ARM and turn the arms.

**C.** Stuff the ARM firmly with stuffing leaving a

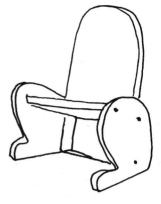

MAKE WOODEN CHAIR

SEW ARMS, TURN, AND STUFF

PIN AND BASTE ARMS TO BEAR FRONT

SEW LEG SEAMS PART WAY

Satin Stitching

APPLIQUÉING

SEW BACK TO FRONT OF BEAR

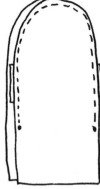

SEW UNDERSEAT TO BEAR FRONT

PAD CHAIR, FIT FABRIC, AND STAPLE TO SEAT

PAD SEAT, COVER WITH FABRIC, STAPLE, AND SEW BOTTOM EDGE

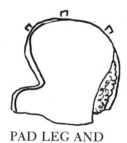

PAD LEG AND FIT FABRIC

SCREW ON LEG, COVER WITH PADDING, STAPLE, AND STITCH BOTTOM EDGE

Assembling Teddy Bear Chair.

space at the top. Fold the front seam to the back seam and pin next to each other with the paw downward. (Don't pin the seams exactly together since the resulting seam will be too bulky.) Machine baste the top of the arm closed.

## STEP 3: APPLIQUÉING

**A.** Pin paper backing on the reverse side behind appliqué pieces, if necessary. Place the MUZZLE, NOSE, EYES, RIBBON, and TUMMY pieces on the bear's BODY according to the pattern guide. Pin these pieces very securely in place since they will slide on the fur readily. Hand or machine baste in place. If a piece wrinkles or slides, or doesn't look right after this step, remove the long machine basting stitches carefully with a seam ripper. Reposition the piece and baste again. It's worth spending time to get just the right expression on your bear's face. A quarter inch can matter!

**B.** When all pieces are basted in place, use machine embroidery thread to satin stitch the outline of the shapes. Sew the EYES, NOSE, MUZZLE, and TUMMY with gold thread. Whenever possible, sew "with the pile," stitching downward on the fur so it won't get stuck in the stitch line. When it does, use a strong needle to pull the fur out of the satin stitching as you sew. If too much fur gets stuck in the stitching line, make a second stitch line to cover the first.

**C.** Sew the red RIBBON with bright pink thread. This makes a livelier outline than a matching red. Remove any paper backing.

## STEP 4: SEWING THE BEAR

**A.** Pin the EARS to the bear BODY FRONT with the gold side forward. Machine baste in place.

**B.** Pin the stuffed ARMS to the sides of the bear FRONT. Machine baste in place.

**C.** Pin the bear BACK to the bear FRONT, face to face. Tuck in the EARS and ARMS. Beginning 7 inches up on the back, sew around the BODY, stopping 7 inches from the end on the other side. Reinforce the EAR seams because you know they will be used as handles to pull the bear.

**D.** Sew the UNDERSEAT to the FRONT of the bear's body.

**E.** Place LEG sections face to face and sew the front seam from toe to knee.

## STEP 5: UPHOLSTERING THE CHAIR

**A.** Remove the screws from the wooden leg sections, four screws each. (Keep track of them.)

**B.** Lay one strip of bonded batting (single or double layer) over the chair's HEAD to cover the front and back of the wooden bear. Slide the fabric covering over the back and batting. This should be a snug fit. If it is not, add more padding or stitch the seams closer.

**C.** Pull the back piece down firmly, eliminating all wrinkles, and staple it to the lower edge of the

BACK. Staple the fabric to the sides, trimming carefully around the screw holes. Trim away any extra fabric from the sides.

**D.** Pull the front fabric down firmly to the SEAT. Staple in three places as close to the joint as possible to hide the staples.

**E.** Lift up the bear TUMMY and add four layers of stuffing to the SEAT and over the front of the SEAT. Pull the fabric over the seat edge firmly. Place a row of staples 1 inch from the seam line (about 2 or 3 inches from the front edge of the chair on the underside of the seat) to hold the seat fabric firmly in place. Put another row of staples at the joining with the back.

**F.** Pull the front fabric to cover the bottom and tack with two loose staples. Sew this seam closed by hand for the neatest appearance, using a sturdy double thread. Remove staple/tacks. Turn a hem if the fabric frays and blind overcast in place. Staple the front fabric to the SIDES and BACK on the edges. Be sure to trim away extra fabric, especially from the screw holes, so you can find them and so the fabric will not bind the screws.

## STEP 6: MAKING THE LEGS

**A.** Lay padding on the wooden LEGS. Staple/tack this in place.

**B.** Fit the partially sewn LEG fabric over the wood. Fit this piece carefully at the toe and knee. Pull only the INSIDE LEG fabric to fit snugly and staple it along the back, top, and bottom edges. Trim away extra fabric.

**C.** Make a ½-inch slit in the inside LEG fabric over the screw holes. Flip up the outside LEG padding and insert screws into the leg, through the fabric slits, and into the bear SEAT and BACK. Screw the LEG firmly in place.

**D.** Replace the outside padding. Add more padding to the LEG and foot to achieve a rounded effect. Be sure added padding lays smoothly in place.

**E.** Pin or staple/tack the outer LEG fabric in place. Pull firmly to remove all wrinkles. Hand sew along the edge to finish. Repeat for the other LEG. Remove all staple/tacks.

**F.** If necessary, sew the body side seams just above the LEG joining by hand if this seam does not entirely cover the wood and stuffing.

*Note:* If you use thin wood or make an adult-size bear, use braces under the seat to join the legs.

Flat mitten-shaped puppets with appliquéd features make up quickly for a cast of *The Three Bears* characters.

# The Three Bears Puppets

These flat puppets are appliquéd by hand or machine on one-piece fronts and backs, then stitched together like mittens. Their bodies are made from brown wool fabric, but any firmly woven fabric or felt would do. Their clothing comes from fabric scraps on hand. Choose materials for all four pieces before you begin so all your color choices will relate in the same way that costume and stage designers carefully coordinate their colors to create an effective performance.

*Note:* These puppets will fit a medium-sized hand. For small children, make them smaller or use a quilted body fabric. Use a backing fabric to make the figures stand up more firmly. Cut them larger if Dad wants to get into the act. To measure, trace around his hand and add at least ¾ inch extra.

Clothing for these bears consists of fabric pieces appliquéd or stitched onto the body, mainly by satin stitching. This satin-stitched line, which can be done by hand or machine, holds the appliqué firmly in place and also provides a colored outline.

Sometimes machine satin stitching ripples the body fabric. To make this fabric firmer, pin it to a piece of typing paper or newspaper for support while stitching. Pin the appliqué pieces to the front side, making a three-layer sandwich. When you are finished, the backing paper will pull off easily along the machine-sewn perforated lines.

## PATTERN PIECES

### PAPA BEAR
**A.** BODY: cut 2 (brown fabric) entire piece
**B.** EARS: cut 4 (brown fabric)
**C.** MUZZLE: cut 1 (tan felt)
**D.** PAW: cut 2 (tan felt)
**E.** VEST: cut 2 front, cut 1 back with STRAP ¾" wide (checkered fabric)
**F.** PANTS: cut 1 front, cut 1 back straight across (striped fabric)

### BABY BEAR
**A.** BODY: cut 2 (brown fabric) entire piece
**B.** EAR: cut 4 (brown fabric)
**C.** MUZZLE: cut 1 (tan felt)
**D.** COLLAR: cut 2 (ecru cotton)
**E.** PAW: cut 2 (tan felt)
**F.** STRAPS: cut 2 front, cut 2 back (blue jeans)
**G.** PANTS: cut 1 front, cut 1 back straight across (blue jeans) *(see p. 109)*

### MAMA BEAR
**A.** BODY: cut 2 (brown fabric) entire piece
**B.** EAR: cut 4 (brown fabric)
**C.** MUZZLE: cut 1 (tan felt)
**D.** PAW: cut 2 (tan felt)
**E.** APRON: cut 1 (striped cotton)
**F.** SKIRT: cut 2 (printed cotton)
**G.** RUFFLE: cut 2 (printed cotton)

### GOLDILOCKS
**A.** BODY: cut 2 (white fabric) entire piece

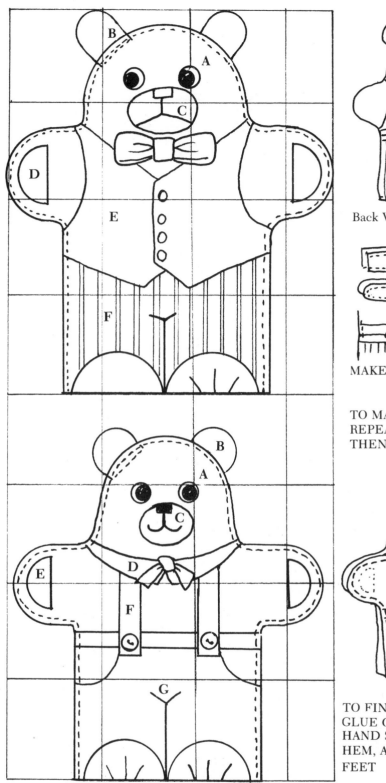

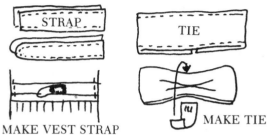

APPLIQUÉ MUZZLE AND
PAWS ON ALL BEARS

Back View of Papa Bear

STRAP

TIE

MAKE VEST STRAP

MAKE TIE

TO MAKE BABY BEAR,
REPEAT STEP 1 **A-C**
THEN APPLIQUÉ CLOTHING AS SHOWN

STITCH ALL BEARS FRONT TO BACK,
WITH EARS AND SKIRTS TUCKED IN

TO FINISH ALL BEARS
GLUE ON EYES, AND
HAND SEW BUTTONS,
HEM, AND CLAWS ON
FEET

SCALE: EACH SQUARE = 3″

Pattern pieces and assembly for Papa and Baby Bears.

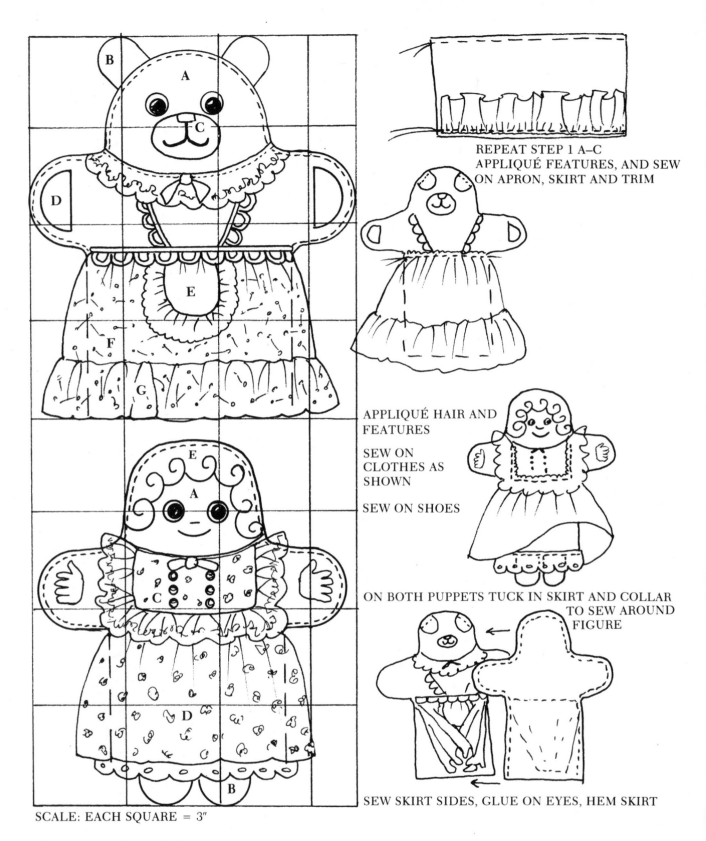

REPEAT STEP 1 A–C
APPLIQUÉ FEATURES, AND SEW
ON APRON, SKIRT AND TRIM

APPLIQUÉ HAIR AND
FEATURES

SEW ON
CLOTHES AS
SHOWN

SEW ON SHOES

ON BOTH PUPPETS TUCK IN SKIRT AND COLLAR
TO SEW AROUND
FIGURE

SEW SKIRT SIDES, GLUE ON EYES, HEM SKIRT

SCALE: EACH SQUARE = 3″

Pattern pieces and assembly for Mama Bear and Goldilocks.

**B.** SHOE: cut 4 (black felt or fabric)
SHOE TRIM: cut 2 (white felt)
**C.** DRESS TOP: cut 2 (printed cotton)
**D.** SKIRT: cut 2 (printed cotton)
**E.** HAIR: cut 1 full head, 1 rim (yellow felt)

## MATERIALS

### Papa Bear

BODY and EARS: 12 by 20 inches of brown fabric
PANTS: 9 by 6 inches of striped fabric
VEST and VEST STRAP: 12 by 6 inches of checkered fabric
PAWS and MUZZLE: 2 by 4 inches of tan felt
TIE: 7 inches of ribbon, 1¼ inches wide
EYES: glue-on movable eyes (or embroider)
THREAD: black, ecru, and rust
BUTTONS: ¼-inch baby buttons

### Mama Bear

BODY and EARS: 11 by 20 inches of brown fabric
SKIRT: 12-inch square of calico
APRON: 2½ by 3 inches of striped cotton
PAWS and MUZZLE: 2 by 4 inches of tan felt
STRAPS: 24 inches of ½-inch-wide braid or trim
APRON TRIM and COLLAR: 28 inches of 1-inch-wide lace
RIBBON: 4 inches of ¼-inch velvet ribbon for bow
EYES: glue-on movable eyes (or embroider)
THREAD: black and ecru

### Baby Bear

BODY and EARS: 10 by 17 inches of brown fabric
PANTS and STRAPS: 5½ by 11 inches of blue jean fabric (used)
COLLAR: 5 by 3 inches of ecru printed cotton
PAWS and MUZZLE: 2 by 4 inches of tan felt
TIE: 4 inches of ¼-inch wide pink velvet ribbon
THREAD: black, light blue, and ecru
BUTTONS: two ¼-inch blue baby buttons

### Goldilocks

BODY: 11 by 17 inches of white or flesh-colored fabric
DRESS: 22 by 4 inches of blue calico fabric
HAIR: 5 by 7 inches of yellow felt or fabric
SHOES: 4 by 5 inches of black felt or fabric
LACE: 26 inches of 1-inch-wide blue lace
RIBBON: 4 inches of ¼-inch-wide pink ribbon
PETTICOAT: 12 inches of 1-inch white eyelet trim.
EYES: glue-on movable eyes (or embroider)
BUTTONS: eight tiny blue buttons
THREAD: gold, pink, white, and blue

## TO MAKE THE PUPPETS

Cut out all pattern pieces and press them flat.

### STEP 1: BEGINNING ALL BEARS

**A.** Pin the bear BODY on paper backing to keep fabric flat.
**B.** Pin the PAWS and MUZZLE in place, then satin stitch appliqué with black thread. Sew the MOUTH expression you want. Machine embroider the EYES, if you prefer.
**C.** Stitch EAR pieces together, then turn and press. Pin the ears to the HEAD with raw edges aligned. Sew in place.

### MAKING PAPA BEAR

**D.** Pin or glue-baste PANTS in place on each body piece. Use rust-colored satin stitching to appliqué edges and to create detailing of the LEGS. Pin on VEST pieces and satin stitch appliqué in place. Sew BUTTONS on by machine or by hand.
**E.** Pin the VEST STRAP pieces face to face and stitch seams ⅛ inch from the edge. Fold TIE piece ends to the center, face to face, and stitch. Turn the straps and tie pieces and press flat.
**F.** Pin the VEST STRAPS on the VEST back, with the finished rounded end over the straight end. Sew in place ½ inch from the rounded end with a square of satin stitching to look like a buckle.
**G.** Sew the end of the small TIE piece to the bear's NECK. Make tucks in the tie, then wrap the BOW around the tie with the end tucked under. Machine or hand stitch in place. Remove all paper backing.
**H.** Pin the front and back BODY pieces together, face to face. Stitch around ⅛ inch from the edge, leaving the bottom open. Clip or trim the seam allowances at the arm corners so the seams will not pull when turned. Turn the bear.
**I.** To finish, glue the EYES in place if you haven't already hand embroidered them. Turn and hand sew a narrow hem at the bottom. Embroider CLAWS on the feet.

### MAKING MAMA BEAR

**D.** Cut two calico SKIRT pieces 3½ by 9 inches and two ruffles 2½ by 12 inches. By hand or machine, run long gathering stitches ¼ inch from the top edge of each piece. Pull the ruffle gathering thread to measure 9 inches and sew to the bottom of the skirt, raw edges aligned.
**E.** Cut the skirt TRIM and STRAPS into 6 pieces: two 6 inches long and four 3 inches long. Pin the

four short shoulder STRAPS in place on the body pieces, then stitch. Pull the skirt gathering thread to the body width and sew in place over the strap ends. The 6-inch TRIM pieces are sewn over the skirt top after the apron is attached.

*F.* Cut the LACE into three pieces, one 8 inches long and two 10 inches long. Run long gathering stitches ⅛ inch from one edge of all the pieces. Gather the longer pieces to fit the NECK with raw ends aligned with raw edges, pin and stitch in place.

*G.* Gather the 8-inch-long lace, then fit and pin it around the APRON. Stitch in place. Unfold the seam, press the apron flat, then top stitch the seam to hold it flat. Gather the top of the apron slightly pin to the top edge of the skirt and stitch. Place the 6-inch TRIM pieces over the raw top edge of the skirt, front and back and stitch in place.

*H.* Remove any paper backing. Pin the finished FRONT to the finished BACK, face to face, with the SKIRT tucked carefully out of the seam. Sew around the bear's BODY except for the bottom. Turn bear right side out after trimming any necessary seam allowances.

*I.* For the skirt HEM, flip up the SKIRT FRONT and BACK, then pin them together at the side seams. Stitch the side seams. (Be sure not to stitch her arms in the seams.) Smooth the skirt down in place. Turn a ¼-inch HEM and machine stitch. Also turn a narrow hem in the bottom of the bear and machine stitch.

*J.* Glue the EYES in place. Tack the velvet ribbon at the neck center, tie it over the stitching.

## MAKING BABY BEAR

*D.* Pin or glue-baste PANTS and STRAPS in place on both BODY pieces. Use blue satin stitch appliqué to hold pieces in place and to delineate the LEGS. Sew on the buttons by hand or machine.

*E.* Pin COLLAR sections in place over the strap ends. Satin stitch appliqué with ecru thread.

*F.* For the TIE, lay pink velvet RIBBON at an angle on the COLLAR ends. Machine stitch in place. Tie the bow over the stitching.

*G.* Remove paper backing. Lay the BODY pieces face to face and seam around all edges very close to the edge (⅛ to ¼ inch), except for bottom edge. Clip or trim the seam allowances at sharp corners

to smooth them. Turn and press. Press a narrow HEM at the bottom. Hand stitch the hem to conceal stitching.

*H.* To finish, glue the EYES in place. (If you plan to machine embroider eyes, do this in step A.)

## MAKING GOLDILOCKS

*A.* Pin her HAIR to HEAD pieces. Mark with tailor's chalk where CURLS, EYES, NOSE, and MOUTH will be sewn. Use gold satin stitching to outline curls in the HAIR, EYES, and NOSE. Change to pink thread to satin stitch the mouth.

*B.* Trace the HAND patterns on tissue paper. Pin the papers on the FRONT BODY ARMS. Set your machine for free-motion sewing. (To do this, reduce the pressure on the presser foot so that your hands guide the fabric in any direction you wish. If your machine will not do this, use an embroidery foot for the same effect.) Sew the hand with tiny stitches, using the pattern drawn on the paper as a guide. Tear off the paper.

*C.* Cut the DRESS fabric for two dress TOPS, each 2½ by 4 inches, and two SKIRTS, each 5 by 8½ inches. Pin the dress tops to the BODY pieces and appliqué in place with satin stitching in blue.

*D.* Run long gathering stitches ¼ inch from the top of the SKIRT. Gather to the body width, pin, and sew in place.

*E.* Divide the LACE in two. Run a gathering thread in each piece of lace. Pin lace on the dress so it fits across the waist and up each arm to the shoulder. Align raw ends with raw edge, and sew in place. Sew the RIBBON on the NECK at an angle, then tie. Sew the BUTTONS in place on the BODICE.

*F.* Lay the front and back BODY pieces face to face and pin together. Be sure the skirt is tucked out of this seam. Sew around the body, except the bottom. Clip the corner seam allowances and turn.

*G.* Flip up front and back SKIRT sections, pin at the sides, and stitch the side seams. Smooth the skirt down in place. Measure the SKIRT 4½ inches long. Turn a ½-inch double hem, then machine stitch.

*H.* Sew a white half-circle to each SHOE front. Sew SHOE pieces together, turn, and press. Sew SHOES to the BODY front bottom. Trim BODY lower edge with ½-inch eyelet lace to create the PETTICOAT and to cover shoetop seams.

Some of the many teddy bears to make shown here range from tiny to huge, from yarn to wood or clay, and from bears to ride on to bears to hug.

Twelve teddy bears appliquéd on a cozy cotton quilt in warm muted colors cavort in cheerful poses.

The Teddy Bear Room contains bears in many forms: toys, puppets (shown framed on the wall), a rug, a chair, curtains, a quilt, a lamp, a pajama bag, and more for you to make.

Traditional toys found in turn-of-the-century nurseries included teddy bears and riding bears. These contemporary versions can be made from patterns and directions given for Carolyn's Bear and the Riding Bear.

Gare's Bear is an oversized zoo bear with lightweight stuffing who can bolster his master's head with his soft body.

Teddy bears made from different materials include the foam bodied Jack-in-the-Box bear and the Teddy Bear Night Light. To make the clay bears shown follow Bread Dough Teddy Bear modeling instructions without flattening the bears, then bake or fire according to instructions on the clay you use.

The choice of fabric—white fur, printed calico, or brown velour—affects the plumpness of "Rand's Bear," shown in three versions of the same pattern.

Decorated Bears done in paint by Leslie Masters. Embroidery by Mary Zdrodowski, appliqué by Susie Whitehouse, and various techniques by the author show the range of possibilities.

Knitted or crocheted teddy bears in synthetic yarns maintain their soft shapes through washing machine cycles or toy box storage. Use other yarns for different effects.

This animated wooden-bead teddy bear jumps over the coat hanger wire jump rope when the little girl's arm is turned.

A well-dressed teddy can choose between blue jeans sewn on permanently or a removable brocade jacket.

The Three Bears and their friend Goldilocks made as mitten puppets can be sewn in felts and fabrics to fit large or small hands.

The Cheerleader Bear and Clown Bear are made from the same pattern as Western Bear and Posh Bear.

The Bear Chair is made from arranging fur fabric and padding over a wooden framework. It has softly stuffed, movable arms for hugging the sitter.

Four different teddy bear patterns that have "articulated" or movable joints include: a homey denim and calico bear, the honey-colored Carolyn's Bear, small bears in plush or calico, and a nylon stocking bear wearing a fur coat.

This cuddly koala made from short and long fur fabric
can act as a puppet or a soft stuffed toy.

# Decorated Bears

A painted bear by Leslie Masters, beaded bear by Mary Zdrodowski, and appliquéd bear by Susie Whitehouse join other decorated bears done in machine embroidery, hand embroidery, and markers.

If you do crossword puzzles, fidget during ceremonies, or nibble too much while you watch TV, you'll enjoy making decorated bears. The simple, one-piece design, cut out twice, just fits on the commercially available felt squares. From there, you are on your own to decorate the bear in any manner you like—embroider, appliqué, bead, paint, glue, or color.

After you've made a collection of busywork bears, use them for quick gifts, package decorations, a bear family of toys, wall decorations, or even table setting decor. The kids might love this project on a rainy day, using materials and tools within their ken.

## TO EMBROIDER

Use embroidery floss, three strands or the full six, to meander in a decorative pattern around the bear, or in a more organized pattern if you wish.

## TO APPLIQUÉ

Cut out appliqué pieces in felt or fabric and sew them in place on the bear. Add touches using other techniques, if you wish.

## TO BEAD

Use the small beading beads or any size or shape on hand that will make a charming bear. Sew the beads on, using a very small needle or the wire needles made especially for beading.

Bead solidly or in decorative patterns. Or use a few beads for trim.

## TO PAINT

Use artist's acrylic paints to paint designs on the bear. The fibers will resist the paint, so you may wish to paint on a base coating of white first. Or use cut-out shapes to block print designs on the bear.

## TO GLUE

Use fabric glue or iron-on patches to decorate the bear. Children might enjoy this easiest technique.

## TO COLOR

Use a firm cotton fabric in a light color as a base. Color on the designs you want with crayons, then press the bear. This will intensify the color as it melts the wax in the crayon colors.

## MATERIALS

FABRIC:   standard 9-by-12 inch felt square or any fabric you wish. For embroidery, use a fabric that the heavy embroidery threads pull through easily. For painting or printing, choose a flat finish in a light color.

STUFFING:   small wad of fiberfill

## TO MAKE THE BEARS

Trace the pattern pieces. Cut them out, unless you think the decorations will distort the fabric. In that case, apply the decoration, machine embroidery, appliqué, or similar technique first, then cut out the bear.

## STEP 1: DECORATING THE BEARS

**A.** With certain techniques, the decorations should be applied first. This allows for fabric contraction that occurs with some techniques—machine embroidery or appliqué, in particular. It also allows for working on a flat surface, which is necessary for machine embroidery, painting, crayoning, block printing, or machine appliqué.
**B.** When the decoration is complete—or if you plan to decorate plain fabric later, pin the front and back pieces together. Pin them face to face if you plan to turn and stuff the figure. Stitch around the edges, leaving ⅛-inch seam allowance and an opening to turn. Use a tiny stitch. Trim the seam allowance or clip at the corners so the seam will not pull when turned. Carefully turn the bear, poking his seams out fully. Stuff the bear softly so he remains somewhat flat. He will begin to wrinkle if he is stuffed too fully. Hand stitch the opening closed. If the bear is not already embellished, embroider, bead, glue, or hand appliqué the designs in place on the stuffed bear.
**C.** If you do not plan to turn the bear to conceal the seams—this works best for when you want to least disturb the embellishment—pin the bear pieces together back to back. Stuff the bear lightly. Sew a seam around the entire bear, leaving a ⅛-inch seam allowance, or overcasting the entire edge with satin stitching. If you used straight stitching, trim the seam allowance to a neat, careful edge.

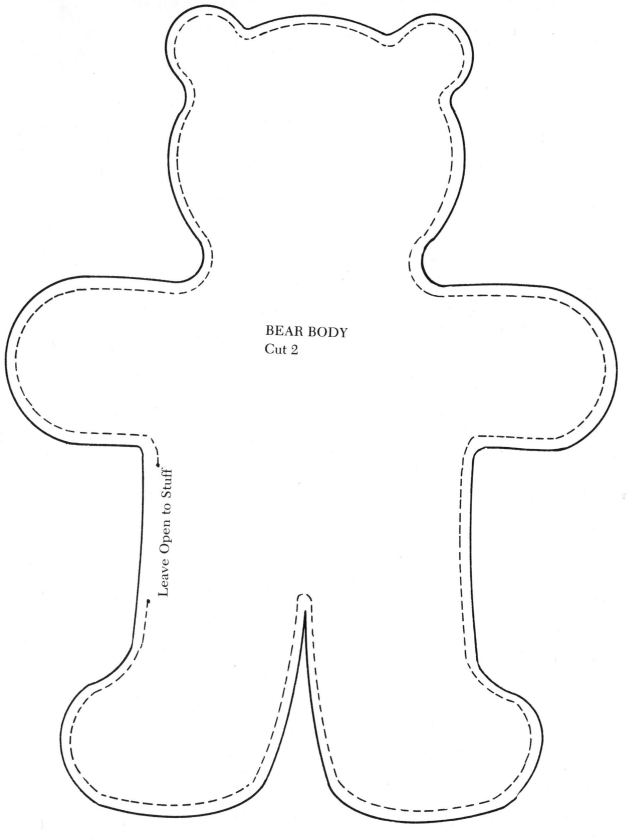

BEAR BODY
Cut 2

Leave Open to Stuff

Pattern pieces for Decorated Bears.

Change from black and white yarns to brown and red to alter this patter from a panda to a honey bear.

# Crocheted Bears

One long TV movie is all the time it takes to crochet this 12-inch-tall soft teddy. This bear weighs only a few ounces, is made from easy-to-obtain yarns of minimal cost, and will wash and wear well. No complex crochet stitches are needed since the entire bear is worked in basic single crochet.

Crochet the bear in black and white to make a panda, brown and red yarn to make a honey bear, all white for a polar bear, all black for the American black bear, or blue for a peculiar bear. Both bears shown here are stuffed with washable polyester fiberfill. Rounded buttons with shanks provide beady black eyes. If the bears are gifts for small children, make embroidered eyes that cannot be pulled off and swallowed. Seated, the bear measures 9 inches tall; standing, 12 inches.

## MATERIALS

PANDA BEAR: 2 ounces black rug yarn, 2 ounces white rug yarn, 2 black shank-back buttons, ½ pound or less of polyester fiberfill stuffing

HONEY BEAR: 3 ounces honey-brown rug yarn, 1 ounce red rug yarn, 2 black shank-back buttons, ½ pound fiberfill stuffing

TOOLS: Size "K" crochet hook, yarn needle, scissors, stitch marker

*Note:* The size of the crochet hook and the bulk of the yarn determine the size of the bears. For these bears, use rug yarn or double-weight knitting yarn, tightly crocheted so the stuffing will not show. If the sample you try is too loose, use a smaller crochet hook, or work more tightly.

## CROCHET ABBREVIATIONS

**Ch**—chain, st(s)—stitch(es)
**Rnd**—once around entire row
**Sc**—single crochet (American), double crochet (English). To single crochet, insert the hook in the next chain. Twist the hook so the wool goes around the hook (called wool round hook—**wrh**), draw the wool through the loop, wool around hook and draw through two loops.
**Hdc**—half double crochet (Amer.), half treble (Eng.). To half double crochet, wool round hook, then insert the hook in the next chain. Draw through a loop. Wool round hook again, then draw through the three loops on the hook.
**Miss one ch**—to decrease, skip a stitch or "chain"
**Crochet 2 sts in 1**—to increase

## TO MAKE THE BEARS

You may crochet the entire bear spiral fashion, marking each row with a piece of yarn or stitch marker (move the marker as you work) or crochet by complete rows, chaining up to the next row. American crochet terms are used.
*Note:* Instructions for the panda are given first, marked by abbreviations for color (W = white, B = black, Br = brown, R = red). Instructions for the honey bear color appear next in parentheses.

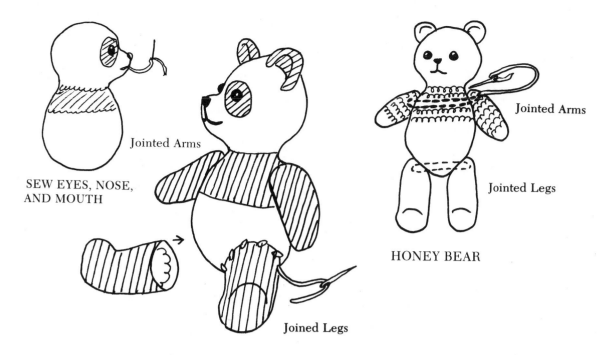

**SEW EYES, NOSE, AND MOUTH**

Jointed Arms

Joined Legs

**PANDA**

**HONEY BEAR**

Jointed Arms

Jointed Legs

Assembling Crocheted Bears.

The number at the end of the round tells how many stitches in the row as a check on progress.

## STEP 1: MAKING THE HEAD AND BODY

**A.** Beginning at the top of the HEAD, Ch 2 W (Br).

*RND 1:* Sc 7 W (Br) in 2nd Ch from hook. 7
*RND 2:* Hdc 2 in each Sc W (Br). 14
*RND 3:* Hdc 2 in each Hdc W (Br). 28
*RND 4:* Sc 28 W (Br).
*RND 5:* Sc 28 W (Br).
*RND 6:* Sc 13, to increase, Sc 4 in 1 st, Sc 4 in next st, Sc 13 W (Br). 34
*RNDS 7 to 10:* Sc 34 W (Br).
*RND 11:* Sc 7, to decrease, miss 1 Ch, Sc 8, miss 1 Ch, Sc 7, miss 1 Ch, Sc 8, miss 1 Ch W (Br). 30
*RND 12:* Sc 14, miss 1 Ch, Sc 14, miss 1 Ch W (Br). 28

**B.** To form the neck, change colors.

*RND 13:* Sc 13, miss 1 Ch, Sc 13, miss 1 Ch B (R). 26
*RND 14:* Sc 26 B (R).

*RND 15:* Sc 6, Sc 2 in 1 to inc. Sc 12, Sc 2 in 1, Sc 6 B (R). 28
*RND 16:* Sc 2 in 1, Sc 13, Sc 2 in 1, Sc 13 B (R). 30
*RND 17:* Sc 7, Sc 2 in 1, Sc 14, Sc 2 in 1, Sc 7 B (R). 32
*RND 18:* Sc 32 B (R).

**C.** Change colors back.

*RND 19:* Sc 2 in 1, Sc 7, Sc 2 in 1, Sc 7, Sc 2 in 1, Sc 7, Sc 2 in 1, Sc 7 W (Br). 36
*RND 20:* Sc 11, Sc 2 in 1, Sc 11, Sc 2 in 1, Sc 11, Sc 2 in 1 W (Br). 39
*RNDS 21 to 28:* Sc 39 W (Br).
*RND 29:* Sc 9, miss 1 Ch, Sc 9, miss 1 Ch, Sc 9, miss 1 Ch, Sc 8 W (Br). 35
*RND 30:* Sc 8, miss 1 Ch, Sc 8, miss 1 Ch, Sc 8, miss 1 Ch, Sc 7, miss 1 Ch W (Br). 31
*RND 31:* Sc 7, miss 1 Ch, Sc 7, miss 1 Ch, Sc 7, miss 1 Ch, Sc 6, miss 1 Ch W (Br). 27
*RND 32:* Sc 6, miss 1 Ch, Sc 6, miss 1 Ch, Sc 6, miss 1 Ch, Sc 5, miss 1 Ch W (Br). 23
*RND 33:* Sc 5, miss 1 Ch, Sc 5, miss 1 Ch, Sc 5, miss 1 Ch, Sc 4, miss 1 Ch W (Br). 19
*RND 34:* Sc 4, miss 1 Ch, Sc 4, miss 1 Ch, Sc 4, miss 1 Ch, Sc 3, miss 1 Ch W (Br). 15

*117*

# Literary Bears

The oldest popular children's story about bears is "The Three Bears," an old folk tale of disputed origin that has been rewritten and newly illustrated many times. In the earliest-known version, the intruder into the bear's house was an old lady the bears tried to destroy. As with many nursery stories, this one has been tamed, shifting emphasis and changing characters in contemporary style. One delightful newer version of the story is found in *Berlitz Italian For Children*, illustrated by Dagmar Wilson and published by Grosset and Dunlap. Another is Fedor Rojankovsky's lively illustrations for *The Tall Book Of Nursery Tales*, published by Harper and Row.

No literary bear is more beloved by generation after generation than Winnie-The-Pooh, who is now nearly 60 years old. A.A. Milne's whimsical yet sophisticated stories combined with E.H. Sheppard's magical drawings produced characters that will live forever. During the 1920s, Sheppard illustrated all of Milne's famous books: *Winnie-The-Pooh* (1926), *The House at Pooh Corner,* and two books of verse, *When We Were Very Young,* and *Now We Are Six,* published by E.P. Dutton & Co. in the United States and by Methuen in the United Kingdom.

The real Pooh teddy bear was owned by Milne's son, Christopher Robin. The idea for Pooh grew from Christopher Robin's remarks about actor Nigel Playfair when he visited his father. "What a funny man. What a funny red face," Christopher Robin said in a gruff voice that he claimed came from his bear. Now Pooh books are printed in every language, and thousands of copies are sold every year.

**D.** To end, stuff the body and head firmly but not tightly, adding small puffs at a time to avoid lumps. When the bear is stuffed fully, draw a loop through all stitches with the crochet hook. Pull the loop to gather the opening closed. Clip the yarn, leaving an end about 6 inches long. Put the end through the loop and pull tightly. Thread the end on a yarn needle. Sew a knot and sew the end into the bear BODY to hide it.

**STEP 2: MAKING THE LEGS**

**A.** Chain on 2 sts B (Br).

*RND 1:* Sc 7 B (Br) in 2nd st from hook. 7
*RND 2:* Hdc 2 in each Sc B (Br). 14
*RNDS 3 to 6:* Sc 14 B (Br).
*RND 7:* Sc 6, miss 1 Ch, Sc 1, miss 1 Ch, Sc 5 B (Br). 12
*RND 8:* Sc 12 B (Br).
*RND 9:* Sc 12 B (Br).
*RND 10:* Sc 5, Sc 2 in 1, Sc 5, Sc 2 in 1 B (Br). 14
*RND 11:* Sc 6, Sc 2 in 1, Sc 6, Sc 2 in 1 B (Br). 16
*RND 12:* Sc 16 B (Br).

**B.** To make an attached LEG, as shown on the panda, clip off the yarn, leaving a strand 12 inches long. Stuff the LEG the same firmness as the body. Thread the strand on a yarn needle and hand sew the LEG to the BODY. To align the LEG, place the back edge of the hole even with the side mid line and the bottom on the fourth or fifth row up from the ending. Repeat step 2, A and B for the second leg, attaching as described. The legs are 7 stitches apart on the body front.
**C.** To make a flexible jointed leg, as shown on the honey bear, continue to crochet as follows:

*RNDS 13 to 15:* Sc 16 (B).
*RND 16:* Sc 7, miss 1 Ch, Sc 7, miss 1 Ch (B). 14
*RND 17:* Sc 6, miss 1 Ch, Sc 6, miss 1 Ch (B). 12

To end, draw a loop through all remaining stitches. Clip off the end 6 inches long. Stuff the LEG firmly. Put the end through the loop and pull tightly to close. Thread the end on a yarn needle and sew a knot, then tuck the end into the leg.
**D.** Make a second LEG following step 2, A and

C, except cut the end 15 inches long and don't tuck it into the leg.

**E.** Next, sew a knot as above, then sew to the outside of the LEG top, emerging down 1 inch in the center of the side of the leg. Insert the needle on the side mid line of the bear BODY, four or five rows up from the ending. Push the needle all the way through the BODY, emerging at the same spot on the opposite side. Insert the needle 1 inch down from the top in the center of the inside of the other LEG, emerging on the outside of the LEG 1 inch down. (Be sure both feet face forward!)

**F.** Reinsert the needle 1 stitch away from where it emerged, running a parallel strand of yarn next to the one through the bear BODY, emerging on the other LEG. Pull the yarn tightly enough to attach the legs but not so tightly as to compress the body. Sew a firm yarn knot and hide the end in the leg.

## STEP 3: MAKING THE ARMS

**A.** Chain on 2 sts B (Br).

*RND 1:* Sc 5 sts in the 2nd Ch from the hook B (Br).
*RND 2:* Hdc 2 sts in 1 B (Br). 10
*RND 3:* Sc 10 B (Br).
*RNDS 4 to 11:* Sc 10 B (R).

To end, draw a loop through all stitches. Clip the yarn, leaving a strand 6 inches long. Stuff the ARM. Put the end through the loop and pull to close. Thread the yarn on a needle, sew a yarn knot. Leave the end until the second arm is done.
**B.** On the second ARM, repeat above, except leave a 12-inch strand of yarn. Stuff and close the end, sew a knot, then insert the yarn needle in the bear BODY two rows from the neck color change on the side mid line. Run the needle through the bear's BODY, emerging at the same spot on the opposite side. Pull the yarn tightly to seat the opposite ARM. Tie the yarn end that passes through the BODY to the yarn end of the other ARM. Tie a firm double knot. Sew the ends into the BODY.

## STEP 4: MAKING THE EARS AND EYE LINERS

**A.** To make the EAR circles, chain on 2 sts B (Br).

The Three Bears come home to find a stranger in their house in *The Tall Book of Nursery Tales,* illustrated by Fedor Rojankovsky and published in 1944 by Harper and Row Publishers, New York and Evanston.

Big Teddy and Little Teddy stirred up all kinds of mischief for British children in stories by Mrs. H.C. Craddock in 1916. Little Teddy, like many a child's bear, was missing an arm and a leg, but this didn't slow him down. (My own teddy was called Little Teddy 15 years later, companion to my sister's Big Teddy. With childlike innocence, we thought we had invented these names.)

*A Bear Called Paddington,* which featured a traveling teddy, was created in 1956 by Michael Bond, with original drawings by Peggy Fortnum. Bond saw a lonely teddy one Christmas eve, the last on the shelf. This planted the seed for Paddington to be found sitting in Paddington station, London, with a tag tied to him reading, "Please look after this bear. Thank you." Paddington zoomed to stardom. Now he is seen everywhere—in toy stores, on television shows, and in 11 books by the author—dressed in his famous duffle coat, Wellingtons, and floppy hat.

Beady Bear and Corduroy are delightful teddy bear stories created by Don Freeman in 1954 and 1968. My children loved feeling scared along with Beady as he searched for the cave where he knew bears were "s'posed to live." Corduroy achieved greater fame and eventually became a real teddy bear toy.

Susanna Gretz created unusual teddy bear books for very young readers. Bears with patched-on faces appear in various whimsical colors, including green and purple. In her 1969 book Teddybears 1 to 10 (Collins Picture Lions, U.K.), her teddy bears clean up for a tea party by putting themselves through the washer, dryer, and cleaners.

Some teddy bear books are aimed at grown-ups. In 1964 Margaret Hutchings, a British toy maker, wrote Teddy Bears and How To Make Them (reissued in 1977 by Dover in the United States and Mills & Boon Ltd. in the United Kingdom). This book gives extensive information about making teddy bears and provides patterns. You can recognize a "Margaret Hutchings" bear made from these patterns by the big ears and shaped legs.

The Teddy Bear Catalogue (Workman Publishing, 1980) by Peggy and Alan Bialosky gives form to the new art of collecting teddy bears. Even if you don't plan to scour antique shows, the book is a delight. It gives historical bear data, pictures of bears from 1902 to the present, and advice on the care and repair of teddy bears.

For additional titles of children's bear stories, check with book stores and libraries. You'll find stories like Gentle Ben by W. Morley, Blueberries for Sal by M.R. McClosky, and How Do I Put It On? by Shigeo Watanabe.

RND 1:    Sc 6 sts in the 2nd Ch from hook B (Br). 6

RND 2:    Sc 2 in 1 for 5 sts, Sc 1 B (Br). 11

To end, leave a strand 8 inches long and clip off yarn. Repeat for the other EAR. Thread the yarn on a yarn needle and sew the EAR on the top side of the head. For the panda's EYE LINERS, crochet circles as for ears. Sew all around each circle to attach it to the head.

## STEP 5: FINISHING THE BEAR

**A.** For the EYES, use a yarn needle or a needle that will fit through the hole in the button shank. Using black yarn, sew through one button shank. Tie a firm double knot around the shank. Insert the needle in the center of the panda's EYE LINER, or on the front of the honey bear's head on the sixth row. Emerge on the other side of the NOSE where the other eye will be placed. Sew through the button shank. Insert the needle and follow the yarn back to the first EYE, going behind some of the stuffing. Pull the yarn to firmly seat the eye. Then tie the yarn around the first eye shank. Sew a knot. Insert the needle and emerge at the NOSE tip.

**B.** To sew the NOSE, make several ½-inch-long stitches vertically at the tip of the nose. Sew the nose about ½ inch square.

**C.** For the MOUTH, sew down ½ inch from the center of the nose. Insert the needle, coming out 1 inch down diagonally for the corner of the mouth. Push the needle under the upper mouth yarn and insert it 1 inch down diagonally, the same place on the opposite side of the MUZZLE as the other mouth corner, emerging under the NOSE yarns. Pull the thread firmly to shape the mouth, then sew a knot under the nose threads to conceal the end and clip.

A bear couple dressed by Marilyn Vickery, is made from patterns in the book Teddy Bears and How To Make Them, by Margaret Hutchings.

This small wooden teddy bear hops over the spinning wire rope when the girl's arm is turned.

# Teddy Bear, Teddy Bear Jump Rope Toy

*Teddy bear, teddy bear, read the news.*
*Teddy bear, teddy bear, shine your shoes.*
*Teddy bear, teddy bear, go upstairs.*
*Teddy bear, teddy bear, say your prayers.*

The little wooden toy was inspired by this rhyme, which little girls have recited for generations while breathlessly leaping over the spinning rope.

Turn the left arm of the little wooden girl on the right and the bear jumps over the spinning wire jump rope. The bear is strung on the coat hanger jump rope wire. This wire pivots in the left girl's bead hand. The wire jump rope threads through the right girl, and her bead arm covers the wire to form the crank handle.

To make this toy, you will need a bag of turned wooden handles and knobs, which are sold in craft stores. If these aren't available, use wooden macramé beads and various-sized dowel sticks; or, carve and sand your own beads. Skilled woodworkers will wince, but I used Plastic Wood to fill joints and bead holes and to model shapes. Hand tools will do for cutting and drilling.

## PATTERN PIECES

No specific pattern is given since most pieces are commercially made wooden parts, altered a bit.

## MATERIALS

BASE BOARD:   one 3½-by-12-inch board, ¾ inch thick

### Left Girl

HEAD:   one 1½-inch-round bead
TORSO:   one 1½-inch-diameter oval bead, 3 inches long, cut in half to 1½ inches long
WAIST:   one flat wooden disk 1½ inches in diameter
SKIRT:   one turned disk 2 inches in diameter and ½ inch thick, one skirt disk 2½ inches in diameter and ¼ inch thick
LEGS:   two ½-inch dowels, 2½ inches long
SHOES:   one 1⅛-inch-diameter disk, ½ inch thick, cut in half to form two semicircles
ARMS:   two 2-inch-long pieces of ⅜-inch dowel, two ⅝-inch beads
HANDS:   two ⅝-inch beads, one cut in half

### Teddy Bear

HEAD:   one 1¼-inch-round bead
MUZZLE:   other half of ⅝-inch bead
EARS:   two ⅝-inch beads
BODY:   one 1¼-inch-diameter oval bead, 2 inches long
ARMS and LEGS:   four ¾-inch-diameter oval beads, 2 inches long, one ⅝-inch bead, cut

121

Half Circle

4½''

3½''

Right Hand

Loop

Twist

Left Hand

ASSEMBLY: BEND WIRE AS SHOWN AND ADJUST IT TO WORK SMOOTHLY

LEFT GIRL

Head

Body

Shoe

BEAR

Ear

Head

Muzzle Filler

Arm

Body

Wire for Legs

Leg

RIGHT GIRL

Head

Skirt

Screw Hole in Feet

Assembling Teddy Bear Jump Rope Toy.

in half to form feet, two 1½-inch heavy screws, 3 inches of florist's wire

JUMP ROPE and CRANK: one lightweight coat hanger wire

**Right Girl**

HEAD: one 1½-inch round bead

BODY: one tapered bead, 1¾ inches in diameter, cut to 2½ inches long

SKIRT: one turned disk 2 inches in diameter and ½ inch thick

LEGS: two turned wooden pegs, 1¾ inches high

ARMS: one ¾-inch-diameter oval bead, 2 inches long, cut in half, two ⅝-inch beads

MISCELLANEOUS: one tube of model builder's glue, one fresh small can of Plastic Wood, two 1¼-inch wood screws, artist's acrylic paints (flesh, black, red, brown, white, honey brown, yellow, blue, red-orange), varnish, needle-nose pliers, regular pliers, coping or band saw, drill, utility knife, sandpaper and sanding disk attachment for the drill

## STEP 1: MAKING THE LEFT GIRL AND BASE

**A.** Cut the base board to size and sand it smooth on all edges. Varnish with several coats.

**B.** Cut the BODY bead to measure 1½ inches long. Drill a ¼-inch-diameter hole ½ inch down from the neck on the front of the body for the ARM.

**C.** Set the bottom SKIRT disk on a flat surface. Glue the turned SKIRT disk on top of it. Next, glue on the WAIST disk. Then glue on the SKIRT disk. Finally, glue the HEAD bead on top. Let dry until the glue is firmly set.

**D.** Saw the SHOE disk in half.

**E.** Cut the ⅜-inch dowel for the LEGS with a slight angle at the top. Cut right ARM angled sharply at the top.

**F.** Fill the HEAD bead hole with Plastic Wood. Do this in two steps: add filler, let it dry firmly, then add a finishing layer to model in shape. Sand smooth and rounded when dry.

**G.** To assemble, glue the LEGS to the SKIRT disk. Let this piece dry upside down. Sand the end of the dowel to fit the ARM hole. Put glue in the hole, then insert the ARM firmly. Glue and push the HAND bead on her left ARM. Sand the wrist if necessary. Glue the half HAND bead to her right ARM. When the hand is dry, glue her right ARM to the body. Hold it in place with tape until it is dry, then remove the tape. Fill the joint with Plastic Wood; sand.

**H.** Position the SHOES on the BASE, ¼ inch from one end, and glue in place. Glue the LEGS to the SHOES, bracing the piece until it is dry. Fill around the joint with Plastic Wood.

**I.** Paint the figure. Paint her face, arms, and legs flesh color. Paint her shoes, eyes, and nose black. Paint her skirt and her mouth red. Paint her hair brown and her torso white.

## STEP 2: MAKING THE TEDDY BEAR

**A.** With the utility knife, cut a notch across the top of the BODY bead large enough to accommodate the coat hanger wire about ¼ inch into the wood.

**B.** Saw off (or sand off with the disk sander) the "hip" sections on each side of the BODY bead at an angle for the legs. Fill the BODY hole at the base with Plastic Wood and let it dry. Add a second layer and model a smooth, rounded bottom for the bear. Sand smooth when dry.

**C.** Glue the HEAD bead on top of the BODY bead, being careful not to fill the notches at the neck. When this glue has set, fill the HEAD hole with Plastic Wood. Dome the Plastic Wood slightly to carry out the roundness of the bead. Sand smooth. Fill the EAR beads with Plastic Wood, sand, then glue to the HEAD bead. Glue on the MUZZLE half bead. Fill around the joint with Plastic Wood and sand smooth when dry.

**D.** Cut off a slice from the top of each LEG bead at the same angle as the BODY hips. Cut the ⅜-inch FOOT bead in half. Glue one half to each leg on the front.

**E.** For added weight push a heavy screw into the LEG bead hole and fill the top and bottom of the hole with Plastic Wood. Fill around the FOOT bead where it joins the LEG. When the Plastic Wood dries, sand the LEG to shape.

**F.** Drill a ⅛-inch hole ⅜ inch down from the top of the LEG from the side. Continue to drill the hole through the BODY ½ inch up. Continue the drilled hole through the top of the other LEG.

**G.** Cut ¼ inch off the ¾-inch ARM beads. Sand them to an angle at the end so they will rotate well. (The ARMS are attached in Step 4.)

**H.** Paint all the pieces a honey brown, with black features.

**I.** To assemble, twist a loop in one end of the florist's wire. Thread the wire through one LEG, the BODY, and then the other LEG. Twist a loop at the other end of the wire and clip off the extra.

## STEP 3: MAKING THE RIGHT GIRL

**A.** Saw the BODY bead to size. Drill a ¼-inch hole through the body ¾-inch down from the neck for the wire.

**B.** Fill the HEAD bead with Plastic Wood, and sand. Glue the HEAD to the BODY. Glue the SKIRT to the BODY.

**C.** Saw the oval ARM bead in half crosswise. Glue her right arm to the BODY, and glue the HAND bead to the arm, leaving the hole open for the wire. Carve or sand the cut end of the other ARM bead round so it will pivot.

**D.** Glue the SKIRT to the LEGS. (Shoes are part of the leg pieces.)

**E.** Paint the girl's face, hands, and legs flesh color. Paint her body yellow and her skirt blue. Paint her hair red-orange, her mouth red, her eyes and nose black, and her shoes brown.

## STEP 4: ASSEMBLING THE TOY

**A.** Using a lightweight all-wire coat hanger, clip off the twist and the hook. Straighten one corner bend. Bend the other corner more sharply, then twist into a small loop. Use one or two pairs of pliers for good grip and leverage.

**B.** Referring to the diagram, bend the long end of the wire up from the loop into a half circle 4½ inches wide and 3⅓ inches tall, or as needed.

**C.** Bend the short end down at a slight angle from the loop and thread the bear's right ARM on it. Bend the wire straight ½ inch past the ARM bead. Thread the BODY bead on the wire. Bend the wire up at the same angle as the other ARM just past the BODY. Thread on the bear's left ARM bead.

**D.** Twist the end of the half circle wire and the end of the bear's BODY wire together ¼ inch past his left ARM. Hold the loop in one hand and the twist in the other. Rotate the wire to see if the bear moves freely and remains upright as the wire spins. If he does not, loosen the twist until he does. When the bear works well, clip off the shorter wire 2 inches from the bear's left paw.

Using two pairs of pliers, twist the long and short ends firmly together to make a 2-inch long tight, even twist. Align this twisted wire so it is straight with the loop and both pivot on center. The axis from the loop all the way to the hand crank must be a straight line for the bear to rotate well.

**E.** Thread the long wire through the right girl's hand and arm, through her body and out the far side. Bend the wire up at a slight angle and thread on her LEFT ARM bead. Bend the wire straight at the end. Thread on a washer and the HAND bead with a washer glued to the end. Insert the loop in the left girl's hand, and see if the mechanism works well. When it is properly adjusted, clip off the wire ½ inch past the right girl's HAND and twist a sharp loop to hold the HAND in place.

**F.** With the loop in the left girl's hand bead, glue and clamp the right girl's feet to the base. Turn the base on its side and drill through the base into the feet. Turn in one screw each to hold the right girl's feet firmly in place.

**G.** Now you can make up your own teddy bear jumping rope verses as your bear jumps over the wire—backward or forward.

# Cookie Bears

"I'm so hungry I could eat a bear!" you've heard people say. So here are bears to eat. To make the cookie cutter, find a commercially available metal cookie cutter similar to a bear. The larger cutter shown was a gingerbread boy, the smaller was a pine tree. Use needle-nose pliers (long, skinny points) to bend the cutter to the shape you want. To keep the metal crisp looking, decide where the bends will go before you begin. Keep adjusting until the teddy looks right. The metal is so flexible that you can make him fatter or thinner using only your fingers.

Next, choose a recipe for rolled cookies. It may suggest that you keep the dough in the refrigerator to firm it for rolling. Decorate cookies with sugar trim before baking, and with squeeze tubes of frosting afterward.

Edible teddy bears can be made from any rolled cookie dough and decorated in a variety of ways.

Bread dough bears, when coated with varnish and trimmed with a ribbon bow, can last for years.

# Bread Dough Teddy Bears

These small bears are made from a simple flour, salt, and water dough, kneaded to a plastic "clay," sculpted into shape, and then baked to bone-dry hardness in the oven. Color or fragrant spices can be mixed into the dough, or applied later. Finishing touches include a sealer coat of varnish and a ribbon trim.

Bread dough teddy bears can be used to liven the Christmas tree, hang on a mobile, glue onto boxes or wall plaques, or even decorate a birthday table.

## MATERIALS

DOUGH:   two (or more) cups of flour, ½ cup of salt, ¾ cup of warm water (optional: food coloring or aromatic spices)

TRIM:   2 inches of ¾-inch-wide ribbon per bear; wire ornament hangers, fine wire, or thread; polyurethane varnish for finishing coat

COATING:   one egg, small bowl of water, dab of cooking oil for cookie sheet.

TOOLS:   pastry brush, kitchen knife, paint brush, round toothpick, Teflon-coated cookie sheet, mixing bowl, mixing spoon or whisk

*Note:* This amount of dough will make about 16 bears, 4 inches tall. Since the dough doesn't store well, mix only the amount you need for one session. Divide the recipe in half for fewer bears, double it for more. Different flours and weather conditions will require that you experiment with amounts in the recipe, which are approximate, to reach the right consistency.

## STEP 1: PREPARING THE DOUGH

**A.** To begin, mix the salt in the warm water to dissolve as much as possible, then add the flour. This stiff mix will become difficult to stir, so use your hands to mold a ball. Add more flour if the dough sticks to your hands. To remove sticky dough from your hands, rub them together and add these little bits to the ball.

**B.** Dump the ball and extra flour out of the bowl onto a hard, flat surface low enough for you to work on easily. Knead the dough for 5 or 10 minutes to make it elastic and as smooth and firm as skin. Even though this may take 5 to 10 minutes, it will not be too tiring if you work above the dough and use your body weight to lean into it.

**C.** To test readiness, roll a long strand of dough. If the strand splits, the dough needs more kneading. Insufficiently kneaded dough may crack or bake unevenly. It will puff up in bubbles, like those lumps on soda crackers, if it is too moist.

## STEP 2: FORMING THE BEARS

**A.** Handle the dough like clay, rolling it into balls and strands as needed for head, body, arms, legs, ears, and muzzle. Moisten added parts and push them firmly together to help "glue" the joints. Follow the diagram to form the bears. Make the bears on the Teflon-coated cookie sheet on which they will be baked.

**B.** Insert the hanging loop into the head and body, making a loop at both ends—one to hang by and the other (in the body) to anchor. Press the completed bear to a ½ inch thickness. Keep the unused dough in a plastic bag since it dries out rapidly.

### STEP 3: FINISHING THE BEARS

**A.** Beat the egg with a spoonful of water, then brush the mixture on the bears so they will bake to a toasty brown color. Bake in a slow oven, 275° or less for 1 hour. You may then increase the heat to brown, or cook for another hour or so at the same temperature. Experiment to see what works best.

**B.** Trim the bears with a small bow tied on with thread or wire. Mix color into the dough, or paint the finished bears with acrylic paint, shoe polish, or cake coloring.

**C.** Brush on several coats of polyurethane varnish to seal out moisture. Store well sealed in a dry place. These bears are *NOT EDIBLE*. They may mold or attract bugs if not preserved and stored well to keep for the following year.

TO KNEAD THE DOUGH, MAKE A BALL, PUSH FLAT, AND FOLD IN

ROLL THESE PIECES

WET JOININGS

INSERT WIRE, TURN HOOK IN END

CUT ARMS AND LEGS

USE WIRE TO MAKE FEATURES

PRESS BEAR ½" FLAT

FINISHED BEARS

Assembling Bread Dough Bears.

# Felt Bears

Some teddy bears in this book take hours or days to make, but these felt bears take only minutes. A finished teddy can last for years: we have a blue felt bear, made 25 years ago, that comes out with our other Christmas tree ornaments every year, and holds up very well.

Only a small amount of felt, in any color you like, is needed for each bear. Use various bits of trim from the sewing box to dress the bears in bits of clothing. Beginning with a basic bear shape, many variations are possible. Decorations can be sewn, glued, or ironed on. Use the bears for ornaments, clothing trim, characters in a cloth book, toys on a mobile, birthday present box decorations, or note card trim.

Collect small scraps of felt, trim, buttons, and beads to make a quick collection of felt teddy bears.

## MATERIALS

For each bear, about 2 by 4 inches of felt in the colors specified or as you choose
assorted trim as shown: ribbon, beads, feathers, sequins, buttons or pieces of felt or fabric

## TO MAKE THE BEARS

Trace the pattern on heavy paper to make a template. Lay it on felt and trace around it with tailor's chalk or pencil. Use small sharp embroidery scissors to cut out pieces with a crisp edge. Cut just inside the trace line with smooth strokes to create the best-shaped bear.

For a more dimensional bear, cut two felt teddys and sew them together with a little stuffing inside. Cut the pattern a little fatter for this since the stuffing takes up the fabric.

Glue or sew the clothing and trim to the bears, taking care to work neatly and to use small details that are in scale with the tiny figures. Pay attention to the back as well, if the bear will also be seen from that side. To sew the features with hidden stitching, sew from the top of the head between the layers of the felt. Use the trailing ends of the embroidery thread for a hanging loop.

For the clown bear and the Santa bear, cut head and body pieces with a small overlap to glue or stitch the joinings. Model builder's glue or fabric glue works well. Weight the glued joint for a firmer joining.

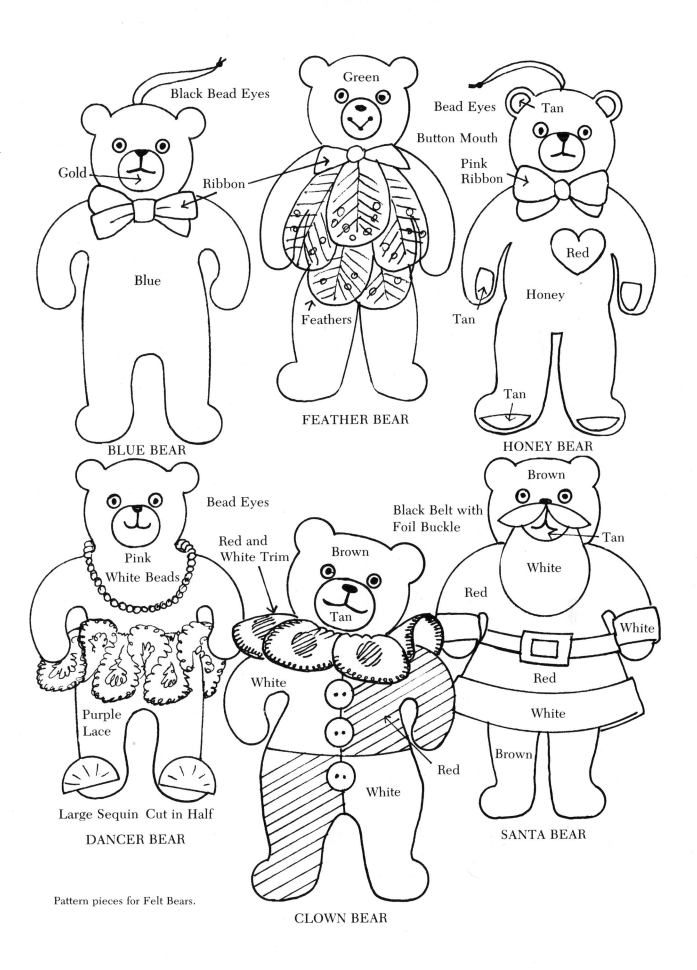

Black Bead Eyes

Green

Bead Eyes — Tan

Button Mouth

Gold

Ribbon

Pink
Ribbon

Blue

Red

Feathers

Honey

Tan

BLUE BEAR

FEATHER BEAR

Tan

HONEY BEAR

Bead Eyes

Black Belt with
Foil Buckle

Brown

Pink
White Beads

Red and
White Trim

Brown

Tan — Tan

Tan

White

Purple
Lace

White

Red

White

Red

White

Red

White

Large Sequin Cut in Half

Brown

DANCER BEAR

Pattern pieces for Felt Bears.

CLOWN BEAR

SANTA BEAR

Be a bear for a day in a fuzzy bear costume. Complete the children's costume with a nose drawn on with eyebrow pencil for a mask.

# Bear Bunting and Bear Costume

To test this bear bunting design, I sent it to my sister, Lois, who sewed the bunting shown for her granddaughter, Andrea. Andrea's mother, Mary, dressed her daughter in the bear bunting and went to the 1982 giant Teddy Bear Rally benefit for the Philadelphia Zoo. Andrea, in "our" bear bunting, won a prize for "Personality Bear" and

appeared on that night's CBS-TV evening news with her dad.

Perhaps your children won't have this much excitement wearing a teddy bear suit, but they're guaranteed to feel cozy and lovable in it.

## PATTERN PIECES

**A.** HOOD TOP: cut 1 (tan)
**B.** SLEEVE: cut 2 (tan)
**C.** BODY FRONT: cut 2, 1 reversed (tan)
**D.** TUMMY: cut 2, 1 reversed (off-white)
**E.** BODY BACK: cut 2, 1 reversed (tan)
**F.** HOOD BACK: cut 1 (tan)
**G.** EAR: cut 4 (tan)
**H.** EAR COLOR: cut 2 (off-white)
**I.** SOLE: cut 2 (off-white)
**J.** MITT: cut 4 (tan)
**K.** PAW: cut 2 (off-white)    (see p. 132)

**A.** CHIN: cut 1 (grizzled fur)
**B.** MUZZLE: cut 1 (tan fur)
**C.** HEAD: cut 2, 1 reversed (grizzled fur)
**D.** EAR: cut 4 (grizzled fur)
**E.** EYE RING: cut 2 (black leather)    (see p. 133)

## MATERIALS

BABY BUNTING BODY AND HOOD: size baby small takes 1¼ yards of 36-inch knitted fleecy fabric, tan or honey color

PAWS, EAR COLORS, and TUMMY: 1 foot of 36-inch fleecy knit, off-white, light tan, or related hue

NOTIONS: 12-inch zipper, matching thread, snap tape, 24 inches of cord for hood

Choose longer, thicker fur fabric for a larger bear costume, and top with a Bear Mask for a complete disguise.

130

BEAR COSTUME HEAD:
HEAD, EARS, and CHIN:   20 by 36 inches of
     grizzled fake fur
MUZZLE:   8 by 16 inches of related tan fake fur
NOSE:   3-by-5-inch oval of black wool
EYE RINGS:   two 2¼-inch circles of black
     leather or suede
THREAD:   black yarn for mouth

## TO MAKE THE BEAR COSTUME
## AND BUNTING

*Note:* The pattern given is a baby bunting, size
small. If you plan to make a larger-sized bear costume scale up the pattern to size, adjusting the
pattern to fit as follows. Measure the wearer for
width of shoulder, length of arms and legs, height
from foot to neck back, and distance around.
Check these points by tape measure on the pattern you scale up. Fold a tuck in the pattern to
decrease width. Slash the pattern and add an insert to lengthen.

Make these changes for a larger bear suit: eliminate the leg opening; use sturdy plastic for the
soles, or, to leave the sole open, hem the foot
edge, and attach an elastic that goes under the
foot. Sew a thumb on the mitt but do leave the
wrist slit for freer use of the hands. Make the costume large enough to fit over warm clothing.
Make the suit loose and floppy in the hips and
with a low crotch so it looks like a bear.

The bigger the costume, the longer haired the
fur you can use. The weight and bulk of a long,
dense fur is too heavy for a child, but desirable
for an adult.

For any size costume you may substitute the
loose costume head for the hood attached to the
body. The head pattern is given adult size, and
may be scaled down to fit smaller heads.

## TO MAKE THE BUNTING

Scale up and cut out all the pattern pieces. To
alter a commercial pattern, add hip fullness, make
an oval of the appropriate size for the tummy, and
enlarge the ear pattern. Make the zipper seam up
the back to make the tummy one piece, if desired.

## STEP 1: MAKING THE BODY

*Note:* The pattern shows ⅝-inch seam allowances.
For sturdy wear, double stitch most seams.
*A.* Pin bias tape across the foot at the ankle. Stitch
along both sides ⅛ inch from the edge of the tape
to form a casing. Insert elastic with raw edges
even. Baste the ends.
*B.* Turn a narrow hem around the curved edges
of the TUMMY. Position it on the BODY FRONT,
raw straight edges aligned, pin, and top stitch in
place. Repeat for the other BODY FRONT and
TUMMY.
*C.* Stitch the center BODY FRONT seams for 3
inches at the bottom. Clip to avoid pulls. Turn
and press a ⅝-inch hem in the center BODY
FRONT seam allowances.
*D.* Center the zipper under the BODY FRONT
opening edges, with the tab pull below the neck
seam line. Sew the zipper in place, using a zipper
foot.
*E.* Place the BODY BACKS together, face to face,
and stitch the back seam. Clip seam allowances
at the crotch.
*F.* Match the BODY FRONT shoulder seams
with the BODY BACK shoulder seams; pin and
stitch.

## STEP 2: MAKING THE EARS AND HOOD

*A.* Turn and press a small hem on the curved
section of the EAR COLOR. Pin the EAR COLOR
to the EAR front, raw straight edges aligned. Top
stitch in place.
*B.* Place the EAR front face to face with the EAR
back. Pin and stitch. Trim the seam allowances
and turn. Repeat A and B for the other EAR.
*C.* Pin the EARS on the HOOD TOP, 4½ inches
apart on the top of the head. Machine baste in
place. For the hood casing cord, sew small buttonholes 1 inch up on the hood front corner. Turn
under a double hem 1 inch wide on the front edge
and stitch.
*D.* Fit the HOOD BACK to the HOOD TOP. Pin
and stitch. This seam includes the EARS. Hand
stitch the front edges of the EARS to the HOOD
TOP ⅜ inch up from the seam. This will hold the
ears erect.
*E.* Pin the HOOD to the BODY neck, matching
centers. Stitch and clip the neck seam allowance.
Press the HOOD seam allowance down on the
BODY and top stitch in place. Trim away extra
seam allowance.

## STEP 3: MAKING THE MITTS AND ARMS

*A.* Turn and press a ½-inch double hem in the
end of both SLEEVES. Stitch.

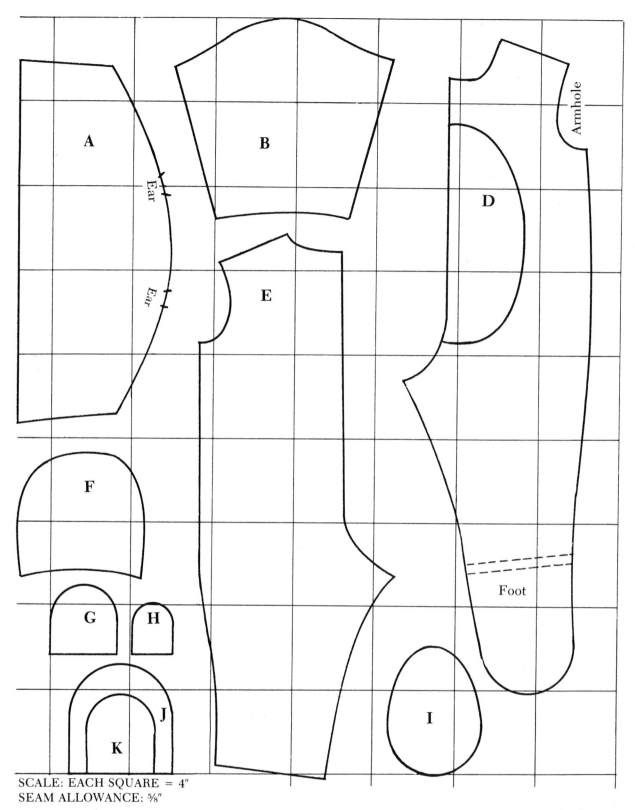

Ear
Ear
Armhole
Foot

SCALE: EACH SQUARE = 4″
SEAM ALLOWANCE: ⅝″

Pattern pieces for Bear Bunting and Bear Costume.

132

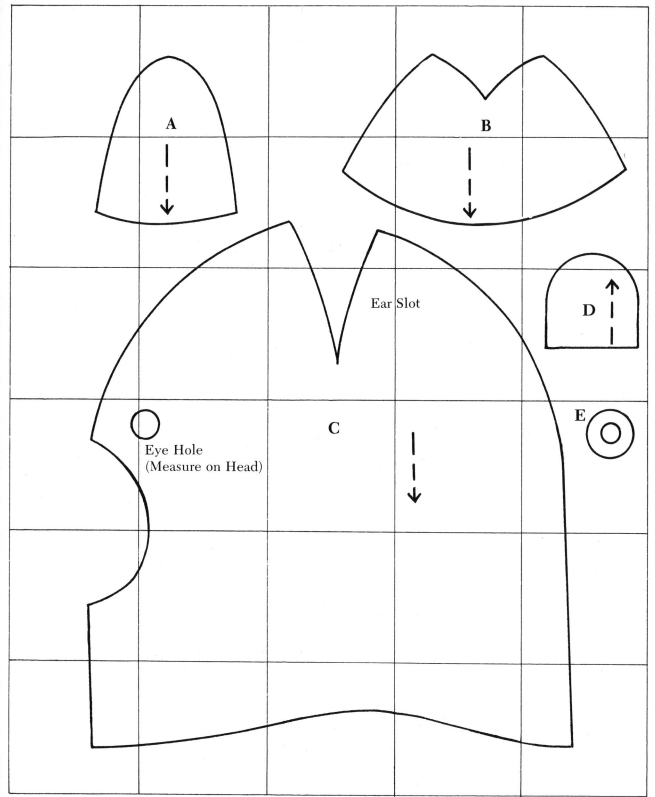

A

B

Ear Slot

D

Eye Hole
(Measure on Head)

C

E

SCALE: EACH SQUARE = 4″
SEAM ALLOWANCE: ⅝″

Pattern pieces for Bear Bunting and Bear Costume.

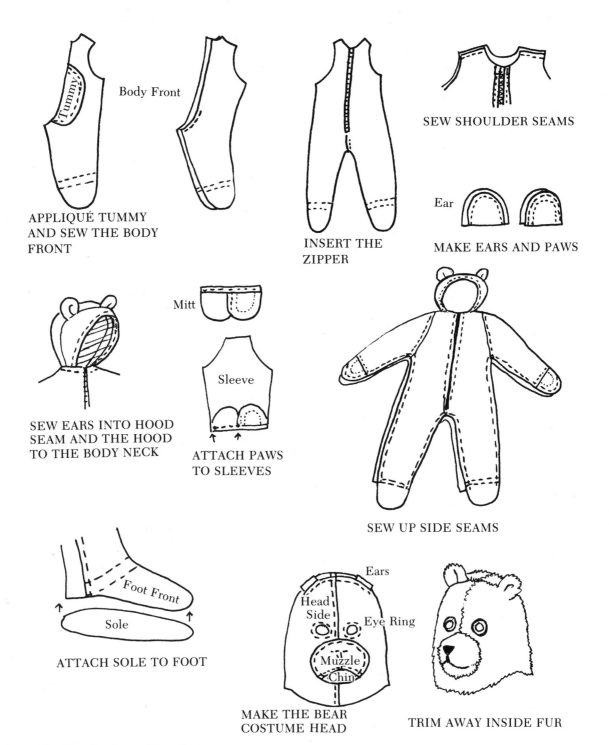

**Body Front**

**APPLIQUÉ TUMMY AND SEW THE BODY FRONT**

**INSERT THE ZIPPER**

**SEW SHOULDER SEAMS**

Ear

**MAKE EARS AND PAWS**

Mitt

**SEW EARS INTO HOOD SEAM AND THE HOOD TO THE BODY NECK**

Sleeve

**ATTACH PAWS TO SLEEVES**

**SEW UP SIDE SEAMS**

Foot Front

Sole

**ATTACH SOLE TO FOOT**

Ears

Head Side

Eye Ring

Muzzle

Chin

**MAKE THE BEAR COSTUME HEAD**

**TRIM AWAY INSIDE FUR**

Assembling Bear Bunting and Bear Costume.

*B.* Turn a narrow hem on the curve of the PAW. Press. Pin onto the front of the MITT, aligning the straight top edges. Top stitch in place. Repeat for the other MITT and PAW.

*C.* Pin the MITT front to the MITT back, face to face, and stitch top side seam. Repeat for the other MITT. Turn a ½-inch double hem on the straight edge of the MITT. Stitch. Pin the wrong side of the MITT to the right side of the SLEEVE front, placing the edge of the MITT on the sleeve line. Stitch the back half of the MITT only, ⅛ inch from the edge. Repeat for the other SLEEVE.

134

*D.* With right sides together, pin the SLEEVE to the armhole edge. Stitch in place.

## STEP 4: MAKING THE SIDE SEAMS AND FEET

*A.* Fold the right sides of the MITTS together with raw edges even. Pin or baste. Pin BODY BACK sides to BODY FRONT sides, including the sleeve edges. Stitch a continuous seam from the FOOT to the MITT, tapering the seam smoothly on the mitt fold to end.
*B.* Pin and stitch the inner legs together on the FOOT for 3 inches, to just past the elastic casing. Pin snap tape to the seam allowances, making sure the snaps on one side of the opening align with those on the other. Sew the snap tape in place. Top stitch the other edge in place close to the edge.
*C.* Pin the SOLE face to face with the FOOT opening. Stitch around the entire sole. Repeat for the other FOOT. Trim the seam allowances.
*D.* Insert a drawstring through the hood casing.

## STEP 5: MAKING THE BEAR COSTUME HEAD

Cut out all pattern pieces. Use interfacing for the muzzle if the fur is not stiff enough.

*A.* Pin the EAR pieces face to face. Stitch and turn. Fold a tuck in the front side and pin.
*B.* Pin the HEAD sections together loosely, try the BEAR HEAD on and mark the eye holes to appear in the right places. Remove the pins. Place the EYE ring back to face over the eye hole mark. Using a short stitch, sew around the inner edge of the EYE ring. Clip out the EYE fur to make an EYE hole. Satin stitch around the edge with dark brown thread. Repeat for the other EYE.
*C.* Pin the EAR in the EAR slot at the top, raw edges aligned. Sew the head dart seams together over the base of the EAR. Repeat for the other side; open flat.
*D.* Pin the HEAD sides together, face to face, aligning the HEAD dart seams. Stitch from the nape to the MUZZLE and the CHIN seam. Use interfacing to stiffen the MUZZLE, if necessary.
*E.* Fold the MUZZLE face to face and stitch the nose seam to the MOUTH. Fold the MUZZLE seam to align with the fold. Insert the nose tip

# Good Bears of the World

The teddy bear club, Good Bears of the World, now has bear dens (local groups) in cities across the United States and England, and aims to go worldwide. What draws members together is their love for teddy bears and the freedom to express this feeling no matter how long ago they left childhood behind. Each recalls the comfort a teddy bear companion can give, so the group's avowed goal is to provide teddy bears for hospitalized children to help them through difficult times.

Founder Jim Ownby, a journalist, owned a teddy bear as a child and then forgot about it for some 50 years—until he met Colonel Bob Henderson and read the book *The Bear with Me*, by British actor Peter Bull. Bull tells how bears have affected men over the years. (Ownby phoned his 90-year-old mother for news of his childhood teddy and learned she had given it to the Salvation Army!)

In England, Colonel Bob Henderson had set out to explore the phenomenon of "The Teddy Bear Consciousness" apparent among many adults. While conducting the research, he began to increase his teddy bear population beginning with his childhood bears, his children's bears, and bears for his grandchildren, and building to an enormous bona fide collection. As cofounder, he joined with Jim Ownby to form the Good Bears of the World movement in 1970.

Now parallel groups exist in the United States and England. Ownby's group, headquartered in Hawaii, produces a quarterly journal of considerable charm. Intentionally folksy in style, the booklet gives information on and encouragement for forming local bear dens. People also write to the letters column requesting information on teddy bear lore.

The journal, *Bear Tracks*, features articles about all aspects of teddy bears: the places where Roosevelt lived, Christopher Robin's feelings about his unintended fame, Michael Bond's views on his creation, Paddington, and personal stories by the bear-owning public. Ads appear for individual teddy bear makers and for craft stores selling all kinds of teddy bear objects: teddy bears, teddy sweatshirts, teddy mugs, teddy ties, teddy stationery, and a catalogue from a store called Bear Necessities.

The winter 1982 issue describes the Great Teddy Bear Rally, organized by the Marquis of Bath and presided over by his teddy bear Clarence. Everyone attending was invited to bring a teddy to the stately grounds of Longleat. "It was a deluge of teddys of every description," bear den leader Jenny George said in *Bear Tracks*. "They were carried in their owners' arms or pockets. They came in haversacks and shopping baskets, in prams, pushcarts and trolley bags. Cherished teddys clutched by children and adults alike."

Unable to attend the 1982 Teddy Bear Rally in America, the Marquis of Bath sent Clarence (escorted by plane) to the event held to benefit the Philadelphia Zoo, America's oldest zoo, which resembles a Victorian garden. Again thousands of people came from near and far, bringing their teddys. Prizes were given in various categories. Everyone marched in the 34th Street parade, all wheeling, pushing, or carrying their teddy bears. Real zoo bear cubs rode in a convertible and people costumed as literary bears—Winnie the Pooh and Paddington, for example—marched with the children.

"In a preliminary ceremony," reports the *Wall Street Journal*, which covered the event, "zoo representatives set free 144 three-inch-tall Paddington bears, each carried by three helium balloons."

Teddy bears are a symbol of love, say the Good Bears of the World organizers. If you don't love one yourself, they advise, give a teddy to someone in need.

from the right side. On the back side, stitch across the corner to stitch the NOSE in place.

*F.* Fit the CHIN to the MUZZLE. Pin and stitch.

*G.* Fit the MUZZLE into the HEAD. Align raw edges. Pin and stitch. Trim carefully, since any fur inside will make the wearer sneeze.

*H.* Turn right side out. Hand sew the bottom of the nose in place. Clip the fur around the MOUTH and NOSE on the MUZZLE to sculpt a good shape. Embroider the MOUTH with black yarn.

*I.* Hand hem the bottom seam if necessary.

The teddy bear club, Good Bears of the World, publishes a newsletter called *Bear Tracks*. One of the club's primary functions is to distribute teddy bears to children in hospitals.

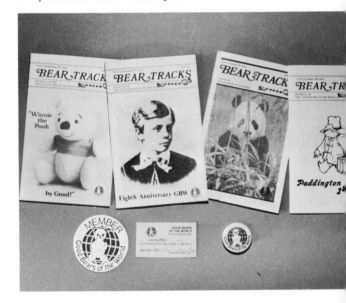

136

The carefully sewn Teddy Bear Quilt of today may be tomorrow's treasured heirloom. Vary the size or number of appliquéd squares for a larger or smaller quilt.

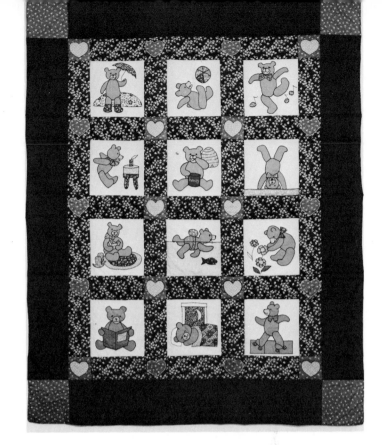

# Teddy Bear Quilt

This quilt may take longer to make than any other project in the book, but it gives much pleasure in the process. How nice it is to participate in the age-old tradition of creating a family folk art form that will last for generations. "Won't my yet-to-come grandchildren love this?" I said, smiling to myself as I stitched.

The quilt, measuring 58½ by 72-inches, is meant to fit a junior bed. Make wider borders than specified if you want the quilt to fit a larger bed, or add more squares, repeating favorites in different colors.

The entire quilt is sewn by machine: the basting, the satin stitch appliqué, the piecing seams, and the quilting of the layers. Machine sewing for me is faster and the result sturdier. However, you may do any or all steps by hand if you prefer.

## TIPS ON FABRICS

Select good quality, colorfast, nonshrinking cotton/polyester fabrics for durability. If you use scraps on hand, wash them first to preshrink them and test for colorfastness. Currently, traditional quilting fabric designs are available widely, but if they should go out of fashion, select your own assortment of colors and prints.

Directions given for appliqué suggest using a fabric glue stick on pieces cut to size, but you may also pin baste these pieces. For traditional appliqué technique, add seam allowances for a narrow hem in cutting, then turn the hem and hand stitch the pieces in place. For smooth machine appliqué, stitch through the pattern, fabric, and square background to anchor pieces, then trim away extra fabric and satin stitch over the cut edges.

## TIPS ON COLORS

Choose colors that project the feeling you want: cozy or bright, traditional or soft. I picked "teddy bear" colors in warm browns and muted colors, but don't get "stuck" trying to find these specific colors. Begin with the bear color and the larger colors, then pick the rest to relate well to these.

## PATTERN PIECES

BEARS (12), PINK HEART (10), RUST HEART (10), ASSORTED APPLIQUÉ PIECES
*Note:* Fabrics are listed by letter. Follow the key in the Materials list and on the patterns to cut pattern pieces. Dimensions given include a ¾-inch seam allowance, except for appliqué pieces.

## MATERIALS

### FABRIC:
BACKGROUND SQUARES: twelve squares of 11-by-11-inch off-white fabric

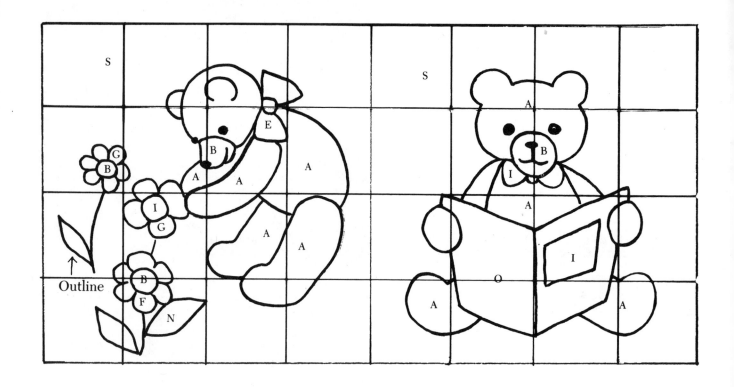

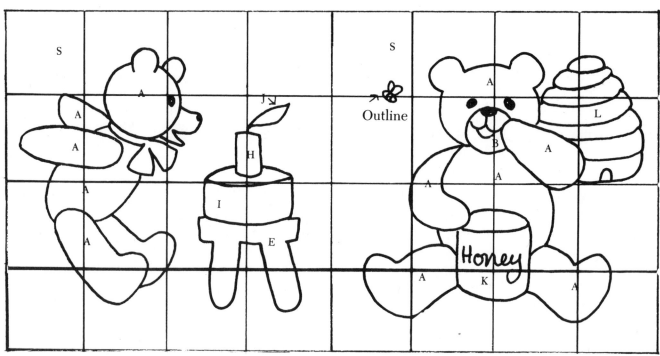

FOR COLOR AND FABRIC KEY SEE MATERIALS
SCALE: EACH SQUARE = ABOUT 2⅖" (See Directions)

Pattern Guide for Teddy Bear Quilt Blocks.

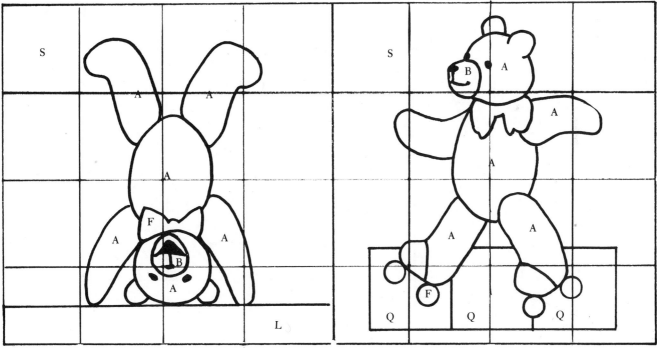

FOR COLOR AND FABRIC KEY SEE MATERIALS
SCALE: EACH SQUARE = ABOUT 2⅗″ (See Directions)

Pattern Guide for Teddy Bear Quilt Blocks.

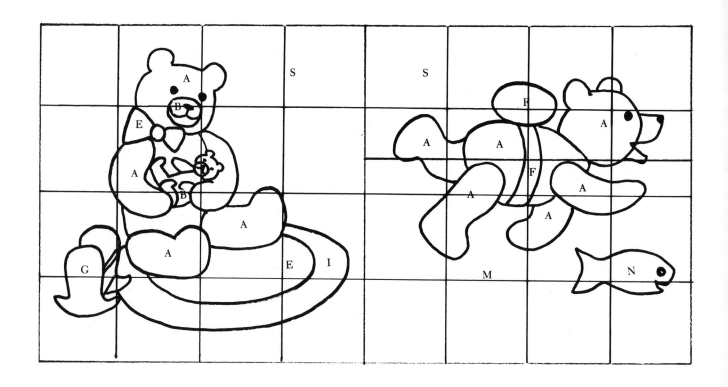

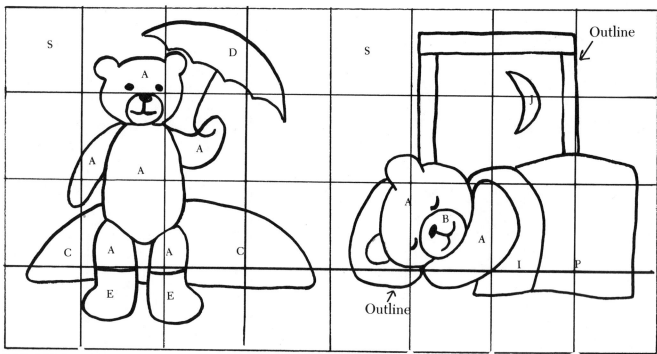

FOR COLOR AND FABRIC KEY SEE MATERIALS
SCALE: EACH SQUARE = ABOUT 2⅖″ (See Directions)

Pattern Guide for Teddy Bear Quilt Blocks.

SPACER BANDS: thirty-one pieces of 5½-by-11-inch black print fabric

SPACER BLOCKS: ten pieces of 5½-by-5½-inch rust print fabric (R) and ten pieces of 5½-by-5½-inch black print fabric (S)

CORNERS: four pieces of 8½-by-8½-inch rust print fabric (R)

BORDERS: two pieces of 65½-by-8½-inch and two pieces of 51½-by-8½-inch solid black fabric (T)

BACKING: one piece 74½-by-45-inch and four strips 9-by-38-inch rust print fabric (R)

STUFFING: bonded quilt batting, cut to a bit larger than the quilt and trimmed later

A. 24 by 36 inches of medium-weight, firmly woven, golden brown fabric for bears (cotton and polyester mix preferred)
B. 4 by 9 inches of solid gold
C. 4 by 10 inches of black and cream print
D. 6 by 9 inches of dark blue with white flowers
E. 4 by 15 inches of dark brown print
F. 6 by 12 inches of medium sky blue print
G. 7 by 9 inches of red print
H. 2 by 4 inches of solid medium purple
I. 12 by 20 inches of pink print
J. 3 by 6 inches of solid light yellow
K. 3 by 3 inches of solid medium brown
L. 4 by 16 inches of tan print
M. 7 by 11 inches of tan stripe
N. 4 by 6 inches of medium greyed green print
O. 6 by 8 inches of magenta with black polka dots
P. 5 by 5 inches of maroon print with squares
Q. 3 by 8 inches of solid warm grey color
R. 4 yards of 45-inch-wide rust print
S. 1½ yards of 45-inch-wide black print with peach
T. 2 yards of 45-inch-wide solid black fabric
U. 1 yard of 45-inch-wide eggshell or off-white fabric

STUFFING: one roll of single-bed-size bonded polyester fiberfill quilt batting

PAPER: eighteen sheets of backing paper (8½ by 11 inches), twelve sheets tracing paper for pattern, carbon paper or tailor's tracing paper, one 9½-by-9½-inch cardboard template for squares

THREAD: black cotton core, polyester wrapped

PINS: safety pins, 2-inch pins, regular pins

FABRIC GLUE STICK: to anchor appliqué pieces

## TO SCALE UP PATTERNS

To enlarge each bear block to full size, begin with a paper 11-inches square. Mark off ¾-inch seam allowances all around. Divide the remaining 9½-inch square into 16 equal squares by measuring or by folding the square in half and in half again in each direction. Copy the drawing square by square.

To make the bear blocks or the entire quilt a different size, refer to Bear Essentials, Scaling Up Teddy Bear Patterns, page 13. Use the quilt diagram for scaling up the entire quilt, and the bear blocks for scaling up the bears in the squares.

## TO BEGIN THE QUILT

Trace the appliqué pattern pieces on tracing paper. Place carbon paper behind the patterns, carbon face down, and trace onto the appliqué fabric identified by letter on the pattern piece.

If you plan to hand sew the quilt, add ¼-inch seam allowances to the appliqué pattern pieces. If you plan to trim seam allowances after stitching, simply pin the fabric to the pattern.

Measure and cut the second group of pattern pieces for the quilt. Press all pieces and store flat.

## STEP 1: APPLIQUÉING THE SQUARES

*A.* Use your pattern as a guide to lay the appliqué sections on the background SQUARE. Complete the entire square. Rub the fabric glue stick around the edges of the appliqué pieces and stick them in place. Work on one square at a time so these pieces will not be rubbed off.

*B.* For machine sewing, pin the paper backing to the back of each SQUARE to keep the appliqué smooth.

*C.* Set the machine to a medium width of solid satin stitch and outline the entire scene. If you find the tracing and placing difficult, lay the pattern over the fabric to be appliquéd and the background, then straight stitch along the pattern lines to outline the pictures; next remove the pattern, trim away the extra fabric, and satin stitch to cover the raw edges.

*D.* Complete all the SQUARES in the same manner. Press each flat with a steam iron.

*E.* Appliqué the HEARTS on the SPACER BLOCKS according to the diagram on page 142.

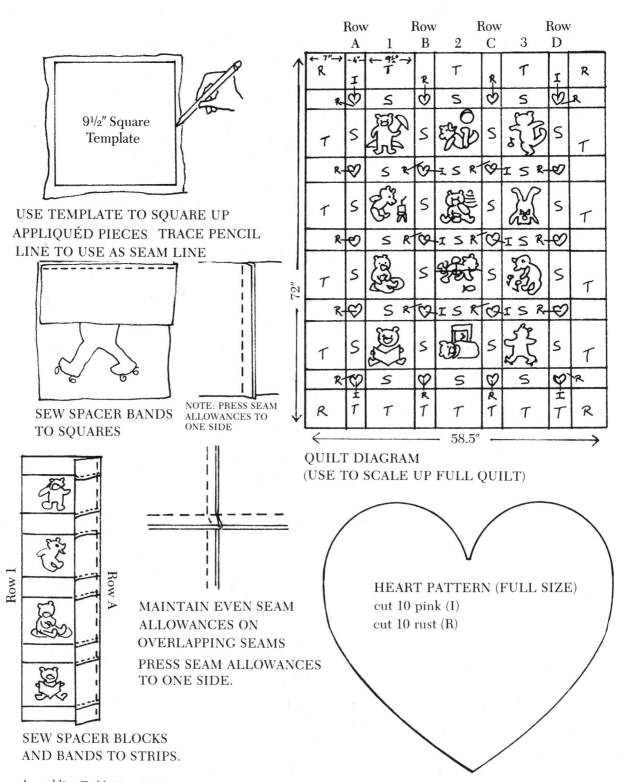

9½" Square Template

USE TEMPLATE TO SQUARE UP
APPLIQUÉD PIECES  TRACE PENCIL
LINE TO USE AS SEAM LINE

SEW SPACER BANDS
TO SQUARES

NOTE: PRESS SEAM
ALLOWANCES TO
ONE SIDE

QUILT DIAGRAM
(USE TO SCALE UP FULL QUILT)

MAINTAIN EVEN SEAM
ALLOWANCES ON
OVERLAPPING SEAMS

PRESS SEAM ALLOWANCES
TO ONE SIDE.

SEW SPACER BLOCKS
AND BANDS TO STRIPS.

Assembling Teddy Bear Quilt.

HEART PATTERN (FULL SIZE)
cut 10 pink (I)
cut 10 rust (R)

## STEP 2: PIECING THE QUILT FACE

**A.** Lay the appliquéd SQUARES face down on a flat surface and smooth them flat. Lay a 9½-by-

9½-inch cardboard template on the back of each aligning it as closely as possible to the grain of the fabric, and draw a pencil line around all edges of the SQUARE. This provides a stitch line that compensates for any amount the appliqué stitching might have contracted the fabric. Measure and trim ¾-inch seam allowances around the edges.

**B.** Sew one 5½ by 11-inch SPACER BAND to the top of each quilt SQUARE, aligning the 11-inch sides and using a ¾-inch seam allowance. Sew along the pencil-marked seam line. Sew another SPACER on the bottom of three quilt squares

*Note:* Press seams to one side after sewing to keep them flat. This makes a stronger seam than pressing them open.

**C.** Sew nine SPACER BANDS sewn to the quilt SQUARES to the SQUARE above, sewing on the pencil-marked seam line. Make sure each spacer now measures 4 inches across. Do this so it results in three vertical rows of squares with spacers above and below each.

**D.** Sew a SPACER BLOCK to one end of each of the remaining SPACER BANDS, matching the 5½-inch sides and using the quilt diagram as a guide. Use a ¾-inch seam allowance. Two black and two rust squares remain. Sew these units into four rows: Attach one of the remaining rust BLOCKS to the end of each row A and D. They now have a rust Block at each end and three black print Blocks in the middle. Attach one of the remaining blade BLOCKS to the end of each row B and C. They now have a blade BLOCK at each end and three rust BLOCKS spaced in the middle.

**E.** Pin row *A* of SPACER BANDS and BLOCKS to the left of row *1* of quilt SQUARES and SPACER BANDS. Match the seams and pin at this point. If the seams do not match, measure all pieces to find the incorrect one and restitch the seams. (All SPACER BLOCKS should measure 4 inches square when seamed. All quilt SQUARES should measure 9½ inches square when seamed. All SPACER BANDS should measure 4 inches wide by 9½ inches long.) Pin and stitch row *B* to the left of quilt row *2*, row *C* to the left of quilt row *3*, row *C* to row *2*, and row *D* to row *3*. Be sure all seams are pressed flat before the next step.

**F.** Pin and stitch the CORNER blocks to the shorter BORDER piece.

**G.** Pin and stitch the longer black BORDER pieces to rows *A* and *D*.

**H.** Sew the two strips of BORDER and CORNERS to each end of the quilt, matching seams. The quilt face is finished and should measure 74½ by 60 inches including seam allowances.

## STEP 3: ASSEMBLING THE QUILT

**A.** Sew the four BACKING strips measuring 38 by 9 inches into two longer strips, 74½ inches long. Sew one strip to each side of the 74½-by-45-inch BACKING, matching the 74½-inch sides. Press the seams flat.

**B.** Spread the bonded quilting batt on the floor. Pat it flat and trim it slightly larger than the quilt.

**C.** Lay the quilt front face side up on the stuffing. Smooth it flat and square. (If you have a tile floor, you could tape the corners to the floor, using the tiles to line up the edges square.) Using 2-inch pins or safety pins, pin the quilt face to the stuffing about every 18 inches. (Safety pins don't stick you unexpectedly when you are sewing.)

**D.** Spread the quilt BACKING face to face with the quilt front. Pin the seams carefully around all the edges about every 6 inches.

**E.** Move the sewing machine away from the wall. It will help to place a card table at the left of the machine to hold the quilt while you work on it. Move the quilt to the sewing machine. It may help to roll it.

Beginning 1 foot from the corner on the bottom, stitch a ¾-inch seam around the entire quilt through the three layers of the face, stuffing, and backing. Angle across or round the corners slightly to allow for the bulk of the stuffing when it is turned. After you round the fourth corner, sew about 24 inches and stop.

**F.** Trim off corner seam allowances at an angle. Trim the stuffing. Be sure to remove pins from around the edges, leaving only those holding the front to the stuffing.

**G.** Carefully turn the quilt right side out and spread it out flat. Pin the edges flat or press them carefully with a steam iron. *Do not* use much heat, since it may fuse the bonding. Reposition the front pins so they pin through the entire quilt, pinning liberally to hold the layers smoothly in place.

**H.** To machine quilt, set the machine for a long stitch: 6 to 10 stitches per inch. Quilt along seam lines. Keep the seams flat and taut as you sew so the backing will not "tuck." Keep checking the back as you sew for tucking or puckering on any seams. Remove any incorrect stitching and resew the seam. If unbonded batting has been used, quilt around the bears' bodies and more closely spaced within other areas to hold the stuffing in place during washing. Wash carefully by hand in cool water and dry carefully to avoid excess wear on the quilt.

This lounging teddy strikes a comfortable pose across a foam bolster or headboard.

# Headboard Bear

Here's a pal to help scare away the things that go bump in the night. This bear is as big as a small child, yet he's soft and furry; he's an assortment of fabrics appliquéd onto a fabric background that slip-covers a large bolster. The plush upholstery body feels furry contrasted with the other fabrics—a smooth cotton background, the ribbed wide wale corduroy boxing, and best of all, real plastic/glass eyes. If sleep comes hard, just reach up and stroke the bear's many textures.

The bolster, a lightweight polyurethane foam, measures as wide as a single bed, but the pattern could be scaled to make crib bumpers or pillows. A zipper on the back allows for removal of the cover for cleaning. If you plan to wash the cover, check all fabrics for shrinkage and colorfastness. The bolster can be made with cloth tabs at the top so it can hang on the wall over the bed.
*Note*: This project presents special appliqué problems. For one, it is difficult to trace a pattern on dark fake fur. Also, knitted fur fabric may stretch or shift in stitching and other fabrics slide on the fur pile. Another special consideration, finally, is that the pattern is large.

To get around these problems, I suggest using the following appliqué method. In this technique, the pattern is pinned to the fake fur and cut out with a wide seam allowance. The pattern and fur are then pinned to the background and stitched in place through the paper/fur/background fabric sandwich. The stitch line perforates the pattern

for easy removal later. The extra seam allowance fabric is trimmed away with sharp scissors. A final satin stitch line covers the edges for a neat finish. If you don't wish to use this technique, cut out the pattern pieces on the seam line, then pin, baste, or glue-stick baste the pieces in place before stitching.

## PATTERN PIECES

**A.** BEAR: cut 1 (brown fake fur)
**B.** FOOT PADS: cut 2 (tan felt)
**C.** PAWS: cut 2 (tan felt)
**D.** MUZZLE: cut 1 (tan felt)
**E.** BOW TIE: cut 1 (red calico)
**F.** STEM: cut 2 (print fabric)
**G.** FLOWER CENTER: cut 1 (yellow fabric)
**H.** PETALS: cut 1 (gold print fabric)
**I.** GRASS: cut 1 (green calico)
**J.** BACKGROUND: cut 1 (creamy fabric)
**K.** BACKING: cut 1 (gold corduroy)
**L.** BOXED EDGING (entire piece): cut 2 (gold corduroy)
**M.** BOXED EDGING SIDES (minus EDGING): cut 2 (gold corduroy)
*(see p. 146)*

## MATERIALS

*Note:* Choose all the fabrics as to color and texture so they relate and look well together. Use fabrics listed or your own choices.
BEAR: 18 by 40 inches of brown fake fur
PAWS, FOOT PADS, and MUZZLE: 12 by 15 inches of tan felt (divided into 5 pieces)
BOW TIE: 4 by 6 inches of red calico print

PETALS: 4 by 4 inches of gold print fabric

STEM: 1 by 4 inches of print fabric

FLOWER CENTER: 1¼-inch circle of yellow fabric

GRASS: 9 by 41½ inches of green calico print

BACKGROUND: one piece, 19½ by 41½ inches, of creamy medium-weight fabric, firmly woven

BACKING: one piece, 19½ by 41½ inches, of wide wale gold corduroy

BOXED EDGING: two pieces, 5½ by 41½ inches, and two pieces, 5 by 19½ inches, of wide wale, heavy-ribbed gold courduroy

EYES: 2 plastic eyes, 1 inch across, that have a post on the back and metal attachment washers. Fabric eyes may be appliquéd in place, if you prefer.

BOLSTER: 19-by-41-by-4-inch bolster. Dimensions should measure an inch larger than the finished cover so it will fit snugly, without wrinkles.

CLOSING: use 18 or 40 inches of upholstery zipper, upholstery snap tape, or Velcro brand tape, or hand stitch the bolster closed

NOTIONS: box of 2-inch-long straight pins, sharp scissors, zigzag sewing machine, yardstick, pencil, 16-by-36-inch paper

## MAKING THE PATTERN

**A.** First, scale up the pattern to the size you want. Pattern amounts are given for an 18-by-40-inch headboard but you can reduce or increase these dimensions for a larger or smaller bear. Draw the pattern on full-sized paper of a medium to light weight. Try tracing paper, wrapping paper, or even newspaper. Trace a second pattern if you wish to save one, since the pattern is destroyed in the appliquéing process.

**B.** Measure and cut the background piece, the boxed edging pieces including ¾ inch seam allowances, and the rectangular grass section. If you tear the fabric for straight lines, make sure this does not pull threads in the fabric. To cut the bear, pin the paper fabric securely on the fake fur. Cut loosely around the pattern of the entire bear about 1 inch or more from the pattern edge to leave a wide seam allowance. Leave the pins in place. Assemble the fabric for the small pieces, which are cut out with 1 inch or more seam allowances and trimmed after stitching.

## STEP 1: APPLIQUÉING THE FRONT

**A.** Place the rectangle of GRASS on the bottom half of the BACKGROUND piece. Pin it liberally and straight stitch it in place around the outside edges. Straight stitch ⅛ inch from the edge across the top of the GRASS. This raw edge, like all others, will be covered with satin stitching later.

**B.** Pin the paper pattern and fake fur BEAR in place on the BACKGROUND and GRASS. Use 2-inch pins, if you have them. If you pin over a seam line, put the pin in at right angles to the line so you can stitch over it without damaging the needle.

**C.** Using a short straight stitch, sew around the outline of the BEAR on the drawn lines. Do not sew the MUZZLE, TOP PAW, FOOT PAD, or FLOWER details yet.

**D.** Remove the paper pattern and set it carefully aside. With sharp scissors or clippers, trim away the wide seam allowances outside of the stitch line. Trim as close as possible to the stitch line without cutting the background fabric or the stitching.

**E.** For the PAWS, FOOT PADS, and MUZZLE, use the reserved paper pattern and pin the pieces of felt on the back of the paper pattern. Keep the pins on the top side of the paper so they won't be sewn inside. Make sure the whole pattern piece is covered by fabric.

**F.** With the felt pieces in place on the back side, reposition the paper pattern onto the BEAR, pin in place, and sew around the PAWS, FOOT PADS, and MUZZLE through the paper. Remove the pattern and save. Trim away the extra felt seam allowances.

**G.** For the TIE and FLOWER, use the reserved paper pattern again. Pin the TIE and FLOWER fabric to the back of the paper pattern with the face side to the back of the pattern piece. For the FLOWER, place the yellow CENTER (cut to the pattern size) first, then the golden PETALS, then the STEM pieces. Reposition the pattern pieces on the BEAR and stitch in place through the paper. Trim away the extra fabric.

**H.** All the appliqué pieces are now straight stitched in place with extra fabric trimmed away. Using black thread (or the color you prefer), set your machine for a wide, solid satin stitch and sew carefully around every appliqué piece, including the background GRASS. For an additional touch, sew a straight stitch line where the seams

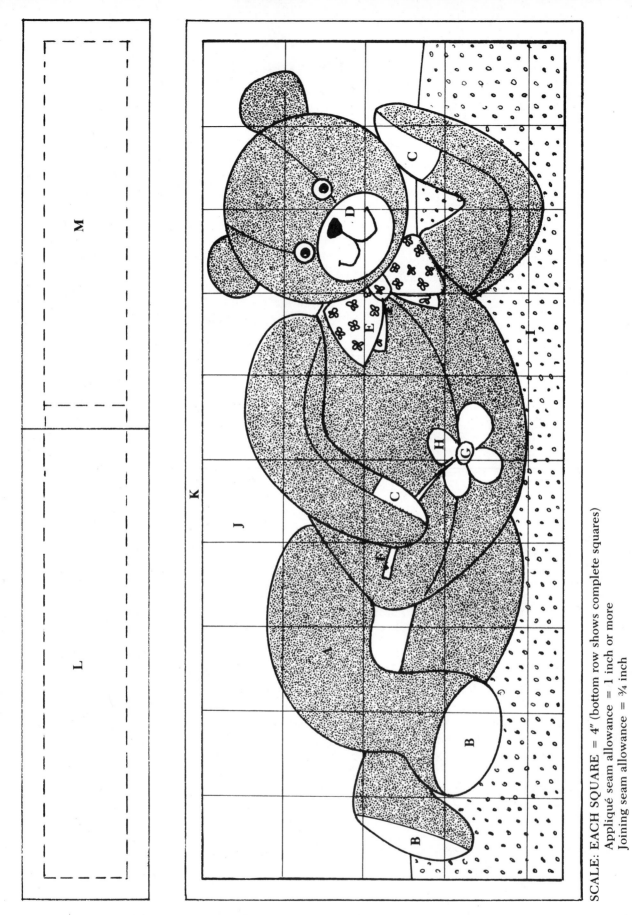

Pattern pieces for Headboard Bear.

SCALE: EACH SQUARE = 4" (bottom row shows complete squares)
Appliqué seam allowance = 1 inch or more
Joining seam allowance = ¾ inch

Paper Pattern

Fur Fabric
Background

TO APPLIQUÉ, SEW THROUGH PAPER PATTERN,
FUR FABRIC, AND BACKGROUND. REMOVE PAPER PATTERN CAREFULLY, ALONG
PERFORATED STITCHING LINES. SAVE THE PATTERN.

Back of Paper Pattern

PIN PAWS, FOOT PADS, AND MUZZLE TO
BACK OF PATTERN, REPOSITION PATTERN,
AND STITCH

TRIM AWAY SEAM ALLOWANCES
FROM ALL FABRIC PIECES

Satin Stitching

SATIN STITCH OVER RAW EDGES
AND STITCH LINE

Assembling Headboard Bear.

ASSEMBLE HEADBOARD AND ADD
TABS TO HANG ON WALL IF NEEDED

on a teddy bear would occur, on the bear's HEAD, TUMMY, and ARMS.

## STEP 2: ASSEMBLING THE BEAR

**A.** Press the completed appliqué with a steam iron. Lay it face down on a flat surface. Ideally, it's flat as a runway, but in fact it probably ripples a bit and the fabric is pulled slightly smaller in places. Measure it with a yardstick to the 18-by-40-inch finished size and draw pencil lines around all the edges on the back side. Trim to an even ¾-inch seam allowance.

**B.** On the BACKING, use an 18-inch zipper on one end or a 40-inch zipper for the length. To insert the zipper (or snap strip), cut the BACKING fabric 6 inches from the end (or side). Sew the zipper to each side of the cut. Close the zipper and measure the BACKING with a yardstick. Draw a seam line all around on the reverse side that measures 18 by 40 inches to match the front. Trim to an even ¾-inch seam allowance.

**C.** Sew the BOXED EDGING into one continuous piece, alternating the long and short pieces.

**D.** Pin each of the four BOXED EDGING seams to a corner of the BACKING with the zipper placed so the long and short sides align. Place pins every few inches so the edges all meet.

**E.** Sew along the pencil line on the BACKING reverse side. Round the corners a bit. Check to

see how this seam looks. Use a seam ripper to remove stitching, if necessary.

**F.** Using a ruler or measuring guide, measure and mark the BOXED EDGING for a seam line 3½ inches from the front seam line all around. Trim the seam allowance to ¾ inch. Use the marked seam line as a stitching guide.

**Note:** If you plan to hang the headboard on the wall, insert tabs in the top of the back seam at this time.

**G.** Pin the BOXED EDGING to the BACKING. Sew the side that includes the top of the zipper first, and then unzip it part way for turning later. Continue sewing around the BACKING. Unzip the zipper and turn the cover right side out.

## STEP 3: FITTING THE COVER

**A.** It's easy to say just pop the bolster into the cover, but if the cover is the right size—a bit too small—this is as easy as wrestling an alligator. Try this. Put the BOLSTER in a thin garbage bag with a hole started in the end. The plastic helps to slide the bolster in. Fold the bolster a bit so it will fit into the opening, then stuff it in and pull the garbage bag out. Keep on rubbing and wrestling the cover until all the edges are properly aligned. You may need to stick your arm inside several places to adjust the bolster.

**B.** Spray the finished headboard with Scotchguard to make it stain resistant.

147

Block printed or stenciled teddy bears, assembled part by part, gambol along the border of curtains, on wrapping paper, stationery, or children's clothing.

# Printed Bear Curtains

This simple bear design can be printed on curtains, as shown, or on stationery, clothing, wrapping paper, birthday cards, wallpaper, toy chests, or any likely surface. You can make these printed teddy bears assume any pose by stamping the different parts in various positions. Two head patterns allow the bear to face either way. By using two feet facing in the same direction, the bear turns sideways. Print teddy bears solidly in a row, as shown, or create an all-over design. By experimenting, you can devise any number of poses and ideas.

### TIPS ON PRINTING TECHNIQUES

Block printing ranks as one of the oldest forms of printing. It is possible that it goes back to the caveman smearing his hand with mud or charcoal to print on the cave walls. The method still remains the same—a shaped object rolled with ink or paint is stamped onto a flat surface. The firm object or block can be made from a variety of materials by being carved or sawed from wood, cut from linoleum block, or cast in metal, as with letters of type.

In the curtain printing shown here, small plywood pieces were sawed and sanded smooth along the edges. Linoleum blocks made especially for block printing can be bought in most art supply departments or stores. Buy or saw blocks to size. Hard foam rubber makes a good printer, too. Buy shoe liners with adhesive backing, cut the design with scissors, stick the foam to a solid backing, and print. To use the old favorite potato print technique, slice a firm potato smoothly in half or slices and carve the shapes.

### TIPS ON STENCILING

Stencil paper is stiff and resistant to moisture so it will not absorb the printing ink and distort. Stiff, thin paper works best to give a good, crisp edge to the print. Special stencil paper can be found in art or office supply stores. To make your own, choose a stiff, thin cardboard, and coat it with varnish or shellac. Dry, then cut out the designs.

A stiff, clear plastic stencil allows you to better place the stencils since you can see through the material—if the paint is cleaned off. The plastic is more difficult to cut but makes a strong, useful stencil.

### PATTERN PIECES

HEAD (2, right and left), BODY (1), ARMS (2, right and left), LEGS (2, right and left), EYE (1)

*Note:* These pattern pieces, presented full size, can be scaled up or down to any size.

148

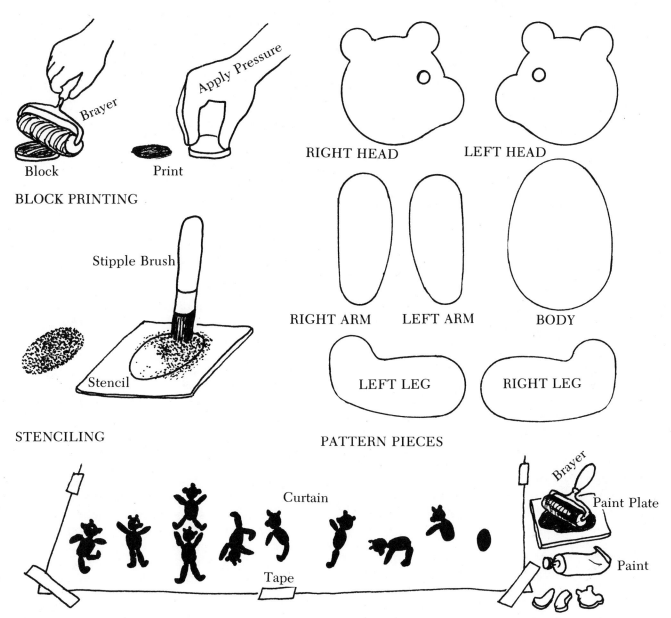

BLOCK PRINTING

STENCILING

RIGHT HEAD  LEFT HEAD

RIGHT ARM  LEFT ARM  BODY

LEFT LEG  RIGHT LEG

PATTERN PIECES

TAPE CURTAIN TAUT OVER PLANNED DESIGN AND DO ALL BODIES FIRST

SOME TEDDY BEAR POSITIONS TO TRY—OVERLAP ALL JOINTS

Making Printed Bear Curtains.

## MATERIALS

CURTAINS:   one set of ready-made curtains, or make your own to fit a certain window. Do not print over seams. (For stationery, use slightly absorbent paper.)

TRIM:   1-inch-wide printed ribbon, large rick rack the width of each curtain

BLOCK:   4 by 5 inches of ¾-inch-thick wood or linoleum block (or ¼-inch thick wood, plus backing), or enough potatoes

DOWEL:   one piece of ⅛-inch dowel 2 inches long

ROLLER:   one brayer—the small, hard rubber roller with a metal handle used to mix ink and roll the blocks. Lacking this, a stiff-bristle brush will do.

STENCIL:   (optional) 6 by 10 inches of stencil board, stiff translucent plastic (thinner than a credit card), or your own coated stencil paper, one blunt round-bristle stippling brush, one small X-acto knife and a package of blades

PAINT:   black, red, and brown (to mix the golden-brown, use ocher and orange, or umber, orange, yellow, and white). Use waterproof paint for textile printing or permanent decorations.

*Note:* block-printing colors are called "inks" even if paint is used. For printing on paper, use block print inks. For printing on textiles, use textile paint or artist's acrylics. These paints are finely ground and viscous (sticky), necessary qualities for good prints.

PALETTE:   one piece of a smooth, hard surface on which to mix and roll paint: cookie sheet, large plate, or 8-by-10-inch piece of Masonite

MASKING TAPE:   enough to hold fabric in place

PAPER:   paper for plan, tracing paper, carbon paper, scrap paper

WATER:   jar of water to use in mixing paint

CLEAN-UP:   pan of soapy water and sponge to remove mistakes from the fabric (if possible)

## STEP 1: MAKING THE WOODEN PRINTER

For a wooden printer, trace the patterns on the wood or Masonite, using carbon paper. Saw out the designs, and sandpaper or carve smooth, sharp edges. Drill a hole for the EYE, using a ⅛-inch drill bit. Mark the names of the pieces on the backs and indicate which is "up." Glue a wooden bead or other small, sturdy handle on the backs of the pieces if needed. To print EYES, cut 2 inches of dowel stick, sanded, to a ⅛-inch-round flat point.

## STEP 1 (optional): MAKING THE STENCIL

Trace the design on the stencil paper or plastic. Place the stencil on scrap cardboard for a cutting pad. Using a new blade in the X-acto knife, carefully cut out the design, achieving the smoothest possible edges. Mark the pieces with the name and an arrow for "up."

## STEP 2: PLANNING THE DESIGN

To get an idea of the size and shape of the bears, mix a small amount of ink and print the bears on scrap paper, in many positions, to see what works best. Try out all the crazy ideas at this point rather than printing on the actual curtain. Measure the area to be printed on the curtains, and tape pieces of paper together to fit for a plan sheet. Draw bear sketches on the plan sheet with a dark outline so they will show through the curtain, or cut out teddy bears from your experiments and tape them on the pattern plan as a guide for printing. This paper also serves as a pad to keep ink from printing on the table or floor. Tape the finished printing plan to the table or floor where you plan to work. Make sure the surface is smooth and firm and that no tape, paper wrinkles, or fabric folds come under a bear. Lay the curtain over the plan and adjust the placement. When this is completed, tape the curtain taut. With a double-width curtain, do one side at a time.

## STEP 3: MIXING THE PAINT/INK

Squeeze out 2 inches of brown paint onto the palette. (If you prefer a warmer color, add ocher and orange, or orange, yellow, and white, until you achieve the color you wish.) Roll the brayer back and forth over the paint to mix the colors. Thin the paint as needed. After each addition be sure to roll it smooth again. Coat the brayer with paint then roll onto the block. Test the block on scrap paper to see how it prints. You may need to print several images to get a good build-up of paint on the block. If the paint is too moist it will squeeze out around the edges of the block, widening and blurring the edges of the image. If the paint is too thick or there is not enough, some areas of the block fail to print. Keep experimenting until you develop a good touch. Try printing on a sample of the fabric since it will accept the paint differently than the paper will. Mix enough paint for the printing you plan to do.

## STEP 4: BLOCK PRINTING

Assemble the printers, the ink and palette, the pan of clean-up water (or other solvent as needed) and sponge, a jar of thinning water or solvent and small brush next to the curtain stretched over the plan. Roll a smooth coating of paint on the BODY piece with the brayer. Carefully place the block on the curtain and push firmly to print. If this does not print well, reroll the block with paint and carefully align the block to reprint. Tiny areas that do not print can be brushed in with a dry, stiff-bristle artist's brush dipped in a small amount of paint. Print all the BODIES first, then other pieces. Look over the curtain to see if you missed any arms or legs.
*Note:* You may need to thin the paint after printing awhile.

Peel off the masking tape and carefully lift the curtain, pulling it up off the paper backing. (If you leave it in place to dry it may stick.) Move it

carefully to avoid smears and drape it to dry.

After all the brown is printed, mix the black. Retape the curtain in place and print the EYES with the dowel stick to complete the bears. When the paint has dried, iron the curtain to smooth the fabric and set the paint. Stitch the printed ribbon and large rickrack in place for trim, or plan your own trim.

## STEP 4 (optional): STENCIL PRINTING

Assemble the stencils, paint and palette, stencil brush, a pan of clean-up water or solvent and sponge, a jar of thinning water or solvent, and a brush next to the curtain stretched over the plan. Mix the paint on the palette as described in step 3, using the brayer to mix if you wish. Using the stippling brush held straight up, dab the brush in the ink to pick up a controlled amount of paint. Hold the stencil in place and dab to fill in the open area. Do not brush the paint on. Stipple the paint until you achieve the color and thickness you want. Practice first on scrap paper and then on fabric scrap to develop the right touch. Stencil the BODIES first, placing them according to the plan. Since the stencil will be laid on a previously printed area for the rest of the design, be sure the paint is dry before placing a stencil on it. Complete the figures part by part. Finish by drying, ironing, and adding trim.

A teddy bear bag sewn in terry cloth provides a durable friend for hiding treasures or pillowing under your head.

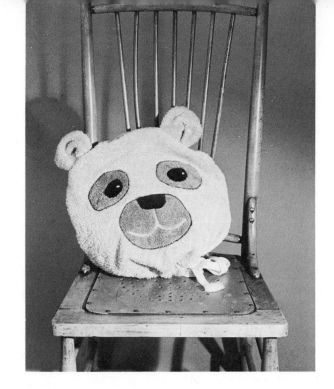

# Claudia's Bear Bag

Anything could fit into this useful bear bag: a pillow, a collection of soft toys, special objects, or a beloved security blanket. Years ago, I found my daughter Claudia's favorite blanket hidden behind her bedroom door. She had an artist's eye even then, recognizing her blanket was too tattered to appear in public but loving it nonetheless. So, I made a bear bag for the remains of the blanket. The drawstrings allowed her easy access. She used the bag for a pillow. When this bear bag grew threadbare, a larger one was made. The finished bear measures about 15 by 16 inches.

## TIPS ON SEWING TERRY CLOTH

Terry is a thick, loopy, softly woven fabric that needs good control when machine stitching. Otherwise, it may stretch, shift on the loops of the other piece, or "tuck" itself when you come to a pin. To cope with this, pin the seams liberally, using 2-inch plastic-headed pins if you have a very thick towel. Pin at right angles to the stitch line. This allows for sewing over the pins with a hinged-foot machine, or hand wheeling over them if not. Hold the pieces firmly with your fingers as you feed the seams to keep the fabric from tucking because of the pressure of the presser foot.

For the appliquéd pieces, pin a sheet of typing or other similar paper to the back and pin the added piece to the front. Hand or machine baste the piece in place; this allows for easy removal

in case it slides out of place. Satin stitch over this line. The paper backing will keep the satin stitching from stretching the terry and making a rippled line of stitching.

## PATTERN PIECES

**A.** HEAD: cut 2 (towel)
**B.** EYE LINER: cut 2 (washcloth)
**C.** EYE: cut 2 (brown or black velveteen)
**D.** MUZZLE: cut 1 (washcloth)
**E.** NOSE: cut 1 (brown or black velveteen)
**F.** EAR: cut 2 folded (towel)
(see p. 153)

## MATERIALS

HEAD:   one bath towel, or ½ yard of terry cloth
MUZZLE and EYE LINERS:   one washcloth, or 9 by 9 inches of similar fabric
EYES and NOSE:   2-by-2 inch squares of velveteen or suede cloth for each in brown or black, the darker the better
DRAWSTRING:   48 inches of braid or cord
THREAD:   black, orange, tan—nonshrinking
PAPER:   sheet of typing paper

## STEP 1: MAKING THE PATTERN

**A.** Make a paper pattern first, if you wish, or measure and draw the pattern directly on the terry. Beginning at the towel border, measure up 19 by 16 inches across. To make the rounded top, measure down 8 inches from the top and 8 inches from the side. Pin a string at this point with a pencil tied on the string 8 inches from the center point . Inscribe a half circle from the side edge to the top to the other side edge. Cut two identical pieces.

**B.** For the EARS, cut two pieces of terry 8 by 5 inches.

**C.** Cut two EYE LINERS, two EYES, and one MUZZLE from a scaled up pattern.

## STEP 2: MAKING THE BEAR BAG

**A.** Pin paper backing behind the EYES and MUZZLE on the reverse side of the terry.

**B.** Pin the EYE LINERS and MUZZLE in place on the front side, using the pattern placement guide. Hand or machine baste in place with long running stitches.

**C.** Pin EYES and NOSE in place and machine baste.

**D.** Using black thread, set the machine for a wide, close satin stitch and outline the appliquéd

pieces. Change to orange thread and satin stitch the MOUTH with a double row of stitching. Remove the paper backing.

**E.** Fold the EAR pieces in half to measure 4 by 5 inches. Beginning 2 inches down from the top on the fold, sew a 4-inch half circle to the other side using a ½-inch seam allowance. Continue the seam to the bottom in a straight line. Trim off the corners and turn right side out. Fold a 2-inch tuck in the EAR so the exposed fold line comes in the middle of the ear on the front.

**F.** Pin the EARS in place on the front. Stitch to anchor them in place.

**G.** Put the FRONT and BACK pieces face to face and pin securely. Stitch nearly all the way around the head, using a ½-inch seam allowance, stopping 4 inches from the end on one side. Do not sew across the towel-hemmed bottom.

**H.** Turn a 2-inch hem in the bottom and machine stitch in place.

**I.** Turn right side out. Run the drawstring through the opening at the side and through the hem. The wide hem is necessary for fabric this thick to compress into gathers, when the string is pulled.

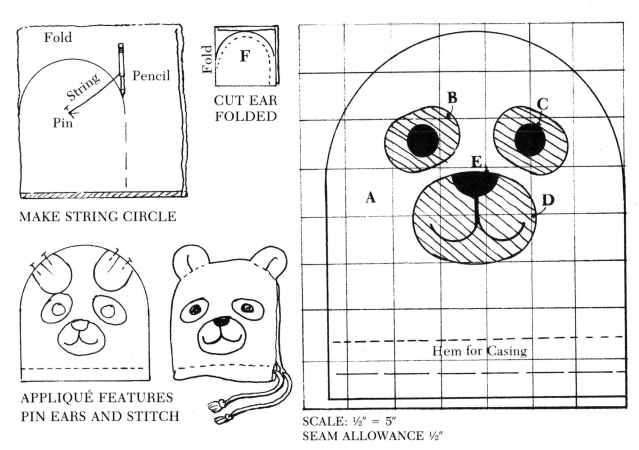

MAKE STRING CIRCLE

CUT EAR FOLDED

APPLIQUÉ FEATURES
PIN EARS AND STITCH

SCALE: ½" = 5"
SEAM ALLOWANCE ½"

Pattern pieces and assembly for Claudia's Bear Bag.

153

# Mail Order Supplies

Most materials and supplies needed to make teddy bears can be found in local craft, fabric, and notions stores or departments. Some are harder to find. For example, fur fabrics are sold to fabric stores in lots containing assorted but unpredictable selections. Unless you buy huge amounts from wholesalers, these fake furs cannot be specifically ordered locally. Tour the various fabric stores to see what they have on hand. To order plushes and velvets consult the upholstery order swatch books.

The following companies stock mail order supplies:

For a complete list of teddy bear supplies, eyes, growlers, joint sets, fur, and more, write to:

Merrily Doll Supply Co.
8542 Ranchito Avenue
Panorama City, California 91402

For eyes, noses, and doll parts write to:

Florida Supply House
P.O. Box 847
Bradenton, Florida 33506

For traditional glass eyes, write to:

G. Schoefer, Inc.
138 West 31st Street
New York, New York 10001

For disk sets, write to:

Build-A-Bear
14809 West Point Drive
Sterling Heights, Michigan 48078

# Metric Conversion Chart

## LINEAR MEASURE

1 inch = 2.54 centimeters

12 inches = 1 foot = 0.3048 meter

3 feet = 1 yard = 0.9144 meter

## SQUARE MEASURE

1 square inch = 6.452 square centimeters

144 square inches = 1 square foot = 929.03 square centimeters

9 square feet = 1 square yard = 0.8361 square meter

# Index